P9-AFK-991

An Exposition of The Gospel of Luke

An Exposition of The Gospel of Luke

By Herschel H. Hobbs

BAKER BOOK HOUSE
GRAND RAPIDS, MICHIGAN

Library of Congress
Catalog Card Number: 66-28804
ISBN: 0-8010-4045-0

First Printing, December, 1966
Second Printing, February, 1972

PHOTOLITHOPRINTED BY CUSHING - MALLOY, INC.
ANN ARBOR, MICHIGAN, UNITED STATES OF AMERICA

Dedicated
to all Christian doctors
who are under-physicians
of The Great Physician

INTRODUCTION

The Gospel of Luke has been called the most beautiful book in the world. It reflects culture and literary finesse in style, language, and contents. This, in turn, reflects the fact that it was written primarily for the Gentile world. It is the universal Gospel which presents Jesus as the Saviour of the world. This is seen further in the author's regard for Samaritans, Gentiles, women, outcasts, the poor, and the down-trodden. Someone has called it "the Gospel of the underdog." Furthermore, it is a Gospel of prayer and praise.

Scholarship is almost universal in attributing this Gospel and the Acts to Luke, whom Paul called "the beloved physician" (Col. 4:14). The use of medical language in both of these works reveals him to be a physician in a class with Galen and Hippocrates. Luke is the only Gentile writer in the New Testament. In all likelihood he was a Greek. Perhaps he was a convert of Paul, and assuredly was his traveling companion during most of his missionary journeys, beginning with Paul's vision at Troas (Acts 16:8 ff.; note the "we" in verse 10 and thereafter). He was with Paul during his more than two years of imprisonment in Caesarea. This period would have afforded him ample opportunity to accumulate the material for his Gospel.

Luke was also a historian. At one time many scholars sought to discredit him in this regard. But largely through the work of Sir William Ramsay he has been thoroughly authenticated as to his historical accuracy. Even at points where his data conflicted with known records of the Roman empire, subsequent archaeological discoveries have shown that Luke is historically accurate. After a lifetime of research Ramsay declared Luke to be the greatest of all historians. The historical accuracy of Luke gives credence to the accounts of all of the records of early Christianity.

What is the date of Luke's Gospel? Both Mark and Acts may be considered as *termini* for determining the date. Luke makes use of Mark, and, therefore, must have been written after it. Mark was written probably not later than A.D. 55. Acts ends with Paul in prison in Rome for two years. It was written probably about A.D. 63. Since Luke precedes Acts this means that this Gospel was written sometime between A.D. 55 and 63. In all likelihood its date would fall sometime during the latter part of Paul's Caesarean imprisonment or during the early part of his Roman imprisonment. This would date it in the period between A.D. 59 and 62. Probably Luke was written after Matthew. But this does not pin down the date other than to suggest that Luke may well have been written during the early part of Paul's Roman imprisonment, perhaps A.D. 61 or 62.

This is the second volume in a series designed to give an exposition of the four Gospels. The first, *An Exposition of the Gospel of Matthew,* is written around certain great themes, following the structure of the Gospel itself. However, *Luke* follows a more chronological order, largely dealing with events in sequence rather than gathering them about topical themes. This within itself has determined the style and arrangement of this present work.

The basic English text followed in this volume is the King James Version. When other versions are employed they are identified. However, in exposition it is desirable to follow rather closely the Greek text (Nestles), but with a minimum use of Greek words. At times the author makes his own translation where it contributes to a better understanding of a given passage.

Quite obviously through the years one gleans many thoughts from many sources. It would be impossible and impractical to cite all of them. However, mention may be made of certain basic volumes which have been consulted.

William Barclay, *The Gospel of Luke,* Westminster, Philadelphia, 1956.

A. B. Bruce, "Luke," *The Expositor's Greek Testament,* Eerdmans, Grand Rapids, 1951.

Herschel H. Hobbs, *Preaching Values from the Papyri,* Baker, Grand Rapids, 1964; *The Crucial Words from Calvary,* Baker, Grand Rapids, 1958; *Who Is This?,* Broadman, Nashville, 1952; *An Exposition of the Gospel of Matthew,* Baker, 1965.

G. Campbell Morgan, *The Gospel According to Luke,* Revell, New York, 1931.

Alfred Plummer, *The Gospel According to St. Luke,* Clark, Edinburgh, 1960.

A. T. Robertson, *Word Pictures in the New Testament,* Volume II, Sunday School Board of Southern Baptist Convention, Nashville, 1930; *Luke the Historian in the Light of Research,* Scribners, New York, 1930; *A Translation of Luke's Gospel,* Sunday School Board of Southern Baptist Convention, 1923.

J. W. Shepard, *The Christ of the Gospels,* Eerdmans, Grand Rapids, 1938.

As Luke wrote his Gospel to present Jesus as the Saviour of all men, this exposition is presented with the prayer that it may point all men to Him in whom alone is salvation. May God bless it to this end!

Herschel H. Hobbs

First Baptist Church
Oklahoma City, Oklahoma

CONTENTS

I. The Dedication of the Gospel

II. The Fulness of the Time

III. The Time of the Beginning

IV. The Galilean Ministry

V. The Period of Withdrawals

VI. The Judean Ministry

VII. The Perean Ministry

VIII. The Gathering Gloom

IX. The Trial, Crucifixion, and Burial of Jesus

X. The Resurrection and Appearances of Jesus

I
The Dedication of the Gospel

Luke 1:1-4

The Result of Inspired Research

The introduction to Luke's Gospel is of the greatest importance with respect to the doctrine of the inspiration of Scripture. "All Scripture is given by inspiration of God" (II Tim. 3:16). Literally, "all Scripture is God-breathed." "Holy men of God spake as they were moved by the Holy Ghost [Spirit]" (II Peter 1:21). Again, literally, "as they were picked up and borne along by the Holy Spirit."

Do these Scriptures mean that a man sits idly while God breathes His message into him or that the Holy Spirit bears him along as an automaton with no effort on his part? Or does God through the indwelling Spirit guide the writer through research and otherwise as his Spirit-controlled mind seeks to comprehend and record God's truth? Luke 1:1-4 says that the latter is true. This does not by any means imply that the Bible is merely the product of men's minds. What it says is that God uses the whole of the personality of the individual writer through which to reveal and record His truth. He guides him in his purpose and research, protects him from error, yet leaves him free to express in terms of his own personality the message involved. An examination of any book in the Bible reveals this to be true.

Dr. E. Y. Mullins suggests that the primary concern of the student of Scripture is not the method but the result of inspiration. And the Bible is its own greatest testimony in this regard.

Turning to Luke's introduction we see that this is true in his experience. The tenses of the verbs involved show that he wrote these verses after he had completed the body of the Gospel itself. Therefore, he is not telling what he plans to do, but what he has already done. In so doing he follows the classical method of ancient historians. For instance, Herodotus begins his Greek history, "These are the researches of Herodotus of Halicarnassus." Much later, Dionysius of the same city began his history, "Before beginning to write I gathered information, partly from the lips of the most learned men with whom I came into contact, and partly from histories written by Romans of whom they spoke with praise." This latter sounds very much like Luke himself, who with the added flavor of divine inspiration uses much more beautiful phraseology as he introduces his Gospel in a splendid literary style which is not exceeded by any Greek writer.

But what of the content of this introduction? As we examine it we note Luke speaks of his sources, his method, and his purpose in writing this Gospel.

The Sources (1:1-2)

Clearly Luke says that his sources were twofold: written and oral. "Forasmuch as many have taken in hand to set forth in order a declaration of those things which are most surely believed among us" (v. 1).

The infinitive rendered "to set forth in order" was basically a military term referring to the lining up of soldiers in an orderly fashion. In the sense as used in this passage it refers to the orderly arrangement of ideas or events. We would say "to compare." So Luke's reference is to previous attempts to compose narratives concerning the life of Jesus. These were not anecdotes or sketchy notes. They were orderly and connected narratives set forth in either topical or chronological fashion. The word "declaration" means something that was declared thoroughly in the sense of a narration or history.

Furthermore, the matters comprising these narratives were "most surely believed among us." This meaning is most certainly true. But the words so translated allow a variety of meanings. Literally, they mean "the things having been fulfilled among us." This could refer to the completed life of Jesus. Or to the finished nature of the narratives. Bruce suggests that it means those things which were widely known among the early Christians. All of these meanings were true. But in any event Luke tells us of the desire of the followers of Jesus carefully to preserve in written form the events in the life of Jesus.

What were these narratives? They did not include the apocryphal gospels which were written after this time. One of these narratives probably was the Gospel of Mark. For Luke in large measure builds his Gospel around the framework of Mark. He could have had access to the Gospel of Matthew, assuming that it was written before Luke. Most likely these narratives include the *Logia* of Jesus, a Hebrew or Aramaic work attributed by Papias to Matthew. This dealt with the teachings of Jesus, and is reflected in both Matthew and Luke.

But even these do not satisfy the word "many." It expresses the extensive literary activity as first one and then another sought to preserve certain cherished incidents in the life of their Lord. How poverty stricken history would be had it not been for the historical sense which found expression in these "many" narratives.

However, these were not all. For there were the oral accounts of those who were eyewitnesses to the life of Jesus. "Even as they delivered them unto us, which from the beginning were eyewitnesses, and ministers of the word" (v. 2).

"Delivered" renders the verb from which comes the word for "tradition." There is one sense in which this word suggests unreliability. But basically the Greek word meant that which was handed over or down from one person to another. The Jews by long training were adept at passing on from father to child the oral traditions of their history or religion. And they did so with marvelous accuracy. It is this custom which is in the usage here. Luke was not an eyewitness to Jesus' life. In a sense he was a second generation Christian. And to him the first generation Christians transmitted their firsthand knowledge of the life of Jesus.

It is of such that the evangelist speaks as "eyewitnesses, and ministers of the word." The "eyewitnesses" were those who with their own eyes had seen Jesus. From the Greek word comes our word "autopsy" *(autoptai)*. It was a medical term. In a post-mortem physicians can see with their own eyes the condition which may have caused death. The thought here, however, is simply that with their own eyes these people had seen the events which they recounted about Jesus. The word "ministers" is also an interesting one. Literally, it means "under-rowers" or one who served in a subordinate position (cf. I Cor. 4:1). But even more to the point this word *(hupēretai)* was used in medical terminology to refer to doctors who served under a principal physician. So Doctor Luke refers to this particular group, perhaps the apostles themselves, who served as lesser *doctors* under the Great Physician.

Now it should be noted that this phrase "which from the beginning were eyewitnesses, and ministers of the word" relates to both those who had written orderly narratives and those who passed on to Luke their oral traditions. So in one terse phrase the author attests the accuracy of both. They had been with Jesus "from the beginning." This does not necessarily mean that each one had been with Jesus during every event of His life. Only Mary had been with Him at the very beginning. And even she was not present on every occasion during His ministry. But those who were responsible for given events had been with Jesus, so that the evidence went back to the very source of information.

The Method (1:3a)

What did Luke do with this wealth of material? He tells us in his own words. "It seemed good to me also, having had perfect understanding of all things from the very first, to write.... in order...."

It is inconceivable that a man of Luke's temperament and training would simply read and hear these things, and then forget them. Instead they presented a challenge to him. Others had sought in their own ways to preserve the precious story. And Luke casts no reflection upon them when he says that it seemed good to him to gather all of these into a more complete narrative. Everything within him, plus the urging of the Holy Spirit, called him to his task.

We have noted that Luke was by training a physician and, therefore, a scientist. He also had the natural instinct of a historian. And this combination perfectly endowed him to be an instrument of the Spirit of God to pen the most beautiful story of the greatest life ever lived. Here then is a by-product of Paul's imprisonment in Caesarea. For how else could God have worked to bring this Greek scientist-historian into firsthand contact with his task? Truly, God works in all things for good to those who love Him, and who are the called according to His purpose. A. T. Robertson reminds us that Luke was the first critic of the life of Christ whose criticism has been preserved for posterity.

One can well imagine that Luke, like every Christian tourist, looked with eager anticipation to the prospect of visiting the land of our Lord. Perhaps he had already read some of the written narratives. From Paul he had heard much about the life of Jesus. It is no wonder then that his extended stay in Palestine was used to seek out other narratives and to talk with everyone who had some choice story to tell. It is possible even that Mary still lived in Palestine, and that Luke talked with her. And with some of the apostles. So that in all likelihood he accumulated voluminous notes.

A person of lesser genius might have been overwhelmed with this abundance of material. But not Luke. For literally he says that "he traced the course of all things accurately from the first."

The King James Version suggests that he "had perfect understanding... from the first." But this was not true. It was his lack of understanding which prompted his study. The Greek word so rendered means to follow alongside a thing which one has in mind, or to trace a thing carefully. It is a perfect participle, meaning that he did a thorough job in his tracing. So Luke thoroughly followed along in his mind every event. And he did not stop until he had determined its unmistakable accuracy. Galen used this word for the investigation of medical symptoms. So as Luke many times had pored over the symptoms to determine the right diagnosis and cure of a disease, he carefully studied the events in the life of Jesus to determine their accuracy and proper chronology. The word "accurately" *(akribōs),* according to Robertson, means to go into minute details. Here was scientific investigation at its best. He did not begin to write until he possessed complete and accurate knowledge of every detail of his subject.

And he made his investigation "from the first." This could mean that he did so beginning with the birth narratives and continuing through the ascension of Jesus. This was true. However, G. Campbell Morgan makes a most challenging suggestion. Noting that the Greek word *anōthen* may mean either "from the first," "again," or "from above" (cf. John 3:3; 19:11), he suggests the last meaning here. Thus Luke claims that his scientific work was under the guidance of heaven itself or the Holy Spirit. Whether one presses this meaning or not, the fact is true nevertheless. There is no reason why both "from the first" and "from above" could not apply here.

Having finished his investigation, Luke says that he began "to write... in order...." The word rendered "order" means in orderly fashion or in chronological order. Morgan notes that this was the word of an artist. Having gathered and sifted his material, he wrote it down in artistic fashion. And Bruce's comments add to the picture. Luke wanted to be exact, and to write in an orderly plan. His historical genius expresses itself in the words *inquiry, accuracy,* and *order.*

How important are these words as we study Luke! He was not one who was caught up in some religious enthusiasm which would lead him to invent stories or to accept those of others without careful examination. Though he worked under the inspiration of the Holy Spirit, he did so with the dedicated spirit of a scientist-historian who did not invent *evidence* but by careful analysis followed where *evidence* led.

This thought should give caution to anyone who proposes to question the trustworthiness of Luke's account. He was in a much better position to judge his evidence than one who is removed from it by almost two thousand years. In every incidence where the science of archaeology has thrown light upon disputed passages in Luke it has corroborated the Gospel record. In this light, if we are to be scholarly and scientific, we shall be wise to trust this scientist-historian in those matters which do not submit themselves to scientific analysis.

The Purpose (1:3b-4)

Why did Luke expend all of this physical, mental, and spiritual energy to write his account of the life of Jesus? He does it for a friend, "most excellent Theophilus, that thou mightest know the certainty of those things, wherein thou hast been instructed."

Who was Theophilus? The term "most excellent" may mean that he was some high official (cf. Acts 23:26; 24:3). It has been suggested that he lived in Antioch, but this is pure conjecture. Of one thing we can be certain. His name means "God-lover," or "God-beloved." Evidently he was a Gentile, and most likely a Christian.

What relation did he have to Luke? Quite often ancient physicians were freed slaves. So someone suggests that Luke had once been a slave of Theophilus, but who had been freed by him. Again, this is in the realm of conjecture. Most likely Theophilus was the patron of Luke. Many ancient writers were supported in their work by men of wealth. It is entirely possible, therefore, that Luke's patron was Theophilus. This would explain why Luke mentions him in the introduction to both his Gospel and the Acts (1:1).

Luke says that his purpose in writing his Gospel was that Theophilus "mightest know the certainty of those things, wherein thou hast been instructed." The word "know" translates a Greek verb which means to have full knowledge. And he must know them with certainty. "Certainty" means without tottering or falling. "The things" mean literally "the words." Theophilus had been "instructed" orally, as the word implies. As a young Christian he had received fragmentary information about the life of Jesus. He had believed in that which he knew. But Luke proposed to give to him a full-knowledge account of Jesus' life and ministry. Plummer notes that "Theophilus shall know that the faith which he has embraced has an impregnable historical foundation." And this Gospel stands as a monument to Luke's successful achievement of his purpose.

However, the Holy Spirit was working through Luke to accomplish more than he knew. Because that which he did for Theophilus he has done for countless multitudes through the centuries who love the Lord Jesus Christ in sincerity.

The Gospel of Luke was written for just such an age as the present one. It is an age which bows before the altar of science. It is one which is iconoclastic in nature. Nothing to it is sacred within itself. Only that which can stand the test of careful criticism and analysis can abide.

The fires of criticism have burned about the whole of the Bible. Yet it has stood the test. And central in this test has been the Gospel of Luke. It is really no wonder that this Gospel stands triumphant in the field of battle. It has stood the stern test of scientific analysis where science is qualified to speak. And where it cannot speak with authority this Gospel itself can. For before this scientist-historian allowed any single item to be honored with a place in his account, he first subjected it to the most critical analysis in every detail. This man of science who possessed a keen appreciation for history surrendered his personality and powers to the Holy Spirit. The result is not only the world's most beautiful story, but one which gives to us the full knowledge of "the certainty of those things, wherein thou hast been instructed."

And for this dual reason we are indebted to Luke beyond measure, a debt which the faithful can never repay.

II
The Fulness of the Time

Luke 1:5-25

The Annunciation to Zacharias

Since Luke's dedication was penned after he had finished the body of his Gospel, we are now at the point where he first began to write his narrative. And in this first event, the announcement by the angel of the forthcoming birth of the forerunner of Jesus, he shows his care for history and the detailed accuracy of his work. It is well to note that whereas the first four verses are written in beautiful literary *Koine* Greek, from verse 5 through Chapter 2 we find the most Hebraistic passage in Luke's writings. This passage is unique to Luke's Gospel. Evidently he relied upon some unknown written source or else he had received it orally from a person or persons who were familiar with the events involved. Was it from the virgin Mary herself?

At any rate these stories are complete within themselves. And an examination of the first one reveals a setting, a message, and a fulfilment.

The Setting (1:5-10)

Luke begins by dating the event. It was "in the days of Herod, the king of Judaea" (v. 5a).

Herod was not a Jew but an Idumean. Thus he was a descendant of Esau. Therefore, he was not a rightful king over the Jews. He received his throne by appointment from the Roman Senate, through the influence of Anthony and Octavius (later called Augustus). This occurred in 37 B.C., and he reigned until his death in 4 B.C. The occasion under consideration happened sometime prior to his death, perhaps in 7 or 6 B.C.

In many respects Herod was an able man. But the manner in which he received his throne, plus his overly suspicious nature, turned him into a crafty and cruel tyrant. His reign was bathed in blood, including that of many members of his own family.

It was a gloomy time for the nation which had been chosen of God to be a priest-nation to the rest of the world. In addition to her woeful political condition, the spiritual life of the Jews had lost its vitality. For the most part it was little more than dry ceremony and rote ritual. But it is all the more significant that in such a condition and time God chose to act in history for the accomplishment of His eternal redemptive purpose. The *fulness of the time* had come; God was ready to act. And despite the existing conditions there were still those faithful ones who were to be the instruments of His will.

There was "a certain priest named Zacharias, of the course of Abia: and his wife was of the daughters of Aaron, and her name was Elisabeth" (v. 5b). Their very names are significant. For Zacharias means "Jehovah remembers," and Elisabeth means "the oath of God." God had solemnly vowed to send the Redeemer, and He remembered His oath.

As a male descendant of Aaron Zacharias automatically became a priest. Hebrew law required that a priest must marry only a Hebrew. But Zacharias had done even more. He had married a daughter of Aaron, or the daughter of another priest. It was as if he were a preacher married to a preacher's daughter.

In the Jewish priestly system there were twenty-four courses of priests, that of Abia (Abijah) being the eighth. Barclay notes that there were approximately twenty thousand priests. This would mean that there were about nine hundred in each course. Each of these courses served for a week twice a year, with various duties allotted to each priest. On the Sabbaths the entire course served. During the great feasts, Passover, Pentecost, and Tabernacles, all twenty-four courses served.

Now Zacharias and Elisabeth were godly people, "walking in all the commandments and ordinances of the Lord blameless" (v. 6). They have been called the "noblest product of Old Testament education." And yet, according to Jewish standards, they were a strange couple. For though they were advanced in years they were childless (v. 7). Such a condition was regarded by the Jews as a curse from God. It is no wonder, therefore, that this was the cause of great sorrow for this righteous couple. And it had also been the object of consistent prayer on their part. But in His wisdom God had not granted their petition, proposing to give to them a blessing far greater than that for which they asked. He did not say "No" or "Yes," but "Wait." And they had waited until "they both were now well stricken in years" (v. 7).

The time came for Zacharias' course to minister in the temple (v. 8). The greatest privilege granted to an ordinary priest was that of burning incense on the altar in the Holy Place before the Holy of Holies. Since this privilege was granted by lots, and since there were so many priests, this opportunity came to few—and that once in a lifetime. It was the good fortune of Zacharias to be chosen for this privilege on this occasion. How excited he must have been as he prepared to do so. "He went into the temple of the Lord" (v. 9). The word "temple" is *naos*. This refers not to the broad temple area *(hieros)* composed of many courts (courts of the Gentiles, of the women, of Israel, of the priests), but to the Holy of Holies in which God was said to dwell with His people. Only the high priest was permitted to enter this most sacred place, and that once each year on the Day of Atonement. So Zacharias was not in the actual Holy of Holies, but in the Holy Place before it.

This was a most solemn occasion. The priests ascended the steps leading to the Holy Place. There they spread coals on the golden altar, arranged the incense, and departed, leaving Zacharias alone before God to await the signal to burn the incense. And all the while, outside in the court of Israel the people waited, bowed down in prayer (v. 10). They were expecting. But they were hardly prepared for what was to take place.

The Message (1:11-22)

Yes, this was the greatest day in Zacharias' life. But it was to be far greater than he imagined. Because as he waited for the signal to burn the incense, suddenly "there appeared unto him an angel of the Lord [Gabriel, v. 19] standing on the right side of the altar of incense" (v. 11). Quite naturally Zacharias "was troubled, and fear fell upon him" (v. 12). There are those who deny the existence of angels. But there is no valid reason for doing so. We know far too little about the spiritual realm to be dogmatic at this point. And Luke, the scientist, was convinced of their reality, a phenomenon which is recognized throughout the Scriptures. We can be certain that Zacharias did not question the reality of this heavenly being.

And then, seeing Zacharias' fear, the angel spoke to him. "Fear not" or "stop being afraid" (v. 13). This was followed by a message of assurance. "For thy prayer is heard." To what prayer did he refer? The people were praying, and Zacharias was praying. But there was a difference as is shown by a different Greek word for the prayer of Zacharias. "The people were praying" (v. 10, *proseuchomenon*). But Zacharias' prayer was a *deēsis*. Trench holds that he was praying for a son, despite advanced age. That this is true is seen in the following words. "And thy wife Elisabeth shall bear thee a son, and thou shalt call his name John" (v. 13). "John" means "God is gracious." This name actually points in two directions: backward to the goodness of God in removing the stigma from this godly couple, and forward toward the purpose for which he was given. For he was to herald the coming of Him who is the gift of God's grace.

Quite naturally there would be great joy at his birth, as was always true when a son was born to a Jew (v. 14). But that joy would know no bounds when it was known for what purpose he was born. He was to be great in God's sight. Because of his divine mission he was to be a Nazirite (Num. 6:3), abstaining from all intoxicating drink. And he would be filled with the Holy Spirit, "even from [*ek,* out of] his mother's womb" (v. 15; cf. v. 41). Because of his ministry many should be turned to the Lord (v. 16).

And then the greatest of all of the angel's words. "And he shall go before him in the spirit and power of Elias, to turn the hearts of the fathers to the children, and the disobedient to the wisdom of the just; to make ready a people prepared for the Lord" (v. 17).

What is so significant about these words? They hark back to the closing verses of Malachi (4:5-6). It had been four hundred years since there had been a revelation from Jehovah to Israel. The Old Testament closes with this promise of Elijah "before the coming of the great and dreadful day of the Lord" (Mal. 4:5). The coming of the Messiah would be both "great" and "dreadful," depending upon how one related himself to Him. The Jews interpreted this to mean that before the Messiah came Elijah must appear (cf. Matt. 17:10-12). John the Baptist denied that he was Elijah the person (John 1:21), but Jesus identified him as one who came in the spirit and power of Elijah. So, in effect, the angel said to Zacharias that his promised son would fulfil the prophecy of Malachi. Thus the story of God's redemptive purpose did not end with Malachi. After a four-century interlude of silence God speaks again. And the story is a continuation of that which He had already spoken. God is not slack concerning His promises.

This was too much for Zacharias. The answer to his prayer was more than he had asked. So immediately his faith gave way to reason. "Whereby shall I know this? for I am an old man, and my wife is well stricken in years" (v. 18). He reckoned with the natural laws of genetics rather than with the divine power of God. And it has ever been thus when men look at God through their problems rather than to view their problems through the power of God.

There was a rebuke in the reply of the angel. "I am Gabriel, that stand in the presence of God; and am sent to speak unto thee, and to shew thee these glad tidings" (v. 19). Gabriel is one of two angels in the Bible who is mentioned by name (cf. Dan. 8:16; 9:21), the other being Michael (cf. Jude 9; Rev. 12:7). He had a gospel from the very presence of God, yea, from God Himself. And did Zacharias dare to question it? Alas, how many have done so to the greatest gospel of all! And to their own infinite hurt.

But Zacharias had asked for a sign that this "gospel" was true. And he received one. He would be unable to speak until God's promise should be fulfilled. And it would be fulfilled in due season (v. 20).

All the while the people waited without, wondering why Zacharias was so long in the Holy Place (v. 21). It was customary for the priest to come forth after burning the incense to pronounce a blessing on the people. When he appeared before them unable to speak they recognized that he had seen a vision (v. 22). A vision indeed! The blessing from the priest was bestowed in silence, as he beckoned back and forth to them, speechless (v. 23). He silently pronounced the traditional blessing upon them. But the greater blessing was yet to come.

The Fulfilment (1:23-25)

Zacharias completed his week of priestly ministry, and then returned to his home (v. 23). Shortly thereafter his wife Elisabeth conceived (v. 24). While it is not stated, in all likelihood her husband told her about his experience. The conception took place by natural means, but, even so, it was supranatural in nature. For both Zacharias and Elisabeth were beyond the age when they might expect to become parents. Of interest is the fact that the word rendered "conceived" *(sunelaben)* appears only sixteen times in the New Testament, eleven of these being by Luke. And only he uses this word in the sense of conceiving offspring (1:24, 31, 36; 2:21; cf. James 1:15). Plummer notes this usage as being common in medical writings and in Aristotle.

Luke adds that Elisabeth "hid herself five months" (v. 24). The word "hid" means that she did so *completely*. Why she did so is not stated. It may have been because of her pregnancy at such an age. Or it could have been due to the sanctity of the entire experience. Even though she was visited by her cousin Mary in her sixth month, there is no evidence that she let her condition be known publicly until the birth of her son (cf. v. 58).

However, it was a blessed experience for Elisabeth and her husband. For in her old age the Lord had removed her "reproach among men" (v. 25). This suggests her own longing for a child, and her sense of failure in not giving to her husband an heir. This reproach also was related to the Messianic hope. For every Jewish mother secretly hoped that her son might be the Messiah. So there was joy, though perhaps a secret joy, in the home of this aged couple. For God not only had answered their prayers; He had done so in a marvelous fashion and for His own divine purpose.

Though it may seem at times that God is silent and conditions are hopeless, He is ever at work to accomplish His own will. And there are always ready at hand those who are the instruments of His will. This was true in the first century. It is true today.

Luke 1:26-38

The Annunciation to the Virgin Mary

With one stroke of his pen Luke shifts the scene in both time and place. It was six months after Gabriel had appeared to Zacharias. This time he was sent from God to the little city of Nazareth in Galilee (v. 26). And the message which he bore was even more wonderful than that which he delivered to the priest in the temple.

Thus we are introduced to Luke's account of the virgin conception of Jesus. The fact that Luke was a physician lends importance to the story beyond measure. Whence came the information which it contains? Obviously it could have come only from Mary herself, either directly or indirectly, to Luke. It is entirely possible, and probable, that Mary was still living in Palestine during Paul's Caesarean imprisonment. If so, Luke could have visited with her. To whom would a woman speak more frankly and in greater detail about the birth of her child than to a physician? Someone has suggested that before writing out a birth certificate the doctor always talks with the mother of the child. So we may regard this account of Luke as the beloved physician's birth certificate of the Son of God.

Everything in Luke's training would lead him to doubt such a story. To record it would subject him to criticism by his colleagues. Yet having traced all things accurately, Luke was so convinced of its truth that he boldly and beautifully penned the most complete account of the virgin birth of Jesus on record. His record is the greatest proof of the virgin birth both historically and scientifically.

Turning to the story itself we note the personalities, the pronouncement, the problem, and the proof.

The Personalities (1:27)

Apart from Gabriel two personalities are involved in the story: Mary, and Joseph to whom she was betrothed. Both were of the lineage of David (cf. 2:4). But the significant point in the story is the fact that Mary was a "virgin" (v. 27). In Matthew 1:19

Joseph is called "her husband." These two facts may seem strange in our modern way of thinking. But to the ancient Jews the language points up no problem.

To them a marriage consisted of three phases: engagement, betrothal, and marriage. The engagement usually took place between children, and was arranged by the parents or by a professional matchmaker. When the engaged couple approached marriageable age, the girl could reject the arrangement. But once she consented the betrothal took place and was binding upon her. Usually a year intervened between betrothal and marriage. During this period the bride lived with either her parents or her friends. However, her property was vested in her husband. Unfaithfulness on her part in this interval was punishable by death (cf. Deut. 22:23). At the end of the year the marriage was completed, and the couple lived as man and wife. However, in the case of Mary and Joseph, Matthew is careful to point out that, though they lived together, they did not enter into sexual union until after the birth of Jesus (Matt. 1:24-25). Thereafter, they entered into normal relationships, and to this marriage were born four sons and at least two daughters (Matt. 13:55-56).[1]

The Pronouncement (1:28-33)

It was during the period between betrothal and marriage that the angel appeared to Mary. In all probability she was in her parents' home, perhaps busy at some household task. "And the angel came in unto her" (v. 28). The words "came in" render an aorist participle *(eiselthōn),* suggesting a sudden appearance.

Simultaneous with Gabriel's appearance was his greeting, "Hail, highly favored, the Lord is with thee" (v. 28). The oldest manuscripts do not contain "blessed art thou among women," but these words are genuine in verse 42. In the Greek "Hail, highly favored" forms an alliteration *(chaire kecharitōmenē).* The latter word is a perfect passive participle meaning that she had been fully endowed with grace from God. In the Vulgate the Latin words are *gratia plena.* One recognizes this as the first phrase in the *Ave Maria,* "Hail, Mary, full of grace." Plummer points out

---

[1] Some holding to the perpetual virginity of Mary insist that these were either Jesus' cousins or else children of Joseph by a previous marriage. But it is more in keeping with the evidence to consider them as half-brothers and half-sisters of Jesus.

the indefinite nature of *gratia plena.* It is wrong if it means "full of grace, *which thou hast to bestow.*" It is right if it means "full of grace, *which thou hast received.*" Mary is not the dispenser of divine grace. She herself had received grace in that she had been chosen to be the mother of Him through whom God's grace is extended to lost men. There is here no basis whatsoever for the system of Mariolatry.

Naturally Mary was both upset and puzzled. She was not thrown into hysteria. Rather she "kept on casting about," or "reckoning up different reasons" *(dielogizeto)* as to this salutation (v. 29). She knew that it had significance, but she did not comprehend it. Seeing this the angel quieted her fears by saying, "Stop being afraid, Mary, for you have found favor [grace] alongside God" (v. 30).

And what was this favor? "Thou shalt conceive in thy womb, and bring forth a son, and thou shalt call his name JESUS" (v. 31). Here again is the virgin birth (cf. Isa. 7:14). In Matthew 1:21 the name "Jesus" is explained, "For he shall save his people from their sins." But to Mary Gabriel simply mentioned the name. However, the name itself was self-explanatory. "Jesus" is the Greek equivalent of the Hebrew "Joshua," or "Yeshua," meaning "Jehovah is salvation."

But the emphasis in Luke is upon Jesus' Kingship. "He shall be great, and shall be called the Son of the Highest" or "Son of the Most High" (v. 32). Here then is expressed the close relationship between the Son and God Himself. Not only shall He be the Son of God, but He *shall be called* or recognized as such. Furthermore as a King on David's throne He shall reign over the house of Jacob in a perpetual kingdom (v. 33). David had been promised an everlasting kingdom. And that promise is to be fulfilled, not in a perpetual political kingdom, but in the spiritual reign of the Christ.

What strange and yet what blessed words these were to Mary. Every Jewish mother, as she nursed her infant son, hoped and prayed that he might be the Messiah. But Mary, a betrothed virgin, was the highly favored one chosen of God to bear His Son.

The Problem (1:34-35)

With what simplicity Luke tells of the greatest birth in history! Mary appears not as the *Queen of Heaven,* but as a simple, wondering peasant girl caught up in the eternal divine purpose of God. That she recognized the problem involved in the words of the angel is quite clear. "How shall this be, seeing I know not a man?" (v. 34).

Some see in this question the fact that Mary had taken or was about to take the vow of perpetual virginity. If "know" were an aorist tense (know at any time) such might be the possible meaning. But its form as an imperfect tense makes this impossible. It simply means that up to this time she had not had sexual relations with any man. Not merely her betrothed husband. The absence of the definite article before "men" *(andra)* means that it refers to *any* man. Furthermore, the fact that she had agreed to the betrothal shows that she had consented to enter into a normal marital relationship with her husband after the completion of the marriage.

Neither should Mary's question be construed as doubt concerning the promised motherhood. It was the natural question as to *how* it should be accomplished. Here is a chaste maiden, knowing of her purity and intending to remain so until after marriage, asking for more light on the subject.

Certainly her problem was a real one. Viewing it purely through natural biological processes, there are those who categorically deny the possibility of a virgin birth. Mary does not make such a denial. Neither does the physician, Luke. But without dodging the problem, he shows us that the first question as to the possibility of a virgin birth came not from the modern critics of a scientific age but from Mary herself.

And Luke records this question with a purpose. For it introduces the response made by Gabriel as to the *how* of the virgin birth. "The Holy Ghost [Spirit] shall come upon thee, and the power of the Highest shall overshadow thee: therefore also that holy thing which shall be born of thee shall be called the Son of God" (v. 35). The figure of *overshadowing* suggests the Shekinah glory or the hovering presence of God (cf. Luke 9:34). So the conception of Jesus took place through the direct action of the Holy Spirit of God in the womb of Mary. Matthew Arnold refused to accept the virgin birth of Jesus because it involved a miracle, something which he denied. Of course it involved a miracle! But to say that miracles are impossible is to walk boldly and brashly where angels fear to tread. A miracle may be regarded as an act of God above law as men understand it, but by laws which are known to God, and which He performs in keeping with His benevolent purposes. Science knows far too little even about the laws of natural birth to state categorically what God can or cannot do.

A modern author states that the "Church does not insist that we believe in this doctrine." But if one accepts Luke 1:26-38 and Matthew 1:18-25 at face value, the Bible does insist that we believe in this doctrine. Matthew 1:16 takes pains to point out that Jesus was born of Mary apart from her husband Joseph. Argument is made that the remainder of the New Testament does not teach the virgin birth. This is to argue from silence, the weakest of all arguments. Certainly John 1:14 and Galatians 4:4 imply it. And *the rest of the New Testament* certainly presents Jesus as the divine Son of God.

It is pointed out that there are other New Testament references which speak of Joseph as Jesus' father. Those who were ignorant of the true facts as to Jesus' birth did so (cf. Matt. 13:55; John 6:42). His enemies even accused Jesus of being born out of wedlock (John 8:41), a fact which in a negative way attests to the truth that Mary was with child before she was married to Joseph. More to the point of the critics, Mary herself referred to Joseph as Jesus' "father" (Luke 2:48). But would not this statement be true even if Joseph were the foster-father or even the stepfather for that matter, the latter of which was not true, of course. But the former was true.

The question is as to whether we shall interpret Matthew 1:18-25 and Luke 1:26-38 by these other occasional verses, or shall we interpret the latter in the light of the former? The weight of an unbiased scholarly approach is definitely on the side of the latter method. If we let the Bible say what it says, then the virgin birth rests upon the two firm foundations of both Matthew and Luke. There is nothing elsewhere in the New Testament which successfully or reasonably contradicts them. And the fact that the record of Luke, the scientist-physician-historian, must rest upon an account from Mary herself stands as a mighty bulwark which the onslaughts of a negative criticism have never been able to breach. Yes, Jesus was/is the virgin-born Son of God!

The Proof (1:36-38)

Mary did not ask for proof, but she received it nevertheless. And that proof was that her kinswoman, Elisabeth, had conceived in her old age (v. 36). Already she was in her sixth month of pregnancy. This within itself was a supranatural phenomenon. If God could accomplish this, why not a virgin conception? It is of interest to note that those who question the manner of Jesus' birth do not bother with that of John the Baptist or of Isaac. Is not the basic problem, then, more related to Jesus' deity than to His birth? On the other hand, if Jesus is the unique Son of God how other than by a virgin birth could He have been born? It requires less faith to believe in the virgin birth than to believe that a naturally born man could be God of very God. Either He was virgin born with God only as His Father, or else He was merely a naturally born man possessing superior qualities and nothing more. The verdict of history rejects the latter position and attests to the former. *The very foundation of the Christian faith rests upon the virgin birth of Jesus!*

Finally Gabriel drove the final nail in the structure of the virgin birth. "For with God nothing shall be impossible" (v. 37). Literally, "For not shall be impossible alongside God any word." God had spoken. And what God said, He could perform, whether it be with Elisabeth or with Mary. Therefore, we are not to gauge the virgin birth of Jesus by man's power or understanding. When seen in the light of God's ability and comprehension, the virgin birth is not only possible but probable. And in view of God's redemptive purpose it is a necessity. God was able to do what He must do in order to provide redemption for man. That redemption must be through One who was sinless in both nature and practice. Only He who was born of the seed of woman, apart from the nature of Adam, could qualify (cf. Gen. 3:15; Rom. 5:14-19). And that One was the virgin-born, unique Son of God, Jesus, who is "Jehovah is salvation."

Mary did not need the proof of sight. She accepted the promise and assurance by faith. "And Mary said, Behold the handmaid of the Lord; be it unto me according to thy word. And the angel departed from her" (v. 38). The word for "handmaid" is *doulē,* a female slave. So as Paul later would delight to call himself a *bond slave* of Jesus Christ, Mary submitted herself to God as His *bond slave* through whom the Saviour would enter the world as a flesh and blood man (cf. John 1:14). She submitted knowing full well the ordeal which awaited her. She placed her social position, her marriage, even her very life in jeopardy for the sake of God's will.

Did Mary reveal her story to her parents? Probably not. For who would have believed it? Certainly she did not tell Joseph (cf. Matt. 1:18-23). But in time he would know her condition. We may well imagine that from him she expected the worst.

But despite that fact she left it all in the hands of Him whose slave she was. Even though the angel departed from her, God did not forsake her. He guarded His chosen vessel to the end for which she was chosen. And in time her greatest shame became her greatest glory.

The submission of Mary is both a challenge and a promise to all who would do the will of God.

Luke 1:39-56

The Blessedness of Motherhood

We are not surprised at the reaction of Mary following the angel's departure. Immediately she "arose" *(anastāsa,* aorist participle of *anistēmi)* and went to visit Elisabeth (v. 39) who lived in a village in the hill country of Judea, perhaps south of Jerusalem. Since this involved a journey of approximately three days, she evidently made the necessary preparations for travel. But she did so without delay. One might say that she went with the purpose of ascertaining the truth of the angel's words. But in the light of her previous submission, this is hardly likely. Was it not rather prompted by a desire to share her joy with another of like happiness? Who better than Elisabeth could understand Mary's experience? It was the kinship of like minds and hearts.

Arriving in the village, Mary entered "the house of Zacharias." But she "saluted Elisabeth" (v. 40). Perhaps Zacharias was not at home upon her arrival. By a divine providence these two women were alone to rejoice in the blessedness of their strange motherhood.

It would be immediately apparent to Mary that the angel's words as to Elisabeth's condition were true. And when Elisabeth's baby leaped in her womb in exultation she was filled with the Holy Spirit so that she also understood Mary's condition (v. 41). The intended forerunner responded to the prenatal presence of Him whom he should proclaim. Thus there began a season of heavenly joy as is seen in the Beatitude of Elisabeth, the Magnificat of Mary, and the fellowship of mutual purpose.

The Beatitude of Elisabeth (1:42-45)

It is of interest to note that Luke alone records the presence of music in connection with the incarnation of the Son of God. Some insist that Luke was an artist. If so, we see that side of his nature expressing itself as he includes in his Gospel the Beatitude of Elisabeth (1:42-45), the Magnificat of Mary (1:46-55), the Benedictus of Zacharias (1:68-79), the Gloria of the angels (2:13-14), and the Nunc Dimittis of Simeon (2:29-32).

It is clear, therefore, that the song of Elisabeth is the first Christian hymn although it is thoroughly Hebraic in nature. G. Campbell Morgan notes that "Elisabeth, the daughter of the old economy, was the first singer of the new." This daughter of a priest who was married to a priest of the old order sang the first song in praise of Him who is the High Priest of the new order that was bursting in full glory upon the world.

In beautiful Hebrew parallelism and in ecstasy Elisabeth utters the first Beatitude of the New Testament. "Blessed art thou among women, and blessed is the fruit of thy womb" (v. 42). In Hebrew thought this twofold "blessed" is equal to the superlative. "Among women thou art the most blessed, and most blessed is the fruit of thy womb." Surely Mary was the most blessed of all women because she alone was chosen to bear the Son of God. So while in one sense this song praises Mary, it does not do so as a person only. It is because she is to bear the Saviour. That, and nothing more. Mary received this blessedness because she believed the promise made through the angel (v. 45). Thereby she became "the mother of my Lord" (v. 43). Even though Elisabeth wondered why so blessed a person should visit her, yet in the Holy Spirit she assured Mary that the promise of the Lord would be fulfilled through her (v. 45).

The Magnificat of Mary (1:46-55)

The word "magnificat" is the Latin for "doth magnify" (v. 46). Thus Mary began her hymn of praise to God. It is fashioned according to the psalms. And as one reads it, it reminds one of the song of Hannah (I Sam. 2:1-10), though it is much more exalted in its moral and spiritual essence. Every phrase of it is filled with Old Testament thought, showing Mary's thorough familiarity with the Scriptures of her people. Plummer notes that "this beautiful lyric is neither a reply to Elisabeth nor an address to God. It is rather a meditation; an expression of personal emotions and experiences. It is more calm and majestic than the utterance of Elisabeth."[1] It may be called a controlled expression of greatest exultation. This utterance by Mary has been called

[1] *The International Critical Commentary,* Clark, Edinburgh, 1960, "Luke," *in loco.*

"the most magnificent cry of Joy that has ever issued from a human breast."

An analysis of the Magnificat divides it naturally into two sections: the first relates to Mary's own experience (vv. 46-49a); the second is a recounting of God's holiness, mercy, greatness, and faithfulness (vv. 49b-55).

First, Mary rejoices in her own experience. "My soul doth magnify the Lord, and my spirit hath rejoiced in God my Saviour" (vv. 46-47). "Soul" *(psuchē)* means her mind in its fulness. "Spirit" *(pneuma)* refers to the innermost being of her personality. In her mind Mary magnifies or esteems God greatly. And all the while her inner being exults in God her Saviour who is also the Saviour of others. She is completely possessed by a holy joy.

And well she might be. For God had chosen one of low estate, His slave, to be called blessed by all generations to come (v. 48). The bride of a peasant carpenter exalted to be the mother of the Son of God! She was blessed indeed. And generations of Christians yet unborn would recognize the great thing which God had done to and through her.

There is no justification in this statement for adoration or worship of Mary. But it does point up the esteem due to this lowly woman who was so highly honored of God. If Roman Catholics have erred in the former, the rest of us have done so in the latter. Jesus honored His mother, and so should we. Not as the Queen of Heaven, the Mother of God, or the Mediatrix of divine grace, but as the human means through whom the Eternal became flesh that He might fully reveal His truth and bestow His grace upon all, including Mary, who would receive it in faith (v. 49a).

Second, Mary declares God's holiness, mercy, greatness, and faithfulness (vv. 49b-55).

"Holy is his name" (v. 49b). There is no direct connection between these words and those which precede or follow. They are an exclamation ascribing holiness to the name of God, and are suggestive of the phrase in the Model Prayer, "Hallowed be thy name" (Matt. 6:9). The verb form *Hagiasthēto to onoma sou* becomes an adjective *Hagion to onoma autou.* Or it could be an adjectival noun, "Holy One is his name." In any case Mary stood in reverent awe before Him who had done so much for her.

From the vantage point of her own state of exultation Mary reviewed the long history of God's dealings with men. Mercifully He had dealt with those who reverenced Him (v. 50). The strength of His arm had been bared toward all who opposed Him (v. 51). With a series of parallels she declared how God had put down the mighty potentates, and lifted up those whom they oppressed (v. 52). He had filled the hungry both physically and spiritually, but had sent away empty those whose material riches left them with no sense of need for God (v. 53). In all ages He had succored Israel as He remembered His promises of mercy (v. 54). This He had done in keeping with the promise made "to Abraham, and *to his seed for ever*" (v. 55, author's italics). This was not a promise based upon the accident of physical birth. Abraham's "seed" are a seed of faith. And the One who then resided in Mary's womb was the true seed (cf. Gal. 3:16). Through Him would the promise of redemption made to Abraham be fully realized.

The Fellowship of Mutual Purpose (1:56)

"And Mary abode with her about three months, and returned to her own house" (v. 56).

The ecstatic joy of their meeting upon Mary's arrival at the home of Elisabeth mellowed into the rich fellowship between these two women of divine purpose. What a blessed experience it must have been for them as for three months they shared spiritual communion.

These three months brought Elisabeth to the time of her delivery. Did Mary remain until after the birth of John the Baptist? It is strange to think that she would leave just prior to it. To be sure Luke records her return to Nazareth immediately before he records John's birth. It could be that he merely completed one story before beginning another. Some of the early church fathers (e.g., Origen, Ambrose, Bede) believed that Mary remained until after John's birth. Plummer suggests that "cousins" in Luke 1:58 could include Mary.

Nevertheless we do know that Mary returned to her home. Perhaps it was at this point that Joseph learned of her condition. Six months of silence settle down about Mary. But they were six months of rich fellowship with God. And from Matthew we know that following God's revelation to Joseph he stood between her and the barbs of village gossip. Together they shared God's secret – and waited. Waited until in God's providence they should journey toward their rendezvous in Bethlehem.

Luke 1:57-80

The Birth of John the Baptist

Life must have moved slowly in the little village where Zacharias and Elisabeth lived. But there was excitement indeed when their promised son was born. This is quite evident as seen in the birth, the naming, the Benedictus, and the childhood of John.

The Birth (1:57-58)

In simple narrative form Luke records the birth of John the Baptist. Elisabeth's time to be delivered having arrived, she brought forth a son (v. 57). When word went out that he was born "her neighbors [dwellers about, *perioikoi*] and her cousins" came to rejoice with her. Bruce notes that the order of the words "neighbors . . . cousins" suggests that they came in that order. The former lived near her home, but the latter perhaps had to come from a distance. At any rate, "they rejoiced with her." "Rejoiced" is an imperfect form. This could mean that they were rejoicing, kept on rejoicing, or rejoiced from time to time as various ones came and went. Any or all of these could be and perhaps were true. This is a beautiful picture of simple Israelite life.

The Naming (1:59-66)

In keeping with the law the baby was circumcised on the eighth day (v. 59). This rite might be performed anywhere and by any Jew, even by a woman (Exod. 4:25). Note that "they came to circumcise the child." This could mean that the family, relatives, and friends came to the place where it was to be done, or the ones who were to circumcise him came to the home.

It was customary to name the child at this time. This probably dated back to the change of Abram's name to Abraham on the occasion of his circumcision. Among the Jews, as among many other people, it was a common practice to name a boy after his father. So the relatives and friends probably figured that this first-born son would be called Zacharias. "They called him Zacharias, after the name of his father." "Called" is an imperfect tense. It could simply denote repeated action, "they kept calling." Or it could be what is called a conative imperfect, meaning that they wished to call him Zacharias but their wish was frustrated. In the light of that which followed, the latter probably is true here.

For his mother said, "Not so; but he shall be called John" (v. 60). Elisabeth used a strong negative *(ouchi)*. Zacharias doubtless had told her of the angel's words (v. 13). And since her husband could not speak, she did so for him. There came the protest that none of their kindred bore that name (v. 61). So they made signs to Zacharias as to his wishes (v. 62). Was he deaf as well as dumb? By signs he asked for a writing tablet, probably one covered with wax. And on it he wrote, "His name is John" (v. 63). Not "shall be," but "is." God had said it, and that was enough. The people "marvelled" at this, probably meaning that they wondered if there were not some reason back of this about which they did not know. If Zacharias were deaf he had not heard his wife's words. Yet they agreed as to the name.

But the people were in for a greater marvel. For "immediately" Zacharias' mouth "was opened" (v. 64, aorist). The aorist tense adds to the sense of immediacy. His tongue was loosed as God removed the sign given when Zacharias had doubted the angel's word. His first utterance was to praise God, not primarily for his speech but because God had fulfilled His promise.

The neighbors were seized with reverential awe as they sensed the divine element in all of this (v. 65). This grand event became the topic of conversation in the hill country of Judea. And all who heard wondered as to the manner of child John was (v. 66). Truly, "the hand of the Lord was with him!"

The Benedictus (1:67-79)

Suddenly Zacharias was filled with the Holy Spirit, and he prophesied concerning the great event which had just taken place (v. 67). That which follows is called The Benedictus, the name taken from the word "blessed" (v. 68). It is also called the Song of Zacharias. Some hold that this is the recorded utterance of praise mentioned in verse 64. Plummer notes that as the Magnificat of Mary (vv. 46-55) was modelled on the psalms, so the Benedictus was modelled on the prophecies. It has been called "the last prophecy of the Old Dispensation and the first in the New." Mary's song is regal, and Zacharias' is sacerdotal. And Plummer adds that the former is as fitting for the daughter of David as the latter is for the son of Aaron.

"Blessed be the Lord God of Israel" (v. 68). The word for "blessed" *(eulogētos)* is always used in the New Testament with reference to God, never to man. And why does he bless God? Because once again He has visited His people. And this time for the purpose of redemption. The word for "redeemed" carries a basic political connotation, but it also has moral and spiritual overtones. That Zacharias was thinking of the political aspect is seen in verses 71-75. Even here, however, the moral and spiritual element is present (v. 75).

This redemption is to be provided through one raised up from the house of David (v. 69). This is a reference to Jesus, not John. So Zacharias was familiar with Mary's experience also. Thus God is fulfilling His promise made to Abraham (vv. 73-75; cf. Gen. 22:16-18). This promise had been heralded by the prophets "which have been since the world began" (vv. 70-72). Literally, "from of old."

Then Zacharias addressed his infant son directly, as he gave a forecast of his life. "And thou, child, shalt be called the prophet of the Highest" (v. 76). Jesus later called John a prophet and more than a prophet. John is to be the Forerunner of the Christ (vv. 76-77). The Christ, like the rising sun, will visit His people. His mission will be "to give light to [shine upon] them that sit in darkness and in the shadow of death, to guide our feet into the way of peace" (v. 79). He did not say that He would immediately remove darkness and the shadow of death completely. For they still remain in the world. But in His mission they will be conquered, and ultimately His victory over them will be complete. In the meantime He will guide those who come to Him into the way of peace.

The Childhood of John (1:80)

Luke closes this beautiful story with a summary statement which extends until John began his public ministry. He simply says that the child "kept on growing, and kept on waxing strong in spirit" (imperfects). This is a picturesque statement of the growth in body and in spirit of this child of destiny.

After the death of his aged parents John lived in the desert places. Luke does not say where. It is enough to note that he lived a solitary life. Nothing is said of him, as of Jesus, that he grew "in favor with man" (Luke 2:52). Evidently he had little contact with other fellow beings. Some would hold that John probably was raised by the Essenes, an ascetic Jewish group which lived just west of the Dead Sea. However, there is no real evidence that this was true. Other than his ascetic life and his opposition to the *status quo* of Judaism there is no resemblance between them. Indeed, in many ways they were quite the opposite of one another. Plummer notes two vital differences: John preached the Kingdom of God; the Essenes preached isolation. The latter abandoned society; the former sought to reform it.

But at this point the curtain of silence drops on John "till the day of his showing unto Israel" (v. 80).

Luke 2:1-39

The Birth of Jesus

Almost six months transpired between Chapters 1 and 2. The time for Mary's delivery was drawing near. She lived in Nazareth in Galilee, but prophecy said that Christ should be born in Bethlehem of Judea (Micah 5:2). A decree from the pagan Augustus Caesar himself brought about the fulfilment of this prophecy. So God works even through those who do not recognize His existence to bring to pass His purposes. Thus "it came to pass in those days, that there went out a decree from Caesar Augustus, that all of the world should be taxed [enroled for taxation]" (v. 1). The events connected with the birth of Jesus may be noted as the enrolment; the nativity; the shepherds and the angels; the naming, purification, and presentation; and the praise in the temple.

The Enrolment (2:1-5)

This is one of the focal points concerning the historical accuracy of Luke. If he should be proved in error here, then every statement in his writings would be subject to suspicion. And the adverse critics for many years had a good case against Luke. For no known Roman records made any reference to such an enrolment. It was not until Sir William Ramsay and others began to study the matter that the tide turned in Luke's favor. For instance, it was pointed out by Ramsay that Clement of Alexandria (third century A.D.) made reference to such a system of enrolment, either in the empire as a whole or at least in the province of Syria. And this enrolment would fit exactly the one mentioned in Luke.

But there is greater evidence still. For archaeological records have revealed that the Roman empire did have a system of census enrolments which were taken every fourteen years. Actual census papers have been found in Egypt. These show that enrolments were made in A.D. 90 and at fourteen-year intervals through A.D. 230. Also papers have been discovered for the years A.D. 34 and

62. Indirect references are made to a census in A.D. 20 and 48. In Acts 5:37 Luke refers to a census which would be in A.D. 6. His reference in Luke 2:1, therefore, would be to the one in 8 B.C.

However, a further problem appears in coinciding this first census (8 B.C.) with the usually accepted date of 6-5 B.C. for the birth of Jesus. We know that He was born prior to Herod's death in 4 B.C., probably one or two years preceding it. How, then, may we harmonize the census of 8 B.C. with the date of Jesus' birth? Josephus relates that the one in A.D. 6 caused an incipient rebellion in Judea. The opposition to such an enrolment for taxation by the Jews probably caused Herod to delay the one set for 8 B.C. as long as he could in order to placate his subjects. Ramsay shows that the enrolment in Syria took place in 8-7 B.C. It is understandable, therefore, that it could have been delayed longer in Palestine, say to 6-5 B.C. This would bring it into the accepted time of the birth of Jesus.

A further problem as to Luke's dating centered about his statement "And this taxing was first made when Cyrenius [Quirinius] was governor of Syria" (v. 2). It was known that he was governor in Syria in A.D. 6. So the conclusion was that Luke had erred in his date. But again archaeology came to Luke's rescue. For Ramsay found two inscriptions which show that Quirinius was also governor in Syria in 10-7 B.C. So he was twice governor in Syria. He was occupying this office when Augustus ordered the first enrolment, which is exactly what Luke says.

It has been questioned whether Luke was correct in saying, "And all went to be taxed [enroled for taxation], every one into his own city" (v. 3). Did the Romans take a household census? And why were Joseph and Mary required to go to Bethlehem instead of being enroled in Nazareth? It has been found that in Egypt the Romans did take a household census. But this does not necessarily clear up the point about the journey to Bethlehem. However, the Jews were accustomed to a tribal census. It is likely, therefore, that Herod himself insisted on such a census, something which would be less objectionable to the Jews.

And since Joseph was of the lineage of David it was necessary that he go to Bethlehem of Judea, the city of David (v. 4). There he, together with Mary, was enroled for taxation (v. 5). This implies that she also was a descendant of David. By this time Mary and Joseph were married (cf. Matt. 1:24). Otherwise, she could not have travelled with him.

Also at this time Mary was "great with child" (v. 5). Questions have been raised as to why she would make such a long journey under this condition. Some, denying that she was a descendant of David, insist that the decree did not require this. But there is no valid reason for this position. The Syriac Sinaitic version clearly says that "they were both of the house of David." Even so, it is hardly likely that Joseph would leave her at home at such a time. So despite the hardships involved, she accompanied him to Bethlehem where most likely she also was required to be enroled.

Little did Augustus know that by his decree he was an instrument in the divine will. But God is the God of history. And in the context of history He was working out His eternal purpose of redemption.

The Nativity (2:6-7)

In two short, simple verses Luke tells of the greatest of all births in history. "While they were there" the time of Mary's delivery came (v. 6). Luke does not say at what specific time. We usually think of it as happening the first night after their arrival. Perhaps so, but the record is not clear at that point.

Bethlehem would be unusually crowded at this time. So when Joseph and Mary arrived the inn was full. The "inn" was either a lodging house or a khan, an enclosed place with recesses. At best, it was a poor place to stay. But there was not even room there for them. So it was necessary for them to find shelter in the place where the animals were kept. Justin Martyr said that it was a cave. Modern tourists are shown such a place underneath the Church of the Nativity. Whether or not this is the place, it was somewhere nearby. Due to the time of year the animals were probably out in the fields (cf. 2:8).

It was in this lowly place that the Son of God was born. With only the help of the gnarled hands of a carpenter made tender by love, "she brought forth her first-born son, and wrapped him in swaddling clothes, and laid him in a manger" (v. 7). Evidently Mary had come prepared for the event, as seen in the swaddling clothes or band. The "manger" *(phatnē)* was a feeding trough for animals.

Note that this was her "first-born son." This means that there were other children born to Mary after this. Had Luke believed in the perpetual virginity of Mary he most likely would have used "only-born" *(monogenē)* rather than "first-born" *(prōtotokon)*.

By the time that Luke wrote it was common knowledge that Joseph and Mary had had other children by natural births.

So read the bare facts about the birth of Jesus. But, oh, the romance of it! God tabernacled in the womb of a woman! God wrapped in a swathing band and laid in a common animal-feeding trough! Born not in a palace, a house, or even a khan, but in the place for the animals. Truly, He emptied Himself as the King of heaven; the Lord of the universe submitted to the lowliest of birth conditions.

The mighty Caesar spoke, and the world obeyed. But in the final verdict of history he fades into insignificance. The world of that day paid scant notice to this peasant carpenter and his wife. But time has placed an aura of glory about them exceeding anything the Caesars ever knew. For God, not Caesar, was guiding their footsteps toward the accomplishment of His purpose. And while this birth passed almost unnoticed by the busy, scrambling crowds in the city of David, heaven bent low to herald this event of the ages.

The Shepherds and the Angels (2:8-20)

Hard by Bethlehem is the Shepherds Field. It was here that young David had tended his flocks, protecting them from the lion and the bear (cf. I Sam. 17:34-35). At the time when Jesus was born there were shepherds in this field "keeping watch [night watches] over their flock by night." The plural suggests that they took turns at guarding the sheep. Tradition says that these sheep were intended for the temple sacrifice. At any rate the shepherds were in a night bivouac tending their sheep.

This fact raises the question as to the time of year when Jesus was born. Of course, the traditional time is December 25. However, the fact that the sheep were in the fields suggests a time between March and November, the time when they were kept out in the open. It is hardly likely that Mary and Joseph would have been required to make this long journey in the winter time which is the rainy season in Palestine. Furthermore, would the rulers disrupt the life of the people during the spring farming season, or during the early or the late harvest in early summer or in the fall? It is more likely that this would have been done between the harvests. If so, then sometime in late August or early September might be the time. But, of course, no date can be set for certain. And the celebration of the birth of Jesus is not so much a date on the calendar as it is a spirit within the heart.

The glorious truth is that He was born and that for a purpose.

This is emphasized in the experience of the shepherds. For as they watched their flocks, suddenly an angel of the Lord appeared to them, and the Shekinah glory of the Lord shone round about them (v. 9). The drab Shepherds Field was alive with the presence of the Lord! The angel did not hover over them, but stood by them *(epestē autois)*. Seeing him, the shepherds "were sore afraid." Literally, "they feared a great fear." "Stop being afraid," said the angel (v. 10). "For, behold, I bring you good tidings of great joy, which shall be to all people." Actually he said, "I evangelize to you a great joy." This verb for "evangelize" *(euaggelizomai)* does not appear in the other Gospels, except in a quotation in Matthew 11:5 (cf. Isa. 61:1). Luke's Gospel uses it ten times. And in Acts he uses it fifteen times. Altogether it appears fifty-five times in the New Testament, mostly in the Pauline epistles. It means to bring good tidings (news) or to preach the gospel. Of further interest is the fact that the noun form *(euaggelion)* does not appear in Luke's Gospel and only twice in Acts (15:7; 20:24), yet it is used seventy-seven times in the New Testament.

But the fact remains that this word in the Christian context was first used by a messenger sent from heaven to men. It expresses what is the most glorious message ever heard on earth. And it is universal in scope, not for the Jews only but for all men.

What was the message? "For was born to you today a Saviour, which is Christ, Lord, in the city of David" (literal rendering, v. 11). Note that there are no definite articles with "Christ, Lord" *(Christos Kurios)*. A. T. Roberston notes that Luke is fond of the word "Lord," where the other Gospels use "Jesus." This is the word used in the Septuagint to translate the Hebrew word for "Jehovah." It came to have this very meaning in the New Testament. So the angel heralded the birth of Him who is "an Anointed One, a Lord," "Lord Messiah," or even "Messiah Jehovah." Jehovah had become flesh in order to save men from their sins. The sign that this was true was that they would find a "babe wrapped in swaddling clothes, lying in a manger" (v. 12).

And then there burst forth heavenly music. For there was with the angel "a multitude of the heavenly host praising God" (v. 13). This praise came not merely from a multitude gathered about the angel. For "host" *(stratias)* is what Plummer calls a partitive genitive. He translates it "a multitude forming part of the heavenly host." Then he adds, "The whole host of heaven was praising God, not merely that portion of it which was visible to the shepherds."

And why were they praising God? Because God had acted to effect His redemptive purpose. The child had been born who would be the Saviour of the world. And it is in God's revelation as redeeming love that He shall express and receive His highest glory.

Thus the heavenly host sang what is called the *Gloria in Excelsis*. "Glory to God in the highest, and on earth peace, good will toward men" (v. 14). This is the reading of the Textus Receptus, a late Greek text (KJV and AV). But the best texts read "of good will," or "of good pleasure." Robertson translates it "among men in whom he is well pleased."

Note the two balancing phrases: "Glory to God in the highest" and "on earth peace." In heaven God's glory, on earth God's peace. And it is not a peace brought about by worldly means.

Some like to point out that at this time the doors of the Temple of Janus in Rome were closed. When there was war the doors were opened; when there was peace they were closed. We speak of the *Pax Romana*. But this has no relation to the song of the heavenly host. Rome's peace was an enforced one which existed because Roman arms had destroyed and crushed all opposition within the empire. But there was no peace in men's hearts. We speak of peace, and try to achieve it by diplomacy and balances of military and political power. But the world will never know true peace thereby.

God says, "Peace among men of good will or good pleasure." This does not mean that men merely by showing good will toward others can produce peace on earth. The good will of which this passage speaks is God's good will or His good pleasure among men. It is "among men in whom he is well pleased." And men are not well pleasing to God outside of Christ. So God's revelation in Christ not only gives to Him glory in heaven, it also produces the kind of men on earth who are well pleasing to Him. Men cannot be at peace with one another until they are at peace with God. It is to this end that the Babe of Bethlehem was born.

The angels returned to heaven (v. 15). Then the shepherds began saying to one another that they should go into Bethlehem and see the wonderful thing which had been told them. They hastened into the town, and found it to be as it had been said. Mary and Joseph. Yes. But most wonderful of all—"the babe lying in a manger" (v. 16). It is little wonder that the shepherds "made known abroad the saying which was told them concerning this child" (v. 17). They not only told Mary and Joseph. They spread the glad news throughout Bethlehem. Those who heard it *were astonished* (v. 18, aorist tense). But apparently they did nothing more. The event of the ages occurred right under their noses, but they only wondered momentarily — and, evidently, ignored it. Perhaps the shepherds' words seemed like an idle tale.

But Mary did not ignore them. She "kept on keeping together" (*suneterei*, imperfect, v. 19) every word. Robertson suggests that Mary may have kept a Baby Book. Why not? And, if so, did she show it to Luke? Furthermore, Mary "pondered them in her heart." Literally, "she set them side by side for comparison." She joined the shepherds' words with those of Gabriel, and compared them. And they became food for the high hopes and joys in a mother's heart.

"The shepherds returned," literally, they "went back to work." They resumed the common chore of tending their flocks. But they would never be the same again. For they returned to work "glorifying and praising God continuously" (present participles). A sense of the nearness of God transformed their work as it will do ours.

The Naming, Purification, and Presentation (2:21-24)

As with John the Baptist so with Jesus, He was circumcised on the eighth day (v. 21). At this time He was formally given the name JESUS, the name which God had bestowed upon Him even before He was conceived in Mary's womb.

According to the law of Moses a mother was considered unclean for forty days after a birth (vv. 22-24; Lev. 12). For her purification she must offer as a sacrifice a lamb, costing about two dollars, and a young pigeon. If she were poor she might offer two pigeons or two turtledoves costing about sixteen cents, one as a sin offering and the other as a burnt offering. So Mary came to the temple in Jerusalem, and being a peasant, offered the two young pigeons.

Furthermore, the Mosaic law required that each first-born male, animal or child, must be redeemed before the Lord (Exod. 13:2-12). This was in recognition of the fact that God had saved the first-born sons of the Israelites in Egypt. This was done by the payment of five shekels or about two dollars and fifty cents (Num. 18:15-16). So Mary and Joseph brought Jesus to the temple, and presented Him before the Lord. The law did not require that the son should be brought to the temple. But due to their proximity to Jerusalem they did so at the time when Mary came to make her offering. It is well to note that as Jesus never broke one of God's laws, also His mother and foster father were careful to observe His laws at the birth of His Son.

The Praise in the Temple (2:25-38)

The world may have been so engrossed in other matters that it had lost its Messianic hope. But there were those who had not done so.

One such was Simeon, a just and devout man (v. 25). He constantly looked for and awaited "the consolation of Israel." The Holy Spirit had kept alive in him this hope. Furthermore, the Spirit had revealed to him that he would not die before he had seen the Lord's Christ (v. 26). Apparently he was now an old man. The Spirit guided him into the temple at the very time when Jesus was brought there. And when he saw Him, he knew that this was He (v. 27). So he took the Babe in his arms, and blessed God that He had kept His word (v. 28). From his lips fell what is called the *Nunc Dimittis,* taken from the words "Now lettest . . . depart" (v. 29).

With intense joy he said literally, "Now let depart [set free from the burden of life] thy slave, Despot [*despota*], according to thy word in peace." He was God's slave, and God was his Despot. A despot was the master of a slave. Simeon's long wait had ended, and he wanted only to die, or to be released from his waiting, in peace. "For mine eyes have seen thy salvation," or "the one bringing salvation." He is to be the Saviour of all the people (v. 31). This is an echo of the angel's word (v. 10). Note how Luke's Gospel stresses the fact that Jesus is the universal Saviour. Having said this, Simeon describes the Christ as One who will be "a light to lighten [a revelation of] the Gentiles, and the glory of thy people Israel" (v. 32). Thus he compounds the universal Saviourhood.

While Mary and Joseph marvelled at all this (v. 33), Simeon blessed them also, pointing out the role of the Messiah (v. 34). Then to Mary he said, "Yea, a sword shall pierce through thy own soul also" (v. 35). What a somber note to inject into such a scene of joy! Robertson calls this "a sharp thorn in their roses, a veritable bitter-sweet." And yet it was true. Mary did not know the meaning of these words then. But the day would come when their stern reality would break upon her, as she saw her first-born nailed to a cross.

Another who had not lost her Messianic hope was the aged Anna (v. 36). She was a prophetess who, after a marriage of seven years, had lived in widowhood eighty-four years (v. 37). She never missed a service in the temple night or day. Coming upon the group in time to hear Simeon's words (v. 38), she joined him in praising the Lord; and "kept on speaking" (imperfect) of Jesus to all those in the temple who likewise were looking for redemption in Israel.

In all likelihood none of these lived to see the crowning acts of Jesus' redemptive death and resurrection. But they had seen the One bringing salvation. And, like Simeon, they departed their life in peace.

Luke 2:40-52

The Years of Preparation

It was probably after Jesus had been presented in the temple that the visit from the Wise Men occurred, that Herod sought to slay Jesus, and that the holy family fled to Egypt (Matt. 2). Perhaps Luke wrote after Matthew, and simply supplemented his account. Therefore, immediately after the presentation in the temple, he records the return of the family to Nazareth (v. 39). Thus began the years of preparation for Jesus before He began His public ministry. These years may be divided into His childhood, boyhood, and young manhood.

Jesus' Childhood (2:40)

How old was Jesus when He returned to Nazareth? Combining Luke's narrative with that of Matthew, He must have been more than one year old, depending on whether He was born in 6 or 5 B.C. Herod died in 4 B.C. It was after his son Archelaus came to the throne that Joseph brought the family back from Egypt (Matt. 2:19-22). In all likelihood Jesus was about three years old at this time, although it is impossible to pinpoint His age.

We are given the barest details about this entire period of preparation. For instance, Luke covers about nine years with one verse. "And the child grew, and waxed strong in spirit, filled with wisdom: and the grace of God was upon him" (v. 40). The phrase, "in spirit," is not found in the oldest and best manuscripts. Later ones evidently borrowed it from Luke 1:80 where it is used of John the Baptist. But most certainly the fact was true of Jesus also.

"The child grew, and waxed strong." Luke calls Jesus a *paidion,* a very young child or infant. In this case the emphasis would be on "young child." So as a young child Jesus grew and developed physically. And in His growth He also gained strength. Both of these verbs "grew . . . waxed strong" are imperfect forms, showing the gradual but continued development.

"Filled with wisdom." The development of His mind kept pace

with that of His body. The present passive participle (filled) speaks of a continuous process of learning under the guidance and teaching of Mary and Joseph.

We should not be shocked by these statements about Jesus. They do not in any sense detract from His deity. Rather they emphasize His complete humanity. Apart from sin, He completely identified Himself with man. He grew, gained strength, and learned as did any other child. It is just as great an error to deny Jesus' humanity as to deny His deity. He was both God and Man, yea, the God-Man.

"The grace of God was upon him." This implies the "in spirit" of Luke 1:80. Plummer *(in loco)* sums up the matter in beautiful and meaningful words. "The intellectual, moral, and spiritual growth of the Child, like the physical, was *real.* His was a perfect humanity developing perfectly, unimpeded by hereditary or acquired defects. It was the first [and only] instance of such a growth in history. For the first time a human infant was realizing the ideal of humanity."

Jesus' Boyhood (2:41-51)

Jesus was now twelve years old (v. 42). At twelve a Jewish lad became a "son of the law" *(Barmitzvah: bar,* son, *mitzvah,* commandment). In a sense he became a man. Thus he was subject to keep the law. To remind him of this he began to wear phylacteries. One of his obligations was to observe the various Jewish feasts. Luke takes note of Jesus' growth when in 1:43 he calls Him "the child [boy] Jesus." Whereas in verse 40 he spoke of Him as a *paidion,* a child, in verse 43 he called Him a *pais,* a boy. The former Greek word is the diminutive form of the latter.

Annually Joseph and Mary went up to Jerusalem to keep the Passover (v. 41). It is possible that they had not taken Jesus with them prior to this time. But when He reached the age of twelve, they did. We can imagine the wonder of it all to Him as He went through the various ceremonies with His parents. As they sat down to eat the paschal meal, from the lips of Joseph He would hear the story of the first Passover in Egypt. The tremendous crowds themselves must have overawed Him. But there was something which interested Him more than the crowds.

At the close of the seven days, Joseph and Mary started the return journey to Galilee. Coming to Jerusalem they probably travelled south through Perea in order to avoid the hostility of the Samaritans who resented anyone's journeying through their land toward Jerusalem. But going north they would not be the objects of Samaritan resentment. So likely they went directly north through Samaria. Tourists stop today at a little town about one day's journey (on foot) from Jerusalem, said to be the spot where they camped for the night.

For protection the pilgrims journeyed in a caravan *(sunodia* from *sun,* with, and *hodos,* way or road), thus a journeying together. In such a caravan the women travelled in front, followed by the men. It is conceivable, therefore, how each parent could have thought that Jesus was with the other. Or in the freedom of such a group the children would be running here and there. But unknown to either Mary or Joseph the lad had remained behind in Jerusalem (v. 43). At the close of the first day's journey families would get together for the night. And when Jesus was found missing His parents sought Him among their kinsmen and friends. "Sought" is an imperfect form. So they kept on seeking Him or made a thorough search (v. 44). Failing to find Him Mary and Joseph returned to Jerusalem, "seeking him." The present tense shows a continuous search, evidently lasting all day (v. 45). For it was on the third day after leaving Jerusalem that they found Him in the temple (v. 46).

He was sitting among members of the Sanhedrin as they gave public instruction. Not only did He listen to them, but He asked repeated questions. His eager mind was alert to seize this opportunity to learn from the "doctors," or "teachers" *(didaskaloi)*. This *Barmitzvah* became a Disciple of the teachers. Heretofore, His religious teaching had been the responsibility of Mary and Joseph. Now of His own volition He sat at the feet of the accredited teachers of Israel.

This was an amazing experience, not for Jesus alone, but for the teachers (v. 47). They were amazed at His questions, understanding, and answers to their questions. He showed an unusual insight into religious matters. He had a grasp and comprehension *(sunesei)* beyond anything that they had ever seen. It was evident that He had been well taught and that "the grace of God was upon him." Also Mary and Joseph were amazed (v. 48). For when they found Him in the temple, His unusual ability surprised even them.

There is a mingled note of anxiety and rebuke in Mary's question to Jesus. "Son [*teknon,* child], why hast thou thus dealt with us? behold, thy father and I have sought thee sorrowing" (v. 48). Actually the word translated "son" is neither "child" nor "boy" (vv.

40, 43). It is *teknon,* the tender word of a mother to one whom she has borne. G. Campbell Morgan says that this word is akin to the Scotch word *bairn.* In effect she asked, "*Bairn* of mine, why hast thou thus dealt with us? behold, thy father and I have sought thee sorrowing."

Some see in Mary's use of the word "father" an argument against the virgin birth. But she was speaking the simple language of the home. Indeed, Joseph was Jesus' foster-father, which perfectly explains the use of this word by the mother. And Alford says that "up to this time Joseph had been so called by the holy child himself, but from this time never."

Why, indeed, had He "thus dealt with" them? Was Jesus a disobedient child? This cannot be, or else He had broken one of the Commandments. To admit such would be to make the "boy Jesus" guilty of sin. And this would be contrary to all that the Bible teaches about Him. In the first place, there is no evidence that either Mary or Joseph had told Him not to remain behind in Jerusalem. Their "sorrowing" was for their sense of failure or neglect to care for Him who was entrusted to their charge. In the second place, the record does not show that they had told Him to come with them. They had assumed that He was in the caravan, when all the while the Boy was absorbed in His experience in the temple. In the third place, as a "Son of the law" Jesus was responsible within Himself for His religious obligations. He had now entered into a new relationship in which He was primarily concerned with the things of His Father. If there was any error here, it was that of Mary and Joseph, not that of Jesus.

This new relationship is expressed in Jesus' reply to His mother. "How is it that ye sought me? wist [know in the soul] ye not that I must be about my Father's business?" (v. 49). These are the first recorded words which fall from Jesus' lips. Literally, "I must be [*dei einai me,* it is necessary me to be] in the things of the Father of me," or "in my Father's house [*en tois tou patros mou*]." This "must" *(dei)* is the moral and spiritual necessity inherent in His Messiahship. It is an expression which was often on His lips with regard to His work. Why did they seek Him, since they should have known that He "must" be in His Father's house, and in the things of His Father? Furthermore, it is of interest to note that Jesus said, ". . . the Father of me." He always used the definite article when speaking of God as His Father; but He never used it when speaking of God as the Father of anyone else.

Thus the Sonship of Jesus is different from that of believers. He *is* the Son of God; and it is only through faith in Him we *become* sons of God.

Notice has been taken that these are the first words of Jesus which have been preserved. Does this mean that here for the first time He became aware of His unique relationship to God? If not, when did He come to have this awareness? It is impossible to pinpoint the answer. But His reply to Mary suggests that they should have known/did know of this relationship prior to this time. And it shows a prior awareness on His part. It is this author's conviction that there never was a time when Jesus was unaware of His unique relationship to God as His Father. And this involves a consciousness of His divine mission also.

But Luke notes that neither Mary nor Joseph understood the import of His words to them. They did know of His unique birth and mission. Perhaps the meaning of verse 50 is that they did not comprehend the full meaning of "in the things of my Father." It was a marvelous thing to them, as it is to us, to see this definite expression of the Messianic consciousness of a twelve-year-old boy. But it is clear to all that at this age, and most probably before, Jesus was aware of it and so declared it.

Nevertheless, Jesus returned to Nazareth with Mary and Joseph, "and was subject unto them" (v. 51). Even though He was the Son of God He remained under the care and guidance of His earthly parents. It was pleasing to His Father that it should be so. And He perfectly did the will of His Father always. And Mary "kept thoroughly" *(dietērei)* all these words in her heart. She had other treasures to *place side by side* with all the other wonders about her Child.

Jesus' Young Manhood (2:52)

"And Jesus increased in wisdom, and stature, and in favor with God and man." With these simple words Luke covers the next eighteen years of Jesus' life until the time arrived for His public ministry.

One cannot help but contrast these simple words of Luke with the accounts found in the pseudo-gospels which abounded in the early Christian era. For instance, one reports that as a child Jesus made birds out of clay, threw them into the air, and they flew away. Another says that because of His superior powers Jesus was a problem to His parents and neighbors. But the divine note is in the simple record of Luke as he pictures Jesus in submission to His parents, growing and developing as an ordinary child, apart from human error.

"Jesus increased." The word "increased" means to cut or chop one's way forward, as one cutting down trees or cutting away underbrush. It speaks of the rigorous effort required of Him as He developed into manhood.

"In wisdom." He learned as others learn. He faced problems, and found the answers. He acquired knowledge, and that knowledge sobered into wisdom. "In stature." This may mean "age" or "bodily size and strength." Either makes sense, and both were true. "In favor [grace] alongside [*para*] God and man." He grew intellectually, physically, and *spiritually*. He cut His way forward in grace alongside God and alongside man. This does not mean merely that both God and man liked Jesus more and more. Rather it means that He increased "in grace" *(chariti)* in the presence of both God and man. This is ideal manhood at its best!

All of this took place in Nazareth. Tradition says that Joseph died when Jesus was perhaps sixteen years of age. Every Jewish lad was required to learn a trade. From Joseph Jesus had learned the carpenter's trade, so that at Joseph's death He became the carpenter of Nazareth (Mark 6:3). Thus He became the breadwinner of the family.

But during these years Jesus did not confine all of His interests to the carpenter's shop. Nazareth was on one of the main highways of Palestine. Caravans passed through this village on their way to Egypt or to the Mesopotamian Valley. From these travellers Jesus, even as a child, learned of the mystery of the world of His day. From the hills about Nazareth He could look eastward beyond the Sea of Galilee or westward at the plain of Esdraelon and at the blue waters of the Mediterranean Sea whose waves lapped the shores of the ancient world. So in truth Jesus grew up in Nazareth to be a citizen of the world.

Because of the polyglot of people passing through His village, Nazareth was a notoriously wicked place. So Jesus viewed life in the raw. He saw firsthand what sin does to men. But He also knew the other and more normal side of life. Roaming the hills about Nazareth He lived close to nature. He saw farmers planting and harvesting their crops, birds building their nests, and foxes running to their holes. He saw His mother kneading dough or patching clothes. All of these things, and more, are reflected in His later teachings.

Thus Jesus increased in wisdom, stature, and grace until the day when His Father said, "The time has arrived for your showing to Israel." And when God spoke, He was ready.

III
The Time of the Beginning

Luke 3:1-22

The Ministry of John the Baptist

Second in importance only to the ministry of Jesus was that of John the Baptist. For he is the connecting link between the Old Covenant and the New. It is for this reason that Luke took such pains to relate both his birth and his public ministry. When John came preaching in the wilderness of Judea he sent a thrill throughout all Jewry. For four hundred years after Malachi God was silent insofar as His revelation was concerned. It was in John's preaching that men recognized the sound of God's voice. Therefore, Jews from far and near flocked to hear him. For "the word of God came unto John . . . in the wilderness" (3:2).

The Date (3:1-2)

With the sense of a true historian Luke relates the event to current history. And he is the only one of the Evangelists who does so. He follows the ancient method of dating by locating it in the context of those in places of rule and leadership. Thus he mentions one emperor, one governor, three tetrarchs, and two high priests. In so doing he began with the outer circle and worked inward.

Specifically Luke places the beginning of John's ministry "in the fifteenth year of the reign of Tiberius Caesar" (v. 1). Tiberius reigned as emperor A.D. 14-37. But assuming that in accordance with Jewish custom John began his ministry at thirty years of age (A.D. 25-26), this immediately poses a problem. For the fifteenth year of Tiberius' reign would mean A.D. 28-29. Did Luke err in his date? Some insist that he did so. But did he figure the reign from the time of Augustus' death (A.D. 14), or is there another possibility?

According to Suetonius, Tiberius shared the reign with Augustus in the provinces for two years prior to the latter's death. If so, then it is possible to begin with A.D. 12, thus arriving at A.D. 25-26 for the fifteenth year. Since Luke lived in the provinces, it is a reasonable assumption that he would so date the reign.

This would agree with the dates of Pontius Pilate's procuratorship of Judea (A.D. 26-36). Greater latitude is allowed in the cases of Herod (Antipas) and Philip. Each came to his tetrarchy upon the death of his father Herod the Great in 4 B.C. A tetrarchy was one-fourth of a kingdom. Herod Antipas was the son of Herod the Great by Malthace the Samaritan. To him his father bequeathed the reign of Galilee and Perea, where he ruled under the Romans until his banishment by the emperor Caligula in A.D. 39 or 40. It was he who beheaded John the Baptist. His rule spanned the entire lifetime of Jesus, and the greater part of Jesus' ministry was carried on in his territory. Herod Philip was the son of Herod the Great by Cleopatra. To him his father bequeathed the tetrarchy of Iturea and Trachonitis. He married Salome, the daughter of Herodias, shortly after she had danced for the head of John the Baptist. It was he who built the city of Caesarea Philippi. He named it in honor of the empress Julia, daughter of Augustus and wife of Tiberius. Philip died in A.D. 33.

Lysanias, the tetrarch of Abilene, poses another problem in dating. At one time it was widely held that Luke had made the mistake of including in his dating pattern a Lysanias, son of Ptolemy, who had reigned as a king prior to 36 B.C., when he was killed by Anthony. But it should be noted that this Lysanias was a king, whereas Luke mentions one who was a tetrarch. However, Plummer notes that the king Lysanias reigned in Chalcis in Coele-Syria, not in Abila in Abilene. And an inscription has been found in Abila bearing the words "on behalf of the salvation of the Lords Imperial and their whole household" by "Nymphaios a freedman of Lysanias the tetrarch." Ramsay insists that the "Lords Imperial" can only be Tiberius and Julia. Julia Augusta died in A.D. 29, so this inscription must be dated sometime in A.D. 14-29. Thus this Lysanias fits into Luke's dating plan. And instead of revealing an error it speaks of the careful accuracy of Luke's writings. For he rescues from oblivion this tetrarch who is mentioned nowhere else in ancient writings other than on the inscriptions.

Annas and Caiaphas are mentioned as being high *priests* at this time. Actually the word "priest" is singular, the "high priesthood" of Annas and Caiaphas. The fact is that Caiaphas alone occupied the office at this time (A.D. 17-35). Annas had been the high priest A.D. 7-14. After he was deposed by the Romans, he was succeeded in turn by four of his sons and finally by his son-in-law Caiaphas. Annas had been a strong high priest, and continued to be the power behind the throne with both Jews and Romans. By including him and placing his name first, Luke takes note of this fact.

Therefore, this dating of the beginning of John's ministry corresponds with the date A.D. 25-26. But Luke notes that for his purpose these reigns are not important within themselves, except as they fix the time when "the word of God came unto John the son of Zacharias in the wilderness." This was the vital note in the story. Emperors, governors, tetrarchs, even high priests, might sit in their places of authority. In their little day they thought themselves important in the schemes of the world. But unknown to them God was moving in history in a fashion which eclipsed them all. God had prepared and was now ready to move in His eternal redemptive purpose. And He by-passed the great of earth to speak through a rugged, uncouth son of the desert who was sent to prepare the way of the Lord.

The Mission (3:3-6)

John suddenly "came [aorist] into all the country about Jordan." This included the plain of Jordan or El Ghor from the Dead Sea as far north as Succoth (II Chron. 4:17). Apparently he had grown up in this general area. So he began his ministry where he was when the word of the Lord came to him. Most of this ministry was spent on the western side of the river, but John 10:40 notes that he also preached on the eastern side. All of his work was done near the Jordan river in which he was baptizing.

John came as a *herald* of God (v. 3). The word rendered "preaching" *(kērussō)* means basically to act as the herald of a king. He went in place of the king, to declare the message of the king, and those who heard were obligated to obey it as though the king had delivered it in person. So John was the herald of God, whose words rang with the authority of God.

He heralded "the baptism of repentance for the remission of sins." The word for "baptism" is *baptisma.* It referred not to the *act* of baptism *(baptismos)* but to the meaning involved in the act. The word *baptismos* never appears in the New Testament in the sense of Christian baptism. The word so rendered is *baptisma.* Of course, Luke's usage here is not with reference to Christian baptism but to that of John (cf. Acts 18:25; 19:3, 5). And what was John's baptism? It was a repentance-baptism "for the remission of sins." It was the inward meaning of the outward act. The word "for" is *eis,* which could mean "for," "unto," "into," "on the basis of," "as the result of," or "with reference to." Sometimes the word was used in the sense of purpose, but not always (cf. Matt. 10:41; 12:41). In this latter reference the men of Nineveh repented "at [*eis*] the preaching of Jonas." They repented not before and in order that Jonah might preach. They repented after he had preached and as the result of it. We even use "for" in the sense of result. "He was executed for murder." Not in order that he might murder, but because he had already done so.

Robertson (*Word Pictures,* Mark, 1:4) concludes that "with reference to" is as good a translation here as is possible. John preached the meaning of repentance-baptism with reference to the remission of sins. The remission came as the result of repentance, and it was symbolized in the meaning of baptism. So actually John's baptism was an evidence of repentance and a willingness to participate in the kingdom which he came to herald.

At this point it is well to note briefly the meaning of Christian baptism (*baptisma*). The noun comes from the verb *baptizō,* to immerse, or to submerge in water. It is also used in the sense of being overwhelmed in trouble or sorrow (Matt. 20:22). But Christian baptism is, in fact, immersion in water and emersion from water. It is a symbol or picture of death, burial, and resurrection (Rom. 6:1-5). It symbolizes that which Jesus did for our salvation, that which happens to one when he believes in Jesus for salvation, and the faith which the believer has in the final resurrection from the dead. Thus, "know ye not, that so many of us as were [are] baptized [the act of baptism] into [*eis,* with reference to] Jesus Christ were [are] baptized into [*eis,* with reference to] his death? Therefore we are buried with him by [*dia,* through] baptism [*baptisma*] into [*eis,* with reference to, the result of] death: that like as Christ was raised up from the dead by the glory of the Father, even so we also should walk in newness of life. For if we have been planted together in the likeness of his death, we shall be also in the likeness of his resurrection" (Rom. 6:3-5).

In Acts 2:38 "into" (*eis*) may well be translated "as the result of" (cf. Matt. 12:41). Through repentance and faith our sins are remitted or carried away. And as the result we are baptized in order to symbolize that fact. We do not bury one in order that he may die, but as the result of death. So we are baptized, not in order to remit sin, but because we have already died to sin which has been remitted.

It is of interest to note that "remission" (*aphesis*) is used by Luke more than by all other New Testament writers combined:

ten times in Luke and Acts; seven times elsewhere. This could reflect Luke's medical training. For in the medical sense it meant the relaxing of diseases.

But returning to Luke's account we note that John based his mission on the words of Isaiah 40:3-4. He is "the voice of one crying in the wilderness, Prepare ye the way of the Lord..." (v. 4). When an Oriental monarch was preparing to visit an area he sent his herald before him, exhorting the people to prepare a road over which he might travel (vv. 4-5). So John, the "voice," is sent to prepare the hearts of the people for the coming of the Messiah. He is more than a person. He is a "voice," or a message, the forerunner of Him who would bring salvation.

"And all flesh shall see the salvation of God" (v. 6). Not the Jews only, but "all flesh" *(sarx),* the entire human, sinful race. "The salvation of God" might well read "the one bringing salvation of the God" *(to sōtērion tou Theou).* So John heralds not only an act of God but the One who will perform that act. "All flesh" shall see the One bringing salvation. But, alas, not all will receive Him.

The Message (3:7-18)

In this section Luke records a sample of John's preaching, but is careful to note that this was not all that he said (cf. 3:18). It is quite evident that the burden of his message had to do with judgment. However, John 1:29 indicates that it also contained the note of mercy and promise. But it is evident that uppermost in John's mind was the picture of the Messiah as presented in the Minor prophets, a Messiah of judgment.

To the multitudes "keeping on coming forth" (present participle) John "kept on saying" (imperfect tense), "O generation of vipers, who hath warned you to flee from the wrath to come?" (v. 7). Matthew 3:7-10 (cf. Luke 3:7-9) shows that this particular word was delivered to the Pharisees and Sadducees who were in the multitude. But there is no conflict here. Luke is summarizing John's general message. Apparently it was evident that the Jewish rulers came to hear John with no good purpose in mind. So he aimed a barrage at them.

His words reflect the imagery of one who was familiar with the desert. When a fire swept across the dry, arid land snakes and other desert creatures would flee before it. These Pharisees and Sadducees were like a brood of snakes running before the wrath of God. The word "wrath" *(orgē)* refers to the abiding opposition of God against evil. Another word *(thumos)* depicts the wrath of God as boiling up in one place but quickly subsiding. But this "wrath to come" is God's abiding opposition to sin everywhere. How do these sinners expect to escape this? Run where they will, but the *orgē* is there also. Carrying out the figure of a sweeping desert fire, the only safe place is where the fire has already burned. The only safe place for a sinner is at the cross or "in Christ" where God's wrath has been fully expressed.

John then exhorts them to "bring forth works worthy of repentance" (v. 8). The word for "worthy" suggests a weight. Their works should be of such weight or quality as to demonstrate true repentance, or a change of mind, heart, and attitude (true meaning of *metanoia,* repentance). He warns them not to presume on a racial relationship to Abraham for salvation. For "God is able of these stones [an abundance of which filled the desert] to raise up children unto Abraham" (v. 8). The Jews considered that as descendants of Abraham they were already the favored of God. Indeed, they taught that he had accumulated more merit with God than was necessary for his own salvation. And every one of his descendants might draw on this excess merit for his salvation (but note Romans 4). The relationship to God is no longer to be thought of as racial and corporate; it is to be spiritual and personal. The time has come when the axe of judgment shall be laid at the root of each tree which does not bring forth good fruit (v. 9). Such shall be cut down and destroyed.

John's reference to "fruits worthy of repentance" brought an immediate response from the crowd. "What shall we do then?" (v. 10). To this question, actually a series of repeated questions ("asked," imperfect, kept on asking), John gave three replies, one general and two specific. Generally he said that they should show their repentance by sharing with the less fortunate. If a man has "two coats," let him share with another who has none. This *coat* was a *chitōn,* an undergarment, not the indispensable outer garment *(himation)*. A man could wear only one *chitōn* at a time, so he should share with the unfortunate. As for "meat," nothing is said about a surplus. A repentant man simply should share his food with the hungry. This is not communism; it is godly charity or love in action.

Among those who came to hear John were some publicans or tax collectors. They were a despised lot among the Jews, being classed with harlots and gross sinners. Under the Roman tax system the privilege of collecting taxes was sold to individuals.

This resulted in political gouging of the worst sort. Among the Jews a publican was regarded as a traitor. He was excommunicated from society, and his family was disgraced. Publicans were called "bloodsuckers."

In reply to these publicans' question, "What shall we do?" John said, "Exact no more than that which is appointed you" (v. 13). A repentant publican would not be guilty of extortion.

Furthermore, certain soldiers asked the same question. These were probably Jewish military men assigned to the publicans to assist in collecting taxes. In doing so they often resorted to violence. Also they served as informers against the wealthy, and for a price. So John told them to do no violence to any man. Neither were they to bring false accusation against them. Instead, they were to be content with their wages (v. 14).

Barclay sums up this advice as saying that these men were to be good tax collectors and good soldiers. Whatever they were doing they were to do it honestly and well. Such advice is universal in scope. It was both timely and timeless. Good deeds were to be evidence of genuine repentance, and not within themselves a means of becoming a part of the kingdom which John proclaimed.

John's preaching had the people in expectation or suspense (v. 15). The Messianic hope was ever present with the Jews. Was John the Christ? Would he establish this new order of which he spoke? The Sanhedrin even sent a delegation to determine if he were the Christ (John 1:19).

Evidently John sensed the excited wondering of the people. A lesser man might have been tempted to capitalize upon it. But so committed to his mission was he that he forthrightly denied that he was the Christ (v. 16). After him came One who was mightier than he was. He was not even worthy to take off His shoes, a service rendered by the most menial of slaves. He was baptizing in water. But the One whom he heralded would baptize them in the Holy Spirit and fire.

What did John mean by the baptism "in the Holy Spirit and fire"? Some see the latter as the phenomenon at Pentecost, "cloven tongues like as of fire" (Acts 2:3). Others would have the two to refer to cleansing and judgment respectively (cf. v. 17). But the fact that the two follow only one preposition *(en)* suggests a connection between them. Both the Spirit and fire suggest cleansing and power. Whereas John's baptism symbolized repentance, the Messianic baptism connotes an inner change of nature.

But there is also a judgment feature in the Messiah's role (v. 17). He will be like a farmer winnowing grain. As both wheat and chaff are thrown into the air, the chaff is blown away and the grain falls to the floor. The former is gathered for fuel, and the latter is gathered in the garner. So those who follow the Messiah will be saved; those who reject Him will be burned in unquenchable fire. "He will thoroughly purge his floor" suggests the thorough work of the Messiah. No *chaff* will be left to clutter up the floor. No single *grain* will be lost. So from this simple Palestinian scene, so common now as then, John draws a grand, eternal truth.

The Interlude (3:19-20)

At this point Luke digresses from the story to relate the final fate of John. Mark and Matthew tell the story in more detail (6:17 ff.; Matt. 14:3 ff.). Luke merely calls attention to the fact that Herod Antipas arrested John and cast him in prison because he condemned his iniquitous marriage to Herodias, his brother Philip's wife. This was not Herod Philip (3:1), but a private citizen who lived in Rome. But Luke notes that John's arrest was also due to the fact that he condemned "all the evils which Herod had done" (v. 19). And they were many.

Josephus confirms the Gospel narrative. He says that Herod imprisoned John because of his popularity with the people, and that the ruler feared a revolt. This could well be Herod's public reason for his action. He would hardly have given the private and real reason, the one reported by Matthew, Mark, and Luke.

This son of the desert may not have been a social being. But as a true herald of God he was concerned with the social evils of his day. No conscientious preacher can afford to do less. John lost his life in the process, but he kept the faith.

The Baptism of Jesus (3:21-22)

Returning to the narrative Luke relates the baptism of Jesus by John (v. 21). News of the Baptist's ministry had reached Nazareth. It was about six months after John had first appeared in the Jordan valley (v. 23). Jesus had reached the age of thirty, the age when a Jewish teacher entered his ministry. So knowing that His time had arrived, Jesus left His carpenter shop to journey southward toward His rendezvous with destiny. Therefore, He appeared before John for baptism.

"Now when all the people were baptized..." (v. 21). Plummer sees this as meaning that Jesus was baptized after all others had been baptized, and probably in private. But Robertson sees no time element in this statement. It is simply a general statement that while others were coming to John, Jesus also came for baptism.

Why was Jesus baptized? Holding to the sinless nature of our Lord, we cannot say that it was a baptism of repentance. Jerome has preserved a fragment of the apocryphal *Gospel according to the Hebrews* which reads, "Lo, the mother of the Lord and His brethren said to Him, John the Baptist baptizeth for the remission of sins: let us go and be baptized by him. But he said to them, Wherein have I sinned that I should go and be baptized by him? except perchance this very thing which I have said is ignorance." This, however, is out of character with everything which we know about Jesus.

Some hold that Jesus' baptism was an authentication of John's ministry. He had foretold the coming of the Messiah, and now He came to him for baptism. In a sense this is true. For at His baptism Jesus began to fulfil that which John had prophesied. In His baptism there was a natural transition from John to Jesus. Hereafter, the former would wane and the latter would increase in position and importance.

Perhaps the most definite thing that can be said is that His baptism marked Jesus' formal entrance into His ministry. Not only did He identify Himself with John's mission but also with the needs of sinful men. Hereafter, Jesus will proceed in the ministry that was redemptive in its purpose and scope. In a sense in His baptism Jesus symbolized His death, burial, and resurrection: that which He did for man's redemption. But whatever else may be said about it, Jesus' baptism marked a definite turn in the events connected with His life.

It is of interest to note that at His baptism Jesus was "praying" (v. 21). The other Gospels repeatedly mention the prayer life of Jesus. But Luke places a greater emphasis upon it than any other. Indeed, on seven significant occasions he mentions the fact that Jesus was praying (3:21; 5:16; 6:12; 9:18; 9:29; 11:1; 23:34, 46). The first of these was at His baptism.

It was while He was praying that "the heaven was opened, and the Holy Ghost [Spirit] descended in a bodily shape like a dove upon him, and a voice came from heaven, which said, Thou art my beloved Son; in thee I am well pleased" (vv. 21-22).

The Cerinthian Gnostics saw the descent of the Spirit upon Jesus as the coming of deity upon the man Jesus. They held that Christ was neither born nor did He die. Rather they insisted that deity came upon Jesus at His baptism and left Him on the cross (cf. Matt. 27:46). But the Gospel writers, especially John (1:1, 14), clearly teach that the eternal Christ became Jesus of Nazareth, and that as such He died. It is impossible to accept Luke's account of the birth of Jesus and hold to any such Gnostic view.

More to the point is the fact that Jesus was anointed by the Holy Spirit. The "dove" has three possible meanings. First, the dove was symbolic of sacrifice. So Jesus was anointed for sacrifice. Second, the Spirit was the revelation of God's power. And Jesus wrought in the power of the Holy Spirit (4:1, 14). Third, the "bodily form" was for John's benefit (cf. John 1:32-33). So in the coming of the Spirit Jesus was made known to John, and He was anointed as a king and a sacrifice for His ministry.

Furthermore, the voice of God gave His approval of the Son (cf. Matt. 17:5). So at Jesus' baptism we see the presence of the Trinity: Jesus (Son); Spirit (dove); Father (voice). The triune God expressed Himself as in the Son He set forth to bear the sin of the world.

John had finished his mission; his message was complete. His words came alive in Him who is the Word. The friend of the Bridegroom is content to recede into the background as the Bridegroom goes forth to claim His bride. For said John literally, "He it is necessary to go on increasing, but me to go on being made inferior" or "to go on declining" (John 3:30). John was glorious as he swayed the crowds with his message. But he was more glorious as he spoke words of finality and self-abnegation to his disciples.

Luke 3:23-38

The Lineage of Jesus

The Jews placed great value upon genealogy. It is understandable, therefore, that Luke would include in his Gospel the lineage of Jesus. Matthew opened his Gospel with Jesus' genealogy. But Luke waits until this point to give it. Plummer suggests that all of the record prior to this time was really preliminary to the Gospel itself. Certainly it is true that Luke is now ready to begin the account of Jesus' public ministry. This could well be the reason why he gives Jesus' genealogy at this point.

A comparison of the genealogies in Matthew and Luke reveals many problems. So much so that many say that it is impossible to harmonize them. However, certain facts may be noted about them which shed light on the over-all problem.

For instance, Matthew begins his genealogy with Abraham and brings it forward to Jesus through Joseph. However, he is careful to point out that Joseph was not Jesus' father (Matt. 1:16). Since he was writing for the Jews, he would naturally give the legal lineage of Joseph.

On the other hand Luke begins his genealogy with Jesus and goes back to "Adam, which was the son of God" (Luke 3:38). Writing for the Gentiles he stresses the universal nature of Jesus.

A further comparison shows that the section after Abraham is peculiar to Luke (3:34-38). The remainder of the genealogies reveals differences, but they agree at certain points also. This would be expected if each Evangelist was giving a different genealogy but within the general family line.

Perhaps a clue to the problem is found in Luke 3:23. "And Jesus himself began to be about thirty years of age, being (as was supposed) the son of Joseph, which was the son of Heli." "As was supposed" suggests that Luke is pointing out a peculiar nature of his genealogy. In the Greek text "Joseph" has no definite article, although all other proper names do have. This could mean that the parenthetical statement should read "as was supposed of Joseph." If so, then the body of the text could read "Jesus...

which was the son [or descendant] of Heli." "Heli" does not appear in Matthew's genealogy. He says that "Jacob begat Joseph" (1:16). Certainly, therefore, Joseph did not have two fathers. There is no reason to say that "Jacob" and "Heli" are two different names for the same man. So who is this "Heli"?

It has been suggested, and with good reasoning, that Heli was the father of Mary. If so, then "son" should read "grandson." And there are grounds for such usage. Thus Jesus would be the son of Mary and the grandson of Heli.

It is reasonable, therefore, to say that Matthew gives the legal genealogy through Joseph, being careful to point out that Joseph was not Jesus' actual father (cf. Matt. 1:16, 18-25). Luke clearly records that Jesus was the virgin-born son of Mary. Therefore, may we not say that he gives the true genealogy of Jesus through His mother. And he traces it back, not to Abraham, but to Adam, the son of God. Thus in His genealogy Jesus is identified not with the Hebrews only but with the entire human race. There is in this no justification for saying that this teaches that Jesus was a son of God only in the sense that Adam was "of God." Luke clearly teaches elsewhere that Jesus is the unique Son of God. The line through Adam simply stresses the universality of His relationship. He was in truth Son of God and Son of Man.

Luke 4:1-13

The Lines of Battle Drawn

Jesus was now ready to embark upon His public ministry, a ministry which was designed to destroy the works of the devil. The battle is ready to be joined. Jesus is the Christ. But what kind of Christ shall He be? Current Messianic ideas pictured Him as a mighty warrior who would destroy the enemies of Israel, and with the Jews establish a reign over all the earth. Would Jesus be this kind of Messiah? Also as the Son of God He possessed great power. How would He use this power? For selfish interest, as earthly kings did? To work mighty wonders with which to startle the people? Or would His be a spiritual reign involving a spiritual use of His power? To misuse His office would be sin. Such would result in the failure of His mission. And it was to this end that the devil was dedicated in his power.

It is to be expected, therefore, that at this juncture the arch-enemy of God and man would manifest himself in the arena of battle. The lines of battle would be drawn. Luke says that "Jesus being full of the Holy Ghost [Spirit] returned from Jordan, and was led by the Spirit into [*en*] the wilderness" (4:1). Shortly after His baptism Jesus retired into the wilderness. Mark says that He was driven into the wilderness by the Spirit (1:12). But Luke says that He "was led by the Spirit in [*en*] the wilderness." While He was there He was constantly led (imperfect) by the Spirit.

Where was this wilderness? It could have been anywhere in this barren, wild country bordering on the western side of the Jordan river. Tradition locates the place as Quarantania, a mountain just west of Jericho. Wherever it was, Jesus was there for forty days. Luke seems to suggest that during this entire period Jesus was tempted by the devil (v. 2). This is possible, of course. "Being tempted" is a present passive participle suggesting a continuous tempting. It corresponds to the imperfect passive verb "was led" *(ēgeto)*. As He was led by the Spirit He was tempted by the devil. However, the whole point of the story centers upon the specific temptations which came at the end of the forty days (cf. Matt. 4:2 f.).

What is meant by *temptation?* The verb *peirazō* means *to test.* Depending upon the one doing the testing, it may mean to test to prove a thing genuine; or it may mean to test to prove a thing false or bad. In the former sense God tests people. But it is in the latter sense that the devil puts them to the test. It is in this dual light that we may understand the temptations of Jesus. God permitted Him to be tried to prove Him genuine; Satan tried Him in an effort to prove Him false. In fact, Matthew says that Jesus was led by the Spirit into the wilderness "to be tempted of the devil." "To be tempted" is an infinitive of purpose. So at the outset of His ministry the Spirit led Jesus into the wilderness for the express purpose of challenging Satan. The lines of battle were drawn indeed. And the initiative was with God, not Satan.

Certain questions naturally arise at this point. Were the temptations subjective and psychological, or were they objective and actual? Did the devil appear in bodily form, or was his approach through Jesus' mind? Were the temptations real? And could Jesus have yielded to them?

There is no reason to think of these temptations other than as objective and actual. As God was in the form of flesh, so the devil could have been so. The adversary (Satan) or slanderer (devil) adapted himself to a bodily form to confront God likewise. In all likelihood he came to Jesus with audible seductive suggestions.

Certainly the temptations were real. This means that Jesus could have yielded to them. Otherwise He was guilty of hypocrisy, the spiritual sin which He condemned more than any other. One rebels at the thought that He merely pretended to endure that which is common to man. The author of Hebrews clearly says that He was tempted in all points like as we are, yet without sin (4:15). He had the power to sin. But, more gloriously, He had the power not to sin!

Jesus' ability to yield to temptation does not mean that He possessed an evil nature, or that He possessed antecedent sins which made other sins possible. Prior to the fall Adam did not possess an evil nature. Nor did he have antecedent sins. He was in a state of innocency but with the possibility of sinning. It was in his yielding to temptation that he acquired a sinful nature and actual sin. Jesus, the second or last Adam, likewise was sinless. But in His free will He was free to choose to yield or not to yield to Satan. *He did not yield!* But He did identify Himself with men, apart from sin. In His triumph over Satan He earned the right to redeem man from his sin.

The very point of Hebrews 4:15-16 is that because Jesus was tempted and did not yield, He not only can sympathize with us in our temptations; He is also the One qualified to be our Saviour. Who knows best the awful fires of temptation? The one who yields to it, or the one who endures its worst without yielding? The answer is obvious. It was this latter which Jesus did for us.

Yes, Jesus was tempted in all points like as we are, yet without sin. In what *points* are we tempted? So often we say that the devil tempts us in our baser nature. But is this the case? To be exact we should recognize that he tempts us in our higher nature in an effort to cause us to give to it a base expression. Take, for instance, the words "desire" and "lust." In the New Testament they translate the same Greek word *(epithumia)*. Luke 22:15 reports Jesus as saying, "With desire I have desired to eat this passover with you before I suffer." Both the noun and verb are this word in their respective forms (cf. Phil. 1:22). Here the words mean a legitimate, God-given desire. But the same noun is also rendered as "lust" (cf. Gal. 5:16). This is *desire* perverted into *lust*. In James 1:14-15 "lust" occurs twice. A man is tempted when he is drawn away, or lured "of his own lust... then when lust hath conceived...." "His own lust" is one's own natural, legitimate desire. But Satan "baits as a fish" (entices) through lust in causing us to give an illegitimate expression to this legitimate desire.

Actually the devil tempts us through three basic and noble desires: physical appetite, aesthetic nature, and spiritual ambition. This is well seen in the first temptation (Gen. 3:6). Eve saw that "the tree was good for food [physical appetite]... pleasant to the eyes [aesthetic nature]... desired to make one wise [spiritual ambition]." It was in an illegitimate expression of these legitimate desires that Eve and Adam sinned. And it was through these three desires that the devil tempted Jesus. He tempted Him in "all the temptation" (Luke 4:13), or in every area in which one can be tempted.

Now before dealing with the temptations themselves one further matter must be considered. Jesus was both tempted and He resisted in the area of His human nature. It is impossible to tempt God to do evil (cf. James 1:13). Jesus was God in the flesh, to be sure. But He was also man. And it was as a man that He was tempted. Furthermore, He resisted temptation as a man. Not once did He call upon His divine power in this struggle. It has been noted that He did not possess a sinful nature. Neither did He have prior sins which bound Him to evil. But otherwise in His resistance to the tempter He relied upon the power of the Holy Spirit and the power of the Scripture. He answered each temptation by quoting from Deuteronomy (8:3; 6:13; 6:16). Thus apart from His freedom from a sinful nature and experience, we can say that all which He relied upon in resisting the devil is available to us when we are tempted. In truth, He submitted Himself unto God, resisted the devil, and he fled from Him (cf. James 4:7).

The first temptation in the wilderness was in the realm of *physical appetite*. For forty days Jesus was so absorbed in prayer and meditation that He apparently was unmindful of food, if indeed any had been available in the barren desert. But "when they [forty days] were ended, he afterward hungered" (v. 2). In such a condition the devil said, "If thou be the Son of God, command this stone that it be made bread" (v. 3). Evidently the devil pointed out one particular stone. In essence he *commanded* Jesus to command. He tempted Him to work a miracle for His own benefit, something which Jesus never did.

"If thou be the Son of God" is a condition of the first class, assuming that it is true. So the devil seeks to turn God's blessed word of approval (3:22) into a snare for Jesus. As the Son of God He possessed divine power. Why not use it? Or why not put it to the test to see if it were real? So this temptation involved distrust as to the Father's word. Furthermore, Jesus was hungry. Would God permit Him to starve? Why should He not take things into His own hands?

Many a man has fallen victim to this temptation to use one's power simply to get bread, even illegitimately. It is the temptation of materialism. Was the purpose of Jesus' life simply to amass material things? And, even more, would He pitch His ministry at this level? Would He be a bread-Messiah for others even as for Himself?

However, Jesus was not taken in by this subtle suggestion. In reply He said, "It is written, That man shall not live by bread alone, but by every word of God" (v. 4). Man must have bread. But he is more than just body. He is a spirit. And his spirit must feed upon God's Word. This, of course, involves God's will. So Jesus chose the will of God rather than the will of Satan.

The second temptation involves *spiritual ambition*. Jesus had come to wrest the world from the clutches of the devil. How would this be done? So Satan "showed unto him all the kingdoms of the world in a moment of time" (v. 5). The King James Version says that the devil took Jesus "up into an high mountain." This does not appear in the best texts. If we suppose that He was already in the mountain, say, Quarantania, this was not necessary. For from such a height He could see far in every direction. But the phrase "in a moment [second] of time" suggests that the devil gave Jesus a mental picture of the kingdoms of the inhabited earth (Matthew says "cosmos").

Then the devil said, "All this power [authority] will I give thee, and the glory of them: for that is delivered unto me; and to whomsoever I will give it" (v. 6). Here Satan claims world authority, a claim which Jesus does not deny. Indeed, Jesus called Satan "the prince of this world" (John 12:31). Also Satan claims that he can give this authority to others. This would be and is true with respect to wicked rulers. Are not such the very agents of the devil? This explains the evil in history.

Now Satan says that if he can give this authority to others, he can do so to Jesus. Had not Jesus come to establish His authority over the nations? To be sure, it is God's will that He shall do so through suffering. But Satan proposes a short-cut, an easy way. "If thou therefore wilt worship [before] me, all shall be thine" (v. 7). Just bow your knee in my presence, said Satan.

Suppose that Jesus had done so. And suppose that thereby He had received the authority of the nations. He would have received it not from God but from Satan. Thus He would have been an agent of Satan, like many other rulers. A satanic scheme indeed! Had Jesus succumbed the very moral structure of the universe would have collapsed. God would have been dethroned, and the devil would have been the archruler of the entire universe! Imagine the Son of God as a vassal of Satan, ruling by graft and not in righteousness. The result of Jesus' yielding to this temptation is too terrible even to contemplate. But He did not yield. And as Plummer says, "He rejects Satan as an ally, and thereby has him as an implacable enemy. The end does not sanctify the means."

And this rejection by Jesus has an infinite meaning for us. For Satan still proposes the short-cut method for us in realizing our spiritual ambitions. God proposes that we shall attain our goals by brain, body, and soul sweat. To take any other route is to reject God's will in favor of Satan's will.

Again Jesus drew the Sword of the Spirit (v. 8). "Get thee behind me, Satan" is genuine in Matthew 4:10. Jesus simply quoted Scripture again. "Thou shalt worship the Lord thy God, and him only shalt thou serve." Satan said, "Worship me." Jesus said, "Worship God." And these are the difference between hell and heaven in both time and eternity.

The third temptation dealt with Jesus' *aesthetic nature* (v. 9). Satan took Jesus to Jerusalem to the pinnacle or wing of the temple area. This was probably the southeast wing looking straight down into the valley far below. Hegesippus says that it was from this lofty point that James the Just was thrown to his death. To look down from this area makes one dizzy. And this fact may have been involved in the temptation.

Again Satan assumes Jesus' deity. "If thou be the Son of God, cast thyself down from hence." Do the spectacular! No harm can befall the Son of God. And besides, the Jews taught that when the Messiah came He would suddenly appear in the temple. A miracle such as this would certainly convince the Jews that He was the Messiah.

Furthermore, "it is written, He shall give his angels charge over thee, to keep [thoroughly to guard] thee: and in their hands they shall bear thee up, lest at any time thou dash thy foot against a stone" (vv. 10-11; cf. Ps. 91:11-12).

Jesus had quoted Scripture, so Satan does the same. Only there are two differences. In the first place, Jesus quoted from Deuteronomy, the law. But Satan quoted from the Psalms or poetry. He quoted poetry as though it were prose. He took a beautiful, poetic promise of God's providence and sought to twist it into a prosaic means whereby Jesus would doubt God or put Him to a test. In the second place, Satan misquoted Scripture by omitting one very important phrase: "to keep thee *in all thy ways*" (Ps. 91:11, author's italics). Jesus' way was God's way. To have done what Satan suggested would have put Him out of *His way* into Satan's way.

This should serve as a warning to every man. Satan may quote Scripture, but he does so out of context or else quotes only that part which suits his evil purpose. And he has snared multitudes of unsuspecting souls thereby.

But he did not snare Jesus. For once again He quoted from Deuteronomy. "Thou shalt not tempt [put to the test] the Lord thy God" (v. 12). We must not crowd God into a corner by our rash acts, and expect God to rescue us by a miracle. Jesus never did so. Neither will we if we follow Him.

Luke concludes the temptation account by saying, "And when the devil had ended all the [every] temptation, he departed from him for a season" (v. 13). Satan tempted Jesus in every kind of temptation: physical appetite, spiritual ambition, aesthetic nature. This he did with Adam and Eve — and succeeded. This he does with us with the same result. This he did with Jesus — and failed. He used every weapon in his arsenal of evil to no avail.

And having failed, he departed for a season. But he came back again and again, only to fail with each attempt. Not one flaw of Jesus appears among his trophies. And in the end he lost the war.

IV
The Galilean Ministry

Luke 4:14-31

The Tragedy of Lost Opportunity

Luke, following the framework of Mark's Gospel, omits from his Gospel that which is called "the year of obscurity" in Jesus' ministry (cf. John 1:19—4:45). Instead he carried Him immediately to Galilee. Did we not know of the other ministry, there would be no break in the story. However, his reference in 4:14 apparently refers to Jesus' return to Galilee after His visit to Jerusalem and His interview with the woman in Samaria (cf. John 4:43-45).

Luke 4:14-15 gives a general account of the beginning of the great Galilean ministry which was to absorb so much of Jesus' efforts. Three things Luke notes: the power of the Holy Spirit in Jesus' ministry; the growing fame of Jesus; and His use of the synagogues in His teaching and work. "And he taught in their synagogues, being glorified of all" (v. 15). "Taught" is an imperfect tense meaning that Jesus had the habit of doing so. The synagogues were open to Him until the rise of the opposition of the Pharisees.

Early in His Galilean ministry Jesus paid a visit to Nazareth (v. 16). Already He had ministered elsewhere including the healing of the son of a nobleman in Capernaum (cf. John 4:46-54). Evidently He delayed visiting Nazareth until news of His work elsewhere was known there.

At any rate, in keeping with His custom, He attended Sabbath services in the synagogue. Usually the service consisted of two parts: the *Parashah,* or reading from the law; and the *Haptarah,* or reading from the prophets. The latter was followed by a sermon. Those who did these things were chosen by the minister in charge. Jesus was chosen for the latter.

In keeping with custom He stood up to read and then sat down to preach. When His time came Jesus stood up, and the minister handed Him the roll of Isaiah. Whether the portion to be read was specified or was of Jesus' own choosing is not stated. Nevertheless He unrolled the roll until He came to Isaiah 61:1-2 (v. 17). And then He read.

"The Spirit of the Lord is upon me, because he hath anointed me to preach the gospel to the poor; he hath sent me to heal the brokenhearted, to preach deliverance to the captives, and recovering of sight to the blind, to set at liberty them that are bruised [broken to pieces], to preach the acceptable year of the Lord" (vv. 18-19).

Having finished the reading Jesus rolled up the roll, returned it to the minister, and sat down. Instead of returning to His former seat, He sat where the speaker would sit. Thus He indicated that He would preach also. Therefore, all eyes were fastened upon Him. Evidently it was more than the normal expectation of an audience before a speaker. They had heard of the fame of this home-town boy. Now what would He say to them?

They heard more than they had expected. For rather than merely explaining the Scripture verse by verse, He made a startling claim. "This day is this scripture fulfilled in your ears" (v. 21). Literally, it "stands fulfilled," a note of completeness and finality.

What did they understand Jesus to be saying? Actually, Isaiah spoke of the Jubilee year when all captives were released, and of the return of Judah from the Babylonian captivity. But through it all ran the Messianic note. It was regarded as a description of the work of the Messiah. So instead of giving a rote exegesis of the passage, Jesus clearly claimed that the real Jubilee had come and that He was its fulfilment. He declared Himself to be the Messiah. As prophets and kings were anointed with oil, He was anointed with the Spirit of the Lord. And the ministry which He set forth would be a spiritual ministry.

As Jesus continued to speak the people were amazed (v. 22). Reports of His teaching had not been exaggerated. A continuous flow of gracious, winning words proceeded out of His mouth. But the people's amazement soon gave way to the question, "Is not this Joseph's son?" They knew Him as such, even though Luke has clearly shown otherwise. However, the import of the question was simply that one who had grown up among them, the village carpenter, could not possibly be the Messiah. To begin with, the popular concept of the Messiah was that of a mighty conqueror. Certainly Jesus did not fit this picture. And in no sense could they conceive of one so well known to them as being this mighty One anointed of God. Like Nathanael, they could not believe that anything so good and great could come from Nazareth (cf. John 1:46).

Jesus met the challenge implied in their question (v. 23). They were quoting in attitude, if not in words, the proverb common to both Jews and Greeks, "Physician, heal thyself." Of interest is the fact that only Luke reports this. In other words, the challenge is to prove His words by His deeds. He anticipates their demand that He should perform a miracle like the one which He had done in Capernaum (cf. John 4:46-54). It was one thing to hear such reports. They wanted to see it done before their eyes.

But Jesus never worked a miracle on demand. And in this case He countered their implied demand with another proverb. "No prophet is accepted in his own country" (v. 24). This statement is of universal import. For no prophet or other leader is accepted among his own people or in his own time. One generation crucifies a man, and the next builds monuments to him. And this is especially true of those who grow up among us. "He can't be so great because I know him" is a statement heard all too often.

By this statement Jesus not only declares a universal principle. He also says that He will not prove to be an exception. He will perform no miracle to gain for Himself that which is not accorded to another. As in the wilderness, so here, He has so completely identified Himself with man that He will live subject to man's limitations and trials.

And then Jesus drove home this principle by two vivid pictures from the history of Israel (vv. 25-27). Even though at Elijah's word it did not rain for three and one-half years, during that drought he was sent, not to a widow in Israel, but to one in Sidon. Also despite the fact that there were many lepers in Israel, only one was healed by Elisha – Naaman, the Syrian. And the controlling factor was faith. Israel rejected Elijah, but through her faith the woman of Sidon received a great blessing from the prophet (cf. I Kings 17:9 ff.). The lepers of Israel ignored Elisha, but through faith in his word Naaman was cleansed (cf. II Kings 5:1ff.). The import of Jesus' words was clear. Others, even Gentiles, through faith in Him would be blessed by Him. But His own people, yea, those of His hometown would through unbelief miss the blessing.

"And all they in the synagogue, when they heard these things, were filled with wrath" (v. 28). The word for "wrath" is *thumos*. This is a wrath which boils up in anger, or a burst of rage, and then subsides. Why did they react so violently? For one thing their town pride had been insulted. Jesus' reference to Capernaum and His works there, coupled with His implied refusal to do the same in Nazareth, touched a tender spot. And that from one of their own fellow-citizens! But perhaps the greater reason for their rage was Jesus' reference to the Gentiles. According to the Jews "God had created the Gentiles to be fuel for the fires of hell." To infer that they were objects of God's favor, even more than the Jews, was an unforgivable affront. They might have overlooked it had it come from some stranger. But for it to come from Jesus was another matter. Why He even compared Himself to Elijah and Elisha! And He was just their town carpenter!

The people's rage burst forth in mob violence. They rose up and cast Jesus out of the town (v. 29). There they sought to throw Him from a cliff to His death. Such an attempt on their part was what the Jews called a "rebel's beating," somewhat akin to lynch law. It was administered without a trial, and on the spot, when anyone was accused of violating their law or tradition (Plummer). Tourists today are shown a cliff just outside Nazareth called the cliff of precipitation, and said to be the place where this enraged mob sought to kill Jesus.

In some way Jesus escaped the mob (v. 30). John records similar escapes in Jerusalem (7:30; 10:39). It may have been due to the very power of His personality. Yet one wonders why this did not prevent them from rushing Him out of the synagogue. At least it was a miraculous escape. But however it was accomplished, it spared Nazareth the dubious honor (?) which was reserved for Jerusalem – the killing of the Son of God.

Jesus left Nazareth to establish His headquarters in Capernaum (v. 31). Had the people of Nazareth received Him would He have made His home city His base of operations? Who can tell? We can only say that because of their town pride, racial prejudice, and failure to give honor to a *prophet* in His own country, Jesus left the scene of His childhood to center His labors elsewhere. Nazareth stands as a fitting example of *the tragedy of lost opportunity*.

Luke 4:32-44

The Authority of Jesus

Following His rejection in Nazareth Jesus came down to Capernaum, a city on the northern shore of the Sea of Galilee. It was probably the Tell Hum which today consists only of ruins. Modern tourists still view the ruins of a later synagogue which was built upon the foundation of one which stood there in Jesus' day. It was Capernaum which served as our Lord's headquarters during His Galilean ministry. Although He journeyed elsewhere He always returned to this city.

Luke notes that Jesus "was teaching" (imperfect) or made it a habit of teaching in the synagogue on the Sabbath days. The people were astonished at His teaching. "For his word was with power" *(exousia,* authority, v. 32). Mark adds that He taught "not as the scribes" (1:22). Their teaching consisted largely of quoting former rabbis. Obviously it was second-hand and quite monotonous. But that of Jesus was refreshing, since it came out of His very being. This is the basic meaning of *exousia (ex,* out of, *ousia,* being) and so with *authority.*

This note of authority is characteristic of this entire passage. For it shows that Jesus not only spoke but also acted with authority.

On a particular Sabbath day He was in the synagogue. Also present was a man who had a spirit of an unclean demon (v. 33). This is the first mention of demon-possession in Luke. And it is all the more significant because this physician records the story without any question raised as to its reality. That the ancients believed in such there can be no doubt. They believed that the air was populated by evil spirits, and that on occasion by either food or drink they entered into men. Barclay notes that the Egyptians held that there were thirty-six parts of the human body, any of which might be entered and controlled by such spirits. Many moderns call such belief an ancient superstition.

But did Jesus believe in demon-possession? From the record we must answer in the affirmative. Some hold that He did not actually believe in it, but that He accommodated Himself to the beliefs of His contemporaries in order to treat them. Others insist that He really believed in it. Therefore, say they, He too was the victim of superstition, possessing no medical knowledge beyond that of His time. A further position is that Jesus believed in it, and that it was a reality. Modern thought is not so certain that demon-possession is a mere superstition. There is no apparent organic reason for many illnesses, as attested by psychiatry and psychosomatic medicine. We know far too little about the relationship between the spiritual and physical realms to deny such a phenomenon. The record is quite clear that Jesus accepted demon-possession as a reality. It is the position of this writer that Jesus was not mistaken. Ignorance on this matter was not in His mind but is in ours.

Luke notes that the demons recognized Jesus as "the Holy One of God" (v. 34). Men might not do so, but demons did. So they cried with a loud voice, "Let us alone; what have we to do with thee?" (v. 34). "Let us alone" renders an interjection *ea*. It expresses wonder, fear, or indignation. Robertson says that here it was "a diabolical screech." So letting out this screech they asked, literally, "What to us and to you?" This may best be rendered, "What have we in common?" The only possible connection was that Jesus had come to destroy them.

"Jesus rebuked *him*" (v. 35, author's italics). Note the plurals in verse 34: "What to us . . . to destroy us." The demon spoke of all demons. But Jesus replied to him alone, since he was the one who spoke to Him. "Hold thy peace, and come out of him," out of the man. "Hold thy peace" is *phimōthēti,* literally, "Stop thy mouth with a *phimos* [muzzle]," or, "be muzzled." The demon did not argue with Jesus. But he did throw the man into a convulsion as he came out of him. He flung the man down, but Luke, the physician, notes that he "hurt him not." This phrase is absent from Mark's account (1:26).

The people were amazed (v. 36). Not only did Jesus teach with authority in contrast to the scribes' rote teaching, He also cast out a demon with only a word or command. This was in direct contrast with the exorcists who *claimed* to cast out demons with incantations, charms, and superstitious ritual. "With authority and power he commandeth the unclean spirits, and they come out."

It is no wonder that Jesus' fame spread throughout the surrounding country (v. 37). Literally, "There went forth a rumor" about Jesus' miracle in Capernaum. The word rendered "rumor" *(ēchos)* is our word "echo." The news reverberated throughout the area as it was told by both those who saw it and those who heard about it. This is the New Testament method of scattering abroad the good news. We may well imagine that the man who was healed was the greatest and happiest evangelist of all. Go thou, and do likewise!

From the synagogue Jesus went to the home of Simon Peter (v. 38). His mother-in-law "was taken with a great fever." The verb tense (imperfect) indicates that it was a continuous fever, maybe chronic. It was also severe as seen in the word "great." Galen divided fevers into "great" and "small." So Luke speaks with medical exactness.

In response to the pleas of perhaps both Peter and his wife ("they"), Jesus stood over her as a sympathetic physician (v. 39). He commanded the fever to leave her. She was healed instantly. "Immediately rising [aorist participle] she kept on ministering [imperfect] to them." This was a miracle. Had the cure been natural the fever would have left her gradually, leaving her weak. But with the sudden cure she was also strong enough to minister to them repeatedly (cook a meal?). So once again Jesus asserted His authority, this time over disease.

All of the foregoing had occurred on the Sabbath which ended at sunset (v. 40). At that time the people of Capernaum came to Jesus with those who were sick with various diseases. It is a beautiful scene as at the close of day Jesus walks among them. Literally, "And the one to the last of them his hands laying upon [present participle], he healed them one by one [imperfect]." In the process demons "one by one came out" (imperfect) of many (v. 41). They were saying repeatedly, "You are the Son of God" ("Christ" not in best manuscripts). The demons declared the deity of Jesus. But He rebuked them and "repeatedly suffered [imperfect] them not to keep on speaking [*lalein,* present infinitive] that they knew him to be the Christ." The tenses really make this scene to live. Jesus did not want the testimony of demons. All too soon His enemies will accuse Him of being in league with the devil. But it is of interest to note that before men recognized Him as the Son of God, demons did. Even though they were evil spirits they were of the spirit world. And they knew Jesus to be the Son of God.

The crowds dwindled away. Evidently Jesus retired for the night. But a great while before day (Mark 1:35) He slipped away to pray. With the return of day the people again "kept on seeking him" (imperfect, v. 42). They sought Him until they found Him. They "kept on trying to hinder [imperfect] him" from leaving them. But He spoke of the necessity of preaching the kingdom of God to other cities (v. 43). He was sent to them also. "And he was [imperfect] of Galilee" (v. 44). The best manuscripts actually read "of the Jews." But in either case this apparently is Luke's notice of Jesus' first tour of Galilee (cf. Matt. 4:23-25; Mark 1:39).

Matthew tells of the growing fame of Jesus extending even into Syria. Multitudes followed Him, having come from Galilee, the Decapolis (area east of the sea of Galilee), Jerusalem, Judea, and from east of the Jordan. The people flocked to Him who not only spoke but worked with authority.

Luke 5:1-11

The Call of Four Fishermen

In all likelihood this is the same event which is recorded by Matthew and Mark prior to Jesus' first tour of Galilee (4:18-22; 1:16-20; cf. Luke 4:43-44). For some unknown reason Luke places the story after the tour. Some would note differences in the accounts, but they may be explained in that Luke furnishes details not given by the others.

Jesus was teaching on the shore of "the lake of Gennesaret" (v. 1). This body of water was called "sea of Galilee," "sea of Tiberias," and "lake of Gennesaret." Technically it was not a "sea" but a "lake" thirteen miles long by about eight miles wide. With characteristic accuracy Luke never calls it a "sea," but a "lake." It rests 680 feet below sea level, a fact which gives to it an almost tropical climate. About it was fertile soil which produced an abundance of grain, fruits, and other foodstuffs. The lake swarmed with fish. Barclay notes that in it were found shoals of fish covering as much as an acre. For this reason this lake swarmed with professional fishermen whose work furnished one of the principal items of the diet of the people.

Josephus contrasts the fertility of this area with the Dead Sea environs as "the Sea of Life," and "the Sea of Death" respectively. The "Sea of Life" is suggestive of the event which Luke records about the call of the four fishermen.

So great were the crowds pressing in upon Jesus that it was impossible for Him to stand where He might be seen and heard. Two boats were anchored nearby, and their owners, after a night of fruitless fishing, were busy washing their nets (v. 2). This is a characteristic scene even today. One of these boats belonged to Simon Peter and, probably, his brother Andrew. Apparently the other boat belonged to their partners James and John. In order to get a more advantageous point from which to speak Jesus entered Simon's boat, and asked him to push it out a short distance from the shore (v. 3). There Jesus sat in the boat and "kept on teaching [imperfect] the people out of the ship." Plummer comments picturesquely that "Christ uses Peter's boat as a pulpit whence to throw the net of the Gospel over His hearers."

Luke does not record what Jesus said. But he mentions the teaching as an introduction to what Jesus did immediately thereafter. He took command of the boat. This is seen in the two imperatives. "*Launch out* into the deep, and *let down* your nets for a draught" (v. 4, author's italics). The first command (singular) He gave to Peter who probably was steering the boat. The second (plural) included some others, perhaps Andrew and the crew, since more than one was needed to let down the net. Here was a *landlubber* telling fishermen how to fish.

It is understandable, therefore, that Simon Peter would offer a protest (v. 5). They had toiled all night with no success. How could they expect to succeed now? Nevertheless, Simon addressed Jesus as "Master" (*epistata*). The word *epistatēs* means one who has the right to command. G. Campbell Morgan gives it the meaning of "Captain, captain of the boat." In the New Testament only Luke uses it, and always in addresses to Christ (5:5; 8:24, 45; 9:33, 49; 17:13). He never uses the word *rabbi* in this sense, a word which would have little meaning to the Gentiles.

Simon, despite their previous failure, takes orders from his Captain. "Nevertheless at thy word I will let down the net." However, it is evident that he expected to catch nothing. The best time for fishing was at night and near the shore. Now it was day and in deep water (Bruce). But he was in for a surprise. For "they inclosed a great multitude of fishes: and their net was breaking [imperfect]" (v. 6). They were in danger of losing the whole catch. So they beckoned to their partners (James and John) in the other boat to come to their aid (v. 7). There were enough fish to fill both boats so that they began to sink.

Obviously this was a miracle. It might be argued that Jesus had seen a large shoal of fish. But to do so at a distance and in deep water was no less a miracle. More likely it was a miracle of Jesus' knowledge. Certainly Simon Peter recognized a miracle. For he fell down at Jesus' knees, saying, "Depart from me; for I am a sinful man, O Lord" (v. 8). Note the change from *epistatēs* to *kurios*. From the "Master" whose orders must be obeyed, he calls Him "Lord" in whose holy presence the sinner is conscious of his unworthiness. "A sinful man" indeed! And one of his sins was to doubt the wisdom of Jesus. But Peter did confess his sin. From self-confidence and pride to humiliation and prayer. This should be the experience of every sinner who comes into the presence of Jesus.

Yes, Peter was astonished at the miraculous draught of fishes. And along with him James and John, and, by implication, Andrew (vv. 9-10; cf. Matt. 4:18-22). But there was a greater surprise in store for them. For Jesus said to Simon, "Fear not; from henceforth thou shalt catch men." Yes, out of fishers of fish Jesus made fishers of men. And He still calls men to use the talents of their professions to serve Him in the greatest adventure and business of all, catching men for the glory of God.

This call came while they were still in the boats. And as soon as they reached land, "they [all four fishermen] forsook all, and followed him" (v. 11). Already they had become Jesus' disciples (John 1). Now they became His disciples indeed. Blessed is every Christian who does the same.

Luke 5:12-26

The Challenge of the Needy

Jesus never turned His back upon a man in need, whether that need be physical or spiritual. This truth is abundantly seen in this passage.

In a certain city in Galilee "behold a man full of leprosy" (v. 12). The word "behold" without a verb suggests his sudden appearance before Jesus. Leprosy was one of the most dreaded of diseases. Two kinds of leprosy were found in Palestine. One was simply a bad skin disease. The other, starting with a small spot, ate away the flesh until the victim would be left with only a stump of a hand or leg. It was a living death which lasted for years.

Lepers were isolated from society, usually living in caves or tombs. They could not enter a walled town or city. They were not allowed to come nearer than one hundred feet to a well person if the wind were blowing from him toward the latter. When anyone approached he was required to give the warning cry "Unclean!" This isolation made leprosy both a physical and a psychological disease. It was regarded as a *type* of sin.

Strangely enough the law regarded advanced stages of leprosy as less unclean than the earlier stages. This man was "full of leprosy." Luke the physician alone notes this. The man's body must have been one mass of ulcers and sores. This advanced stage probably explains the man's presence in the crowd.

It was believed that leprosy could be cured only by God. This is expressive of the man's faith as he fell before Jesus begging or praying, "Lord, if thou wilt, thou canst make me clean." Apparently he had more faith in Jesus' power than in His goodness. "If you may will" you can do it.

And Jesus was willing. Much more, He touched the leper. Barclay calls this "Touching the Untouchable." The crowd must have gasped when Jesus laid His hand on him. Such was unheard of. One rabbi even boasted that he had driven a leper from him with stones. But not this Rabbi. He touched him, and said, "I will

[I am willing]: be thou clean" (v. 13). "And *immediately* the leprosy *departed* [aorist] from him" (author's italics). With double emphasis Luke notes the immediacy of the healing. "Immediately the leprosy departed at once from him." A miracle to be sure.

Even though Jesus worked a miracle, He did not ignore the law of His people. He never broke a law of God (cf. Matt. 5:17). Leviticus 14 required that healed lepers should go to the priest, make certain sacrifices, and be pronounced clean before he could re-enter society. Jesus told this man to comply with this law "for a testimony [evidence of healing] unto them" (v. 14).

Also He charged that the man should not tell others of his healing. Evidently Jesus did not want to precipitate undue excitement concerning His work. The people did not yet comprehend the nature of His person and mission. Whether the man told it or not, evidently those who had seen this miracle did so (v. 15). For great multitudes flocked to Jesus to hear Him and to be healed. The pressure of His ministry was so great that Jesus "was repeatedly [imperfect] withdrawing in the desert places and praying" (v. 16). If Jesus felt the need for such, how much greater is that need for those who serve Him.

On another occasion Jesus was in a house teaching (v. 17). For the first time Luke notes the presence of Pharisees and teachers of the law. The spreading fame of Jesus had brought these critics from throughout Galilee, Judea, and Jerusalem. The Pharisees were the *separatists* in the Jewish religion. They came into being sometime during the period between the Old and New Testaments. Beginning as a group of purists who opposed deviation from the Jewish religion in favor of Greek religion and customs, they rendered a valuable service in Judaism. In contrast to the liberal Sadducees they were the orthodox party. They regarded all of the Old Testament as Scripture, whereas the Sadducees adhered only to the five books of Moses. The latter group did not believe in angels, miracles, or the resurrection from the dead; the former group believed in all of these. In their zeal for the Scriptures they went to seed in devising myriads of rote rules designed to interpret the Scriptures and to direct people in observing them. By the time of Jesus their religious expressions had degenerated to empty rote rules, rites, and ceremonies. Although not all Pharisees were teachers or scribes of the law, this group was composed of Pharisees. Hence Luke's distinction of "Pharisees and doctors of the law."

Obviously they were present to oppose Jesus. John 4:1-4 shows that Jesus had aroused their opposition in Jerusalem. It was for that reason that He returned to Galilee. But they followed Him to dog His steps wherever He went.

While Jesus was teaching, some men brought a palsied man to be healed by Him (v. 18). Matthew 9:2 and Mark 2:3 call him a *paralutikon,* a paralytic – a vernacular term. But Luke, using the technical medical term, says that he was *paralelumenos.* But the meaning is the same.

The men who brought the paralytic to Jesus were a determined lot (v. 19). When they could not get him into the house because of the crowd, they took him up an outside stairway to the flat roof. There they tore a hole through the tile, and lowered the man on a pallet into the presence of Jesus. This was an act of faith (on the sick man's part also?), a faith which Jesus honored. For He said, "Man, thy sins are forgiven thee" (v. 20).

Why did Jesus forgive the man's sins before healing his body? For one thing, the former is more important. Again, it is possible that his physical condition was due to his sinful life, although this is not necessarily true in every case. Some hold that it was to increase the man's faith. But the reverse order would seem to be the more logical if that were true. In view of the persistent effort to get the man to Jesus, it appears that the faith of the man and of his friends was already quite powerful. Noting what follows immediately, did not Jesus first forgive the man's sins as a direct challenge to the critical Pharisees?

For upon hearing Jesus' words they began to reason, "Who is this which speaketh blasphemies? Who can forgive sins, but God alone?" (v. 21). Jesus had not said that God had forgiven the man's sins. He spoke directly out of His own authority. The Pharisees interpreted this to mean that He was usurping the authority of God, thus speaking blasphemy.

Jesus knew their innermost thoughts (v. 22). So He challenged them as to which was the easier, to speak words of spiritual forgiveness or to speak words of physical healing (v. 23). And then He threw down the gauntlet. "But that ye may know that the Son of man [Jesus' favorite designation of Himself, but never used by the Evangelists in direct reference to Him] hath power [authority] upon earth to forgive sins, (he saith unto the sick of the palsy,) I say unto thee, Arise, and take up thy couch [pallet], and go into thine house" (v. 24). "I say unto thee." Instead of calling upon God the Father to forgive, Jesus emphatically assumes this authority Himself. Of course, all that He did, He did within the will of the Father. But in His challenge to the critics, and upon their own word that "God alone" can forgive sins, He assumed deity for Himself.

"And immediately *rising up* [aorist participle] *before them* [before the critics' eyes], and *taking up immediately* [aorist participle] that whereon he *was lying* [imperfect], he *departed immediately* [aorist] to his own house glorifying God" (v. 25, author's italics). The verb tenses make this a vivid picture. A miracle indeed! And the critical Pharisees saw it.

Luke adds that "they were *all* amazed, and they glorified God" (v. 26, author's italics). Note the "all." This included the Pharisees. But not "all" glorified God. Its absence in the second clause is significant. All saw the same amazing thing. But the critics did not glorify God. They were still closed in mind and heart toward Jesus. The people had "seen strange things today," but one of the strangest was the refusal of the Pharisees to accept as true that which they had seen. Alas, it is ever true of obstinate unbelief!

Luke 5:27-32

The Response of a Publican

The Pharisees may not have received Jesus. But a publican did. It would be difficult to imagine two groups that were further apart in Jewish society in the first century. The Pharisees regarded themselves as the righteous elite. The publicans were classed with the lowest of sinners. The Pharisees were strong nationalists who hated Rome with a passion. The publicans were tools of the Romans, and were regarded as traitors among their people.

In Capernaum Jesus passed by the receipt of customs, and saw Levi the publican (v. 27). Levi is elsewhere called Matthew (Matt. 9:9). In Galilee it was common for one to have two names. Actually there were two kinds of publicans: the *Gabbai,* or tax-gatherer (income or poll tax); and the *Mokhes,* or customs-house officer. The latter was especially hated, since his position would lend itself to a greater abuse, especially among the poor. Levi was a *Mokhes.*

He could have been a Roman customs-officer, but more likely he was under the direct supervision of the tetrarch Herod Antipas. The great commercial route from Acre to Damascus ran through or near Capernaum. Caravans travelling either way would be subject to customs as they passed through Herod's domain. Some suppose that Levi may have been charged with collecting a tax from fishermen on the sea of Galilee. But the term "receipt of custom" more nearly fits the trade route.

When Jesus saw Levi He simply said, "Follow me." The present imperative means a command to follow Jesus permanently as a disciple. The Lord challenged him to change his occupation. While not stated we may assume that Levi had already received Jesus as the Christ. But as with the four fishermen so with him, Jesus called him to a more intimate discipleship.

Why did Jesus call Levi? To be a disciple? Yes. To be a preacher and soul-winner? Yes. But may we surmise another and particular reason? Plummer notes that the word for "saw" *(etheasato)* suggests to see with enjoyment. He looked attentively at him as if reading his character. Or, perhaps, beyond character to ability. As a customs-officer Levi would have to keep records. It is even possible that he wrote shorthand, for such was done then. What a prize for Jesus' purpose! Levi or Matthew wrote what is regarded as perhaps the earliest record of Jesus' teachings, the *Logia*. It is generally regarded as the Aramaic source of much of Jesus' teachings as found in the Gospels of Matthew and Luke. Certainly Matthew contains an abundance of His teachings. One can almost see this former customs-officer taking down in shorthand what he had heard Jesus teach.

At any rate when Jesus called him "he left all, rose up, and followed him" (v. 28). The verb tenses make this sentence come alive. "And immediately leaving [aorist participle] all, standing up [aorist participle], he went on following [imperfect] him." Without hesitation he turned his back on the customs-house and kept following Jesus in his new calling.

It was a significant day in Levi's life. In fact it called for a celebration. So in Jesus' honor he gave a "great feast," actually a *reception (dochē),* which included a dinner (v. 29). Of course, he invited his friends, "a great company of publicans and of others," social outcasts all. Robertson notes that the crowd was so great that this may have been a garden party.

Naturally the Pharisees were not invited. But in keeping with custom they stood about and watched the festivities (v. 30). Had they been invited they would have refused to come. But they stood about buzzing like angry bees (murmured, *egogguzon,* imperfect, note the sound of the word). And what were they buzzing? "Why do ye [Jesus and His disciples] eat and drink with *the* publicans and sinners?" (author's italics). The one definite article links "publicans and sinners" as one group. To them it was an outrage that one who claimed to be a teacher should do so.

Jesus ignored the charge against His disciples. For He alone was responsible. So His answer to this criticism involved Himself alone. "They that are whole [in good health] need not a physician; but they that are sick" (v. 31). Where else would you expect to find a physician but among the sick? Jesus took the Pharisees at their word. They were spiritually in good health; the publicans and sinners were spiritually sick. So the Physician of souls was where He was needed. Alas, the Pharisees needed Him equally as much. But the Physician was helpless before their obstinate wills. Jesus stood ready to heal them, but He, like any ethical doctor, would not force Himself upon them. And it is ever thus.

And then Jesus plainly applied His figure of speech. "I came not to call the righteous, but sinners to repentance" (v. 32). "Repentance" *(metanoia)* means a change of heart, mind, and attitude, or the entire direction of one's life. The "righteous" Pharisees saw no need to change. So Jesus could do nothing for them. The "sinners," recognizing their need, found in Jesus the power to effect that to which He called them.

How many of these "sinners" repented is not told. But Levi in his festive reception gave them the opportunity both to hear and to heed the call. It was a social occasion dedicated to the cause of evangelism.

Luke 5:33-39

The Old and the New

The critics now turned their barbs on Jesus' disciples. In Mark's account (2:18) the critics include both Pharisees and the disciples of John the Baptist. Matthew (9:14) singles out the latter. But Luke's "they" (5:33) would include both. So apparently some of John's disciples were also uninvited *guests* at the feast given by Levi.

This combination asked Jesus, "Why do the disciples of John fast often, and make prayers, and likewise the disciples of the Pharisees; but thine eat and drink?" (v. 33). The occasion may have been on one of the Jewish fast days, hence the Pharisees' criticism. John's disciples may have joined them because, while their teacher was in prison, Jesus and His disciples were enjoying a banquet. It might be noted that had the ascetic John been free he would not have attended such an affair. But, unlike him, Jesus was a social being. However, the problem here was not one of food but of religious ceremonialism.

In reply Jesus asked if it were proper to fast at a wedding feast (v. 34). His reference to the "bridegroom" would have special meaning to John's disciples. For he had called Jesus by that name, stating that he was the friend of the bridegroom (John 3:29). The disciples as "children of the bridechamber" certainly should not fast or mourn while the bridegroom was with them. The time will come when He will be taken from them (crucifixion). Then they will fast. But even that mourning will be of short duration. For joy will return after the resurrection, when He will be with them forever.

It is at this point that we see the difference between Judaism and Christianity. Mourning and joy, bondage and freedom respectively. Even today some Christians feel that to be religious one must be miserable. Such have missed the true meaning of the Christian faith. There is a place in the Christian's life for fasting, for Jesus Himself fasted. But it should not be done by the calendar or merely as an outward expression. It should be the result of an inner compulsion in which one is so absorbed in the things of God that he even loses the desire for food.

In His reply Jesus had already used one parable (bridegroom), even though Luke does not so name it. But then He adds three more parables, the new cloth on an old garment, the new wine in old wineskins, and the drinking of old wine.

Jesus said, "No one taking a patch from a new garment puts it on an old garment. Even if he does he will tear the new, and with the old will not agree the patch from the new" (v. 36). This translation follows the best Greek text.

What is Jesus saying? Obviously the new garment is the Christian revelation; the old is Judaism. Judaism is old and ragged. Should He tear off a piece of the former to patch up the latter? To do so would be to injure and to take away from the new; and even the new patch would be incompatible with the old garment. You cannot harmonize law and grace. The freedom in Christ must not be torn away in order to try to remedy the failure of Judaism or to preserve it. The old order will go on fasting and failing; the new will increase in joy and blessed ministry.

Furthermore, "no one puts new wine into old wineskins. Even if he does, the new wine will burst the wineskins, and it will be poured out and the wineskins will be lost" (v. 37). Again, the new wine is the Christian revelation; the old wineskins are the forms of Judaism. Old wineskins become brittle and lose their elasticity. If new or unfermented wine be put in them, as it ferments it gives off gases. Eventually the old skins will burst, thus losing both the wine and the skins. The proper thing to do is to put new wine in new skins (v. 38). Then when the gases form, the new skins stretch to meet the situation. Thus neither is lost.

The meaning of this parable is quite obvious. The Christian revelation cannot be contained in the forms of the old revelation. Grace cannot be expressed in terms of law. Each negates the other. Alas, how often men try to do this to the loss of all. The Christian revelation calls for new ways to express its truth. These ways are not to be found in rote rules, rites, and ceremonies of the Old Testament or of Judaism. They are found in the freedom which is in Christ: in grace, not law; in faith, not ritual; in joy, not mourning.

But Jesus ends this lesson on a sad note. "No one drinking old [wine] wants new. For he says, The old is good" (v. 39). The Pharisees were satisfied with their "old wine." The old is good or pleasant, so why even try the new? It was easier to win Levi, who probably had not been too concerned with the exact requirements of Judaism, than to win the Pharisees whose prejudiced minds closed their hearts to the new revelation in Christ. How often does the "good" become the enemy of the *best!*

Luke 6:1-11

The Sabbath Controversy

It is impossible to understand the conflict between Jesus and the Pharisees without taking into account the Jewish position concerning the Sabbath. Therefore, this passage is a key section in Luke's Gospel.

Three of the most sacred things to the Jews were the temple, the law, and the Sabbath. But other religions had temples and scriptures. The Sabbath was peculiar to Judaism. Hence this was their most sensitive spot.

The law of the Sabbath as stated in the Decalogue is quite simple (Exod. 20:8-11). But the ancient Jews devised literally hundreds of rules which interpreted and regulated this law. For instance, a Sabbath-day's journey was less than a mile. On the Sabbath one should not drag a stick on the ground, for that was plowing. A woman should not look in a mirror on the Sabbath. Seeing a grey hair she might pluck it out, and that was shearing. Learned (?) debates were held as to what one could or could not do on the Sabbath. Should one eat an egg laid on the Sabbath day? For in laying it the hen worked. A man got off his donkey at sunset on Friday, the beginning of the Sabbath. Should he remove the saddle from the donkey? If so, he worked; if not, the donkey worked. Should a man with a sore throat gargle with oil on the Sabbath? It was decided that he might drink oil for food. If it helped his throat that was incidental. Jesus never broke the commandment regarding the Sabbath. But He cared nothing for this multitude of man-made rules concerning that day.

Actually the question of the Sabbath came to a head in Jerusalem. Previously Jesus had healed on the Sabbath day (Luke 4:31-39). But this was in Capernaum prior to the time when the Pharisees began hounding His steps. John 5 records a subsequent visit to Jerusalem where He healed a man on the Sabbath. While the Pharisees in Judea had long opposed Jesus, this act of healing gave them an issue. And they played it to the hilt.

The incidents in Luke 6:1-11 occurred immediately after this visit to Jerusalem. On the way back to Galilee Jesus and His disciples were passing through a grain field (v. 1). Farmers left hard paths over which travelers might walk through their fields. It was the Sabbath day. The King James Version reads "the second sabbath after the first" *(en sabbatōi deuteroprōtōi)*. This last Greek word does not appear in the best manuscripts. Literally it means "secondfirst." In all likelihood some scribe wrote "first" *(prōtōi)* on the margin, because of the Sabbath miracle in Luke 6:6-11. A later scribe noting the prior Sabbath miracle in Luke 4:31 also wrote "second" *(deuterōi)* on the margin. A third scribe combined the two into *deuteroprōtōi* (Robertson). Robertson also notes that if this word were genuine, we do not know what it means.

Assuming, therefore, that this word does not belong in the true text, the picture is clear. On a Sabbath day Jesus' disciples were plucking heads of grain, rubbing them in their hands, and eating the grain. This was permissible as long as they did not actually cut the grain (Deut. 23:25). But certain Pharisees challenged them for their action. "Why do ye that which is not lawful to do on the sabbath days?" (v. 2). The illegality lay in the day, not in the act.

Why did they consider it illegal? To them plucking was reaping, rubbing was threshing, blowing away the chaff was winnowing, and the entire process was preparation of food. So all four acts were work on the Sabbath day. This shows how ridiculous was their interpretation of a simple law. It is no wonder that Jesus both ignored and condemned it.

Matthew records a longer answer to this charge (12:3-7). But Luke follows Mark (2:25-26) in citing only the case of David. Said Jesus, "Have ye not read so much as this, what David did . . .?" (v. 3). So absorbed were they in their own rule that they were ignorant of or had ignored this simple story (cf. I Sam. 21:1ff.). David and his men were without bread. So they ate the holy showbread in the tabernacle (v. 4). It was lawful only for the priests to eat this bread. But in such a necessity hungry men came before the law. If this were true, how much more so did the hungry disciples come before the man-made rules of the scribes?

Then Jesus made a statement of infinite moment. "The Son of man is Lord also of the sabbath" (v. 5). In the Greek "Lord" comes first in the sentence, and so is emphatic. He controls the Sabbath instead of being controlled by it. In the Jewish mind this was tantamount to claiming deity. Jesus did not in these words set aside the law. He interpreted it in its true meaning. Mark adds that the Sabbath was made for man, not man for the Sabbath (2:27). It was to be a blessing, not a burden. Plummer says, "Ritual must give way to charity. The Divine character of the law is best vindicated by making it lovable; and the Pharisees had made it an iron taskmaster. And, if the sabbath gives way to man, much more to the Son of Man."

Another Sabbath controversy occurred on a later Sabbath day (v. 6). Jesus was teaching in a synagogue. Present was a man whose right hand was withered. Only Luke with a physician's care notes that it was the *right* hand, the working hand (cf. Matt. 12:9; Mark 3:1). Scribes and Pharisees were on hand to spy on Jesus (v. 7). They "kept watching on the side" *(paretērounto,* imperfect). Would He heal on the Sabbath day? They were interested only in finding grounds for an accusation against Him.

Knowing their thoughts, Jesus told the man to rise and stand forth in the midst (v. 8). He read their minds, and threw down a challenge that all might see. The spies thought secretly, but Jesus worked openly. Righteousness has nothing to hide.

Thus it was that Jesus brought the whole issue of Sabbath observance out into the open. Heretofore, the Pharisees had criticized Him among themselves and before His disciples. Now with the crowded synagogue to witness, He asked them a question. "Is it lawful on the sabbath to do good, or to do evil? to save life, or to destroy it?" (v. 9). Which does the law of the Sabbath permit? Obviously the Pharisees would say that it was illegal to do evil or to destroy life. But what about doing a good deed or saving a life? Was the law indifferent to these things? Jesus had crowded His critics into a corner.

Strange to say, the Pharisees and scribes were more considerate of an animal than of a man in this regard. Some said that if an animal fell into a pit it was permissible to get it out on the Sabbath. Others said that you could only make it comfortable in the pit. But there was no relief for a man (cf. Matt. 12:11-12, parallel to Luke's passage).

However, there is more in Jesus' question than meets the eye. Here was a man whose working hand was incapacitated. You did not need to thrust a sword into his heart to destroy him. To leave him in his deformed condition was to destroy him insofar as a full, complete life was concerned. And is it not evil not to do good? So simply to do nothing for the poor man was to do evil, to destroy him.

The critics had no answer. So Jesus, looking about over the crowd (Mark 3:5 says, "With anger." Jesus searched the crowd for an answer and for emphasis.), said to the man, "Stretch forth thy hand" (v. 10). This was both a test of the man's faith and in order to enable all to see what was about to happen. The man did as Jesus said. And without a further word from Him the hand *"immediately was completely restored"* (aorist) to its former state of wholeness. They had seen a miracle before their very eyes!

Did this convince the critics? It did not. Instead "they were filled [aorist] with madness" (v. 11). The immediacy (aorist tense) of healing was matched by that of their being filled with madness. This was more than mere anger. The word "madness" is *anoias (a,* alpha privative, and *nous,* mind, or "no mind"). This was a senseless rage akin to insanity. In such a state they discussed among themselves what they might do with Jesus. Mark 2:6 puts it stronger. They rushed out of the synagogue, and plotted with the Herodians how they might destroy Jesus. Almost two years before His death His enemies were determined to kill Him. The question was how. For One who so defied them and their rules of conduct must be destroyed.

What a strange coalition, the Pharisees and the Herodians. Politically they were archenemies. The former hated the Herods; the latter were dedicated to restoring the Herodian kingdom. Later these will be joined by the Sadducees whose allegiance was to the Romans. Politics and vengeance make strange bedfellows indeed!

Luke 6:12-16

The Choice of the Twelve Apostles

Jesus had reached a moment of great import in His ministry. The number of His disciples (learners or pupils) had steadily increased. Certain of them He had called to follow Him in a special way. His ministry was approaching the half-way point. So He was now ready to choose a small group for a very definite purpose. Mark says that this purpose was threefold: that they might be with Him (for training), that He might send them forth, and that they might have authority to cast out demons (3:14-15). In a very real sense He was preparing this little band to be able to carry on after He left the earth.

Naturally such a choice was of the greatest importance. So He retired into the mountain to pray. All night long He continued in prayer to God (v. 12). The phrase "continued all night" was used by medical writers to express the whole night vigil of a physician at the bedside of a patient.

When morning came Jesus called His disciples to Him. And out of this group He "chose" (of Himself, and for Himself, indirect middle voice, Robertson) twelve, to whom He gave the title "apostles" (v. 13). The word "apostle" comes from the Greek verb *apostellō,* to send forth. It is equivalent to the Latin *mitto,* whence comes the word "missionary."

Luke's listing of the Twelve is found in verses 14-16 (cf. Matt. 10:1-4; Mark 3:17-19; Acts 1:13). A comparison of these lists is most interesting. The first four names are the same in each list, but the order varies. Mark and Acts: Simon Peter, James, John, Andrew. Matthew and Luke: Simon Peter, Andrew, James, John. Philip is number five in all four lists. In the three Gospels (no list in John) the sixth name is Bartholomew, who appears seventh in Acts. His is probably another name of Nathanael, a name which appears only in John where he is connected with Philip. Matthew and Thomas appear in all four lists, though in varying order. James the Son of Alpheus is ninth in each grouping. Thaddeus (Matthew and Mark) is also called Judas the brother of James (Luke and Acts). Simon the Cananaean (Matthew and Mark) is also called Simon the Zealot (Luke and Acts). It was common for a man to have two names. Judas Iscariot appears last in the Gospels and is absent from Acts.

The three groupings of four each are headed by Simon Peter, Philip, and James the son of Alpheus respectively. What significance this has is not known. These lists were made sometime after they were chosen. Peter's name at the head of the list certainly does not mean that he was the formal leader of the group before Christ's death. Jesus Himself was the leader. Peter's forward nature naturally thrust him to the front. In that sense he was a leader but it was not a divinely bestowed position. The New Testament does not support such a claim.

What a motley group was this band. At least four were fishermen. James and John were "sons of thunder" (Mark 13:17). Matthew was a despised publican. Bartholomew (Nathanael) was a combined cynic and idealist. Simon the Zealot was a former member of a terrorist group which was dedicated to the overthrow of Rome. And Judas Iscariot became *(egeneto,* Luke 6:16) a traitor. We can only say that each of these men must have had qualities which, if dedicated to Jesus, would prove valuable in the kingdom. Judas Iscariot was never really a true follower of Jesus. Jesus knew that he was a devil (John 6:70). Why did He choose him? Lange held that he was forced upon Jesus by the pleas of the other apostles. But He chose them of Himself and for Himself (Luke 6:13). Certainly it was not for the express purpose of betrayal. God does not deal with men as puppets. All that we can say is that Jesus offered him his chance, and he did not take it. It will forever remain a mystery. But it serves as a warning to all.

Luke 6:17-49

The Sermon on the Mount

According to Robertson's *A Harmony of the Gospels,* the Sermon on the Mount comes at about the middle of Jesus' ministry. Many different positions have been taken as to the relationship between the accounts in Matthew and Luke. Some insist that Luke's account is no sermon at all, but a collection of Jesus' sayings uttered at various times. To be sure, elements of both records are found elsewhere. But there is no reason why a Teacher like Jesus would not repeat lessons as the occasion demanded. Certainly Luke presents his material as an extended discourse.

Others hold that Matthew and Luke give two distinct sermons delivered to different audiences in two different places. There are slight differences in the audiences, but they may be considered as general statements which do not warrant such position. As to the place, Matthew says that Jesus went up into a mountain (5:1), while Luke says that He came *down* to a *level place* (6:17). But both mention the mountain. Luke simply means that Jesus came down the mountain, not to a plain, but to a level place in the mountain which made it possible for Him to be seen and heard. Where this mountain was we cannot say with certainty. Jerome mentions a tradition that it was the Horns of Hattin located some distance west of Capernaum. There is a level place on this mountain which could be Luke's "plain" or "level place" (6:17).

To be sure, there are decided differences between the two accounts. But they begin and end alike, and make contacts throughout the sermon. Matthew, writing for Jews, naturally stresses certain elements of the law in relation to the Christian revelation. Such matters would be of little interest to Luke's Gentile readers, so they are omitted by him. There is a difference in style. Matthew is smoother and in more detail, though each has material not found in the other. This could reflect a difference in sources of material. Robertson suggests that neither gives a complete account of what Jesus said on this occasion. Certainly this author is hesitant to differ with his great teacher. But in view of the smoother style and greater detail of Matthew, he dares a suggestion. Luke obtained his material second-hand, in rougher style, and lacking in detail. But Matthew actually heard the sermon. We have noted the possibility that he wrote shorthand. Could it be that he took down the sermon verbatim, and has reproduced it exactly as it was given by Jesus? It is an intriguing thought, to say the least.

Following His choice of the Twelve Jesus came down to a level place on the mountain. The crowds flocked to Him from everywhere. And He healed those who were diseased (vv. 17-19). Then He delivered the sermon. According to Matthew it was spoken to the disciples (5:1). But the multitudes were there and heard Him also. Following Luke's account we note the beatitudes and woes, Christian ethics, the question of judgment, and the conclusion.

The Beatitudes and Woes (6:20-26)

The *beatitudes* in Matthew are spoken in general address, and deal with the qualities pertaining to the Christian's *being*. Those in Luke are given in direct address, and point up the happiness in the Christian life as outward and present circumstances affect the inward and future condition. Conversely, the "woes" of Luke (not in Matthew) point up opposite conditions with opposite results. The four beatitudes in Luke correspond to the first, second, fourth, and eighth in Matthew, though not in that exact order.

"Blessed are ye poor: for yours is the kingdom of God" (v. 20). "Poor" *(hoi ptōchoi)* means deep poverty. Matthew reads "poor in spirit" (5:3). But Luke speaks of actual poverty. G. Campbell Morgan insists that we must read Matthew's "in spirit" into Luke. Robertson suggests that either may be true. Certainly Matthew's thought is not foreign to Luke's meaning. For poverty within itself is no virtue as wealth is no vice. In both Gospels the thought is that of contrast between the respective values of the world and of the kingdom of God. In interpreting Luke we must keep in mind that he is reporting Jesus' sermon to the Gentile mind. For this reason we take his emphasis to be upon actual poverty.

The world thinks of riches as a sign of God's approval upon a man. Jesus says that this is not necessarily so. Deep poverty may prove to be a greater blessing. For thereby one is stripped of all self-reliance. Rightly taken it leads one to trust utterly in God both spiritually and for material necessities. To such a person his "is the kingdom of God." Note that it "is," not "shall be." He is not in the kingdom because of poverty. But his poverty makes it easier for him to trust in Christ through whom his "is the kingdom of God." Jesus Himself noted how hard it is for a rich man to enter into the kingdom (Luke 18:24 f.). Not because of his riches, but because of his reliance upon them.

"Blessed are ye that hunger now: for ye shall be filled" (v. 21). There is a natural succession between this and the foregoing beatitude. Poverty produces hunger or actual want in this life. But the Christian not only finds help in such a state, he also has the glorious prospect of being filled (shall be filled) with all spiritual blessings in the life hereafter. Scoffers may sneer at "pie in the sky by and by." But Jesus never did.

"Blessed are ye that weep now: for ye shall laugh" (v. 21). This is audible weeping and laughing. Note the word "now," and "shall," present condition and future prospect. The succession continues. Poverty, want, weeping. And the succession in result obtains. In the kingdom of God they shall be filled, and, therefore, will laugh. Both beatitudes in verse 21 emphasize the contrast between present sufferings and future blessings.

"Blessed are ye, when men shall hate you . . . for the Son of man's sake" (v. 22). The poor and needy will have a rough time in life. They may be cut off from social intercourse ("separate you"). This could even mean to be cut off from the congregation. Their names may be "cast out as evil." Greek writers used this word *(ekballō)* for hissing an actor off the stage. Of course, any of these things could happen to a Christian in more favorable material circumstances. In either case this experience must be due to his faithfulness to Christ. When they experience such the Christians are to "rejoice . . . in that day," even "leap for joy: for, behold, your reward is great in heaven" (v. 23). Again, present sufferings, future blessings. True servants of God have always had to endure present hardships. But they have also had the blessed prospect of rewards in heaven.

But there is another side to the picture of present condition and future prospect. This is seen in the four "woes" which counter-balance the four "blesseds." Note the word "but" (v. 24).

"Woe unto you that are rich! for ye have received your consolation" (v. 24). This, of course, means the non-Christian "rich." Their riches are all the "consolation" *(paraklēsin),* help, cheer, or encouragement which they shall receive. Their riches were all that they had, and they received only that which they could give.

"Receive" *(apechete)* is *apechō* which in the papyri means "paid-in-full" (cf. Matt. 6:2, 5). They receive all that is coming to them in this life. The future prospect is "woe."

"Woe unto you that are full now [in best manuscripts]! for ye shall hunger [know want]. Woe unto you that laugh now! for ye shall mourn and weep" (v. 25). Note the two uses of "now" in contrast to the corresponding uses in verse 21. The situations are reversed both here and hereafter. These are perfect illustrations of The Rich Man and Lazarus in this life and the life to come (Luke 16:19-31).

"Woe unto you, when men shall speak well of you" (v. 26). Here again is the opposite of verses 22-23. For whereas the (true) prophets were mistreated, the "false prophets" were acclaimed. How true! How true! We should always measure values on the scales of God, not on the scales of men.

Christian Ethics (6:27-36)

The conduct of a Christian should exceed in moral quality that of the non-Christian. This thought is implied in the words "but I say unto you" (v. 27). "To you" in contrast to those addressed in verses 24-26.

The governing principle is Christian "love" *(agapate)* as over against the law of retaliation (vv. 27-29). Love for one's enemies, good deeds toward those who hate, invoking blessings upon one's abusers call for more than stoical self-control. There must be the positive outgoing of the kind of love which God in Christ has shown toward us *(agapē)*. A pugnacious world finds great difficulty in verse 29. To a blow on the face with a fist we want to reply in kind. Jesus says to turn the other cheek. This is not an argument for national disarmament. Jesus is talking about personal relationships. And the fact that He Himself reproved the officer who struck Him (cf. John 18:22 f.) suggests that this does not apply on all occasions. It should be noted, however, that Jesus did not strike back. Plummer has a helpful note at this point. "When love resists or refuses, it is because compliance would be a violation of love, not because it would involve loss of suffering." The case of taking one's cloak (outer garment, *himation)* suggests armed robbery. Instead of resisting, let him also take your under garment *(chitōn)*. To resist would be useless anyway, and could result in personal harm.

Furthermore, the Christian should have the habit of giving (present tense) to those who ask for help (v. 30). This does not forbid discriminate giving. But it does place the burden of motive on the giver. If the receiver misuses the gift, that is his responsibility. And when you give, says Jesus, "stop asking [*mē apaitei*]" it back. This implies that such was the custom. Love gives for the sake of giving with no thought of return.

And then Jesus gave a general rule to cover all cases. "And as ye would [plural, *thelete,* wish] that men should do to you, do ye also to them ['you' and 'do,' plural] likewise" (v. 31). This is Luke's version of the Golden Rule. Other teachers had *silver* rules stated in the negative. Do not do to others what you do not want others to do to you. But this is worlds removed from the positive teaching of Jesus. Simply act toward others as you would want them to act toward you were the situation reversed. If this simple rule were followed, what a multitude of problems in personal relationships would be avoided or solved!

Verses 32-36 simply explain verses 27-30 in the light of verse 31. There is no Christian virtue in acting kindly toward those who do the same to you, or to give in hope of a reward. Even non-Christians do this. The Christian under all circumstances should act in love, not for his own benefit but in order to demonstrate the quality of being a child of God and for God's glory (cf. Matt. 5:16). As God is abundantly merciful to us, even so we should be abundantly merciful toward others.

The Question of Judgment (6:37-45)

From outward relationships Jesus now turns to inward attitudes. "Judge not, and ye shall not be judged" (v. 37). Literally, "Stop having the habit of judging." The word "judge" *(krinō)* means to separate or to discern between two things. Jesus does not prohibit the forming of opinions. But they must not be formed rashly. We should not prejudge (prejudice) without sufficient evidence. Even then man's judgment is incomplete, for only God can know all the facts or the thoughts and intents of another's heart. If we are considerate of others, they will be considerate of us. It is the simple law of return.

Furthermore, the Christian should not "condemn" others. This is simply a greater degree of judgment in which one sets himself up as both judge and jury. Instead, one should "forgive" if he would receive forgiveness.

The positive side of such an attitude is to have a charitable nature (v. 38). The law of return works here also. Only the return will be exceedingly abundant beyond that which is given.

Jesus summarizes this entire thought in the words, "For with the same measure that ye mete withal it shall be measured to you again" (v. 38). This is true whether you measure good or evil. You fill a measure and send its contents to another. He simply takes your measure, fills it with the same, and returns it to you. You reap what you sow. You get back what you give. If you give good without measure, not counting the cost but giving out of love, you will receive without measure from both God and man.

With a series of parables Jesus drives home His lesson about judging (vv. 39-45). The blind cannot lead the blind, or else both will fall into a ditch (v. 39). At best we are all blind, and therefore are not capable of guiding or judging others. This is the duty of the Master; only as we are perfected in Him can we perform such a task (v. 40). Before judging others we should first judge ourselves. A man with a beam in his eye cannot remove a speck of dust from the eye of another (vv. 41-42). A tree is known by its fruits, whether they be good or bad (vv. 43-44). That which comes from a man's mouth reveals what is in his heart. "For of the abundance of the heart his mouth speaketh" (v. 45).

The Conclusion (6:46-49)

The Christian should recognize Jesus as Lord. Therefore, Jesus asked, "And why call ye me, Lord, Lord, and do not the things which I say?" (v. 46). A man is not saved by his deeds. But his deeds will reflect his salvation or the lack of it. And his life will stand or fall in accord to how he hears and does Jesus' words or fails to do so.

So Jesus closes the Sermon with the parable of the two builders (vv. 48-49). Note that both heard, but only one acted in accord with what he heard. The latter is as a man who built his house on a foundation of rock. His house withstood the storms of life. But the other is as a man who simply built his house on the flat, soft earth. When the stream came it ate away the earthy foundation. And his house fell. And the "ruin" was great. Like a giant tree falling in the forest, its crash echoed far and wide.

Storms will come. Most any shanty will stand in the sunshine. But what about the storm? Be sure that the house of your life is so grounded in Christ that it will endure the rigors of time, and continue in eternity.

Luke 7:1-10

The Faith of a Roman

Following the Sermon on the Mount Jesus returned to His headquarters in Capernaum (v. 1). How long He had been back there is not stated. Perhaps He had just arrived.

In Capernaum there was a Roman centurion (v. 2). A "centurion" was the military commander of a hundred soldiers. Polybius says that the best men in the army held this position. This could be true, for in the New Testament they always appear in a good light. This particular one must have been unusually fine, as seen in three statements made about him.

In the first place, he was a kind and considerate man (v. 2). He had a "servant [slave, *doulos*], who was dear to him." The word "dear" *(entimos)* means honored and respected, esteemed, valuable and precious. The last two words could mean that he was a valuable piece of property. But the over-all picture suggests the warmth of the other words. The centurion owned him, but evidently there was a much higher and warmer relationship between them.

The slave was sick, hovering between life and death. Apparently he had been ill for some time during Jesus' absence from the city. So hearing of Jesus' return the centurion sent the elders of the city, probably highly respected citizens but not priests, requesting that He come and heal his slave (v. 3). Matthew says that the centurion came (8:5). There is no need to see a conflict here. What one does through another he does himself. The fact that the elders came speaks for the character of the man.

In the second place, the centurion was a loving and generous man (vv. 4-5). For the elders described him as "worthy" *(axios)* or deserving of Jesus' help: "For he loveth our nation, and he hath built us a synagogue." An officer in the Roman army, yet he loved *(agapaō,* highest love) the Jewish nation. This could mean his esteem for their worship of one God. (There is no evidence that he was a proselyte to that religion.)

And he had shown his love by building a synagogue in Capernaum. "He himself" suggests that he not only built it but paid for it. He must have been a man of means. Modern tourists still see the ruins of a synagogue which was probably built upon the foundation of the one erected by the centurion. Jesus Himself had taught and worked miracles in it.

In the third place, the centurion was a man of faith (vv. 6-10). In response to the elders' request "Jesus went [was going, imperfect] with them." But while He was still some distance from the centurion's home, he sent friends to Him, saying, "Lord, trouble not thyself: for I am not worthy [*hikanos,* sufficient] that thou shouldest enter under my roof. Wherefore neither thought I myself worthy [*ēxiōsa*] to come unto thee." The elders had said that he was *axios* or deserving. But he said that he was not of sufficient importance *(hikanos)* for Jesus to enter his house. Neither did he consider himself to be deserving of Jesus' help *(ēxiōsa).* Quite a humble attitude for a Roman!

Thus he showed his faith in Jesus to heal miraculously. "But say in a word, and my servant [*pais,* boy, an affectionate word for his *doulos,* slave] shall be healed." Jesus need not trouble to come to the boy. His spoken word would be sufficient. Furthermore, he recognized Jesus' authority. The centurion himself acted under the authority of his superiors. And he exercised authority over those under his command. He spoke, and men obeyed. Was he hinting at a faith that Jesus acted under God's authority? At any rate, he took account of Jesus' authority by which He could speak a word, and his servant would be healed.

Jesus responded with His own evaluation of the Roman's faith. He marvelled that a pagan Gentile would believe that He had such authority. Not even an Israelite had dared to believe that He could heal in such a manner. So He said, "I have not found so great faith, no, not in Israel." When the centurion's messengers returned to his house, they found the servant healed. Jesus had honored his faith.

It is so easy to classify men. It is so common to think of the Romans in terms of a corrupt Caesar or a proud Pilate. But do not forget this remarkable centurion. For he was also a Roman.

Luke 7:11-17

The Raising of the Dead

The authority of which the centurion spoke extended also into the realm of the dead. This record is one of three such which are found in the Gospels (cf. daughter of Jairus and Lazarus). Luke alone tells of this present incident. And his record of accuracy certainly supports its genuineness. A physician would hardly record such a story without checking out all details.

Soon after He had healed the centurion's slave Jesus, along with His disciples and "much people," journeyed to the village of Nain (v. 11). Nain is not mentioned elsewhere in the Bible. Josephus mentions a Nain on the eastern side of the Jordan, but it is not this one. A village called Nein was found by Robinson about two miles west of Endor, on the northern slope of Little Hermon. This is exactly where Eusebius and Jerome located Nain. It is about a day's journey from Capernaum.

As Jesus neared the gate of the village He met a funeral procession coming out. Perhaps they were on their way to a rock cemetery which still may be seen. Since there is but one entrance to Nain, it is possible to locate the approximate spot where Jesus met the procession.

Luke says, "Behold, there was a dead man carried out" (v. 12). Literally, "one that was dead." This renders a perfect participle, the perfect tense telling us that the man was really dead, not just in a coma. Death is always sad. But this one was unusually so. For he was the only *(monogenēs,* only born, cf. John 3:16, 18) son of a widowed mother. One could hardly imagine a greater grief than hers.

Perhaps she was walking at the head of the procession, followed by a great crowd of grieving friends and professional mourners. Thus Jesus met her first. In compassion He said, "Stop weeping" (v. 13). So sure was He of the result of what He would do that He said this to her before proceeding. It is of interest to note that here Luke calls Him "Lord." He is the Lord of life and Lord over death.

Then Jesus came and touched the bier (v. 14). He did this in order to stop the procession. When death met its Lord there was no need to proceed farther toward the cemetery. So the bearers stood still. Then Jesus spoke to the dead man. He expected him to hear him and respond. "I say unto thee, Arise." It was death's Lord speaking.

The man *immediately sat up* (aorist) and *himself immediately spoke* (aorist middle) (v. 15). The verb "sat up" is used by medical writers of the sick sitting up in bed. Then Jesus "delivered [gave] him to his mother." She had lost him in death, but Jesus gave him to her in life.

It is no wonder that an immediate "fear seized all" (v. 16, aorist). But their fear gave way to joy as they "went on glorifying God" (imperfect). They began and increased in glorifying God. For this miracle told them that a prophet was among them. Truly "God hath visited his people." The report of this miracle spread throughout the surrounding country, reaching even as far away as Judea (v. 17). Did the Judeans believe it? Or did they simply shrug it off as an idle tale coming from the country folks of Galilee?

But one thing is sure. This was the harbinger of that day when all in the realm of the dead will hear His voice of authority.

Luke 7:18-35

The Confusion of John the Baptist

During all of this time, perhaps eighteen months, John the Baptist was in a dungeon in Herod's castle at Machaerus (cf. Luke 3:20). Evidently his disciples were permitted to visit him on occasion. So they reported to him the things which Jesus was doing (v. 18). Hearing the report, John sent two of his followers to inquire of Jesus, "Art thou he that should come? or look we for another?" (v. 19). So they performed their mission (v. 20).

Nestle, and Westcott and Hort accept the reading of "another" as *allon,* another of the same kind. But they place *heteron,* another of a different kind, in the margin. This is the reading of certain manuscripts. The reading *heteros* is unquestioned in Matthew's account of this event (11:3). Robertson accepts the reading of *heteron* as the true text here. This author agrees with him. As will be seen, this fine point of textual criticism is important in determining the meaning of John's inquiry.

Why did John ask this question? Some say that it was for the sake of his disciples. But Jesus' reply was directed to John, not to his disciples. Others hold that John's own faith in Jesus as the Messiah was failing. Had he been mistaken in identifying Jesus as such? Still others see an impatience in John's question. Where was the program of the Messiah? He was not challenging world powers, organizing a government, or setting up a program for world rule. How like many today who say that the church has failed by pursuing a spiritual ministry instead of becoming simply a crusading organization in the name of social justice!

But Jesus did not interpret John's question in keeping with any of these positions. True, John was in prison while Jesus remained free. And we could understand how such confinement might react on this freedom-loving son of the desert. But was this the case?

An examination of John's question and of Jesus' reply reveals otherwise. What actually did John ask? Literally, "Are *you* the

Coming One [*ho erchomenos*], or are we to keep on looking for another [Messiah] of a different kind?" (author's italics). "The Coming One" was a designation for the Messiah in the Minor Prophets. "You" is written out, and so, emphatic. So John asked if Jesus Himself were that kind of Messiah, or was there to be another of a different kind?

The picture of the Messiah in the Minor Prophets was definitely one of judgment. That in the Major Prophets was one of a Suffering Servant and a reigning King. An examination of John's preaching shows a definite emphasis upon the former, although the latter picture is also present but in a minor key (cf. John 1:29). Now John hears of Jesus' works: preaching, teaching, and healing. Where is the judgment of evil? And this question is being asked to this very day.

To be sure, we can read into John's question an attitude of impatience. His very condition could produce such as in a dungeon he waited for the expected judgment. But is not his inquiry more one of confusion on his part? He had been so certain that Jesus was the Messiah. And He was fulfilling the role of the Major Prophets. But was this to be all? Was there to be another of a different kind who would fulfil the role of the Minor Prophets? So, in effect, John asked whether or not there were to be two Messiahs.

We must not judge John from our vantage point. We know that, in addition to His tender ministry, Jesus also preached judgment. Especially was this true in His portrayal of the end of the age. But John asked his question on the basis of what he had heard from his disciples. It was not a question born of doubt but of perplexity. He expected the two pictures of the Messiah to be fulfilled simultaneously. Both pictures are true, but they are fulfilled within God's will and according to His purpose.

Note Jesus' answer to the disciples of John. He went right on performing His ministry of mercy (v. 21). The Messiah will not alter His mission for the sake of His forerunner. Then He told them to report to John what they had seen and heard (v. 22). Clearly Jesus had Isaiah in mind (cf. 35:5-6; 61:1). The Suffering Servant must meet the needs at hand. Judgment will come, but it will come according to God's plan, not man's.

"And blessed is he, whosoever shall not be offended in me" (v. 23). "Offended" renders a Greek word *(skandalizomai)* which means to trip up, entrap, or to stumble. Jesus' ministry should not be a stumblingblock. This is a mild rebuke of John, but it is one of tenderness and mercy.

After the departure of John's disciples Jesus began to speak to the crowd concerning John (v. 24). And one could wish that his disciples had heard what Jesus said. Perhaps the people were tending to censure John. So Jesus asked them a series of questions.

Did they go into the wilderness to hear John, expecting to see a reed shaken by every passing wind? Certainly John was not so frail. Or one clothed in soft raiment and living in luxury (v. 25)? Such lived in king's courts and bowed to their every wish. John was in the king's *dungeon* because he dared to condemn the king's conduct. Did they go out to see a prophet (v. 26)? The people regarded John as such. "Yea," said Jesus, as He Himself agreed with them. But he was more than a prophet. He was the forerunner of the Christ (v. 27). Certainly Jesus did not agree with those who look upon John as a doubter.

But He reserved His greatest tribute to John until the last (v. 28). "Among those that are born of women, there is not a greater ['prophet' not in best manuscripts] than John." Not just the greatest prophet. "There is none greater than John." What a tribute for anyone to pay to another! This is especially great coming from Jesus. It is the Lord's epitaph to a faithful servant (cf. Matt. 25:21).

But then Jesus added a strange statement. "But he that is least in the kingdom is greater than he." None born of woman is greater. Yet the *least in the kingdom* is greater. Not in character or function, but in privilege. This does not mean that John was not a part of God's kingdom. He stood on the shoulders of all foregoing prophets as the one forerunner of Him whom they foresaw. But those coming thereafter stand on John's shoulders. His very perplexity testifies to this. He saw only one picture of the Christ. But those who have come after him see the whole: death, resurrection, promised return and coming judgment. We see the end from the beginning. And with this we are satisfied.

Some interpreters see verses 29-30 as comments by Luke injected into Jesus' teaching. It is more natural, however, to see them as a part of Jesus' own words. He is simply pointing out the division created by John's ministry. And that division continues in the people's regard for John and Jesus.

To what will He liken the men of His generation (v. 31)? They are like children playing in the marketplace, a scene which could have been transpiring before them at that very moment.

They keep sitting and calling one group to the other. One group wants to play and dance. But the other will not. Then they suggest that they mourn. But the other group will not weep. They neither want to dance nor play funeral. They simply do not want to play. They were interested in other things.

Then Jesus applied the lesson. John the Baptist was a stern ascetic (v. 33). And people called him insane ("He hath a demon"). On the other hand, Jesus was a social being (v. 34). Yet His enemies called Him a glutton, a winebibber, a friend of publicans and sinners. Such diverse roles, yet they rejected both. They just did not want to play. They were so absorbed in other matters that they were indifferent to the whole affair. How true then. And, alas, how true today!

"But wisdom is justified of all her children" (v. 35). In essence, the results justify the wisdom of God. Both John and Jesus lived and wrought according to God's will. Men may reject them now. But time and eternity will testify to their places in God's plan. We must not judge a play by one scene, but must see it to its finale. Hours may seem to tell one story. But the true meaning is in the centuries. We must wait to see what the centuries have to say against the hours.

John saw only the beginning of God's drama of redemption, and was confused. God grant that we shall see it fully, in fact and experience, and in faith realize its glorious prospect.

Luke 7:36-50

The Anointing of Jesus

There are few instances in the life of Jesus which have caused greater dispute. Some would identify this story with John 12:3, thus making Mary of Bethany a sinful woman. And this in spite of Luke's portrayal to the contrary (10:38 ff.). Others see the woman in the story as Mary Magdalene, simply because of Luke's description of her in Luke 8:2. Both of these positions are built upon fancy, not fact. But what of the story itself?

It probably took place in Capernaum. Jesus was the dinner guest of a Pharisee (v. 36). While the man was coldly polite he apparently was not hostile to Jesus. He may have invited Him out of curiosity. Luke has two other incidents where Jesus ate with Pharisees (11:37; 14:1). So He ate with both Pharisees and publicans. Ragg calls Luke the Gospel of Hospitality.

They were reclining at the table. According to custom, upon arrival Jesus had removed His sandals. Now He was reclining on His left side with His feet outward. As usual there were uninvited guests standing about and looking on. Suddenly out of this group there came a woman bearing an alabaster cruse of ointment (v. 37). It was evidently a precious possession. Now Luke notes that she was a "sinner" *(hamartōlos)*. Literally, "which was in the city a sinner." Evidently she was (had been) a notorious woman of the town or a public woman.

She stood behind Jesus alongside *(para)* His feet (v. 38). Overcome by emotion she wept, and her tears fell on His feet. (This was not a part of her original purpose to anoint Him.) It was a shame for a Jewish woman to let down her hair in public. But forgetting the shame she did so, and kept wiping (imperfect) His feet with her hair. Furthermore, as an act of supreme devotion she "kept kissing his feet, and kept anointing them with the ointment" (imperfects). Plummer notes that kissing a rabbi's feet was a sign of deep reverence. With vivid style Luke describes this scene of utter devotion.

Then suddenly the tone changes (v. 39). For the Pharisee-host, seeing this, spoke inwardly or in his thoughts. "This man [*houtos,* this one; he does not dignify Jesus by name], if he were a prophet, would have known who and what manner of woman this is that toucheth him: for she is a sinner." "If he were" is a condition of the second class, stating something that is determined as being unfulfilled. The Pharisee assumes that Jesus is not "a prophet." Some manuscripts read "the prophet." If this be a true reading it means the "Prophet" or Messiah (cf. Deut. 18:15). In any case, reasoned the Pharisee, Jesus is not who He claims to be. For a prophet would know who (person) and what (character) she was. And no prophet would contaminate himself by permitting her to touch him. So reasons proud ceremonialism.

But not Jesus. Knowing the man's cynical thoughts, He said that He had something to say to him (v. 40). Jesus courteously asked permission to speak. Godet rightly sees a note of irony in His request. For Jesus would show that He knew not only about the woman, but also the thoughts of His host.

Receiving permission to speak, Jesus related a parable (vv. 41-42).

A certain money lender had two debtors. One owed him five hundred *dēnaria* or about ninety dollars (a *denarius* was worth about eighteen cents). The other owed nine dollars. Since neither had the ability to pay, he "forgave them both" (v. 42). "Forgave" *(echarisato)* comes from the word for "grace" *(charis).* So "he graced both."

What a picture of salvation! Regardless of the amount owed, both men were in debt, apparently a debt which neither could pay. The lender might have put them in prison or have sold them into slavery. It was not the amount but the debt that mattered. But he dealt with them, not according to law, but according to grace. He graciously forgave the debts, even though it cost him personally to do so. This is what God in Christ does for everyone who comes to Him in repentance and faith.

The Pharisee was in no position fully to understand the grace of God. But he was familiar with law, God's law and man's law. And we may well imagine that he saw, at least partially, the point of Jesus' story. The Lord will not deal with this woman according to law, especially man's ceremonial law, but according to God's grace.

Love is the natural response to grace. So Jesus asked, "Which of them will love him [creditor] most?" The Pharisee may have seen the point. But his heart was not touched. Note his cautious indifference. "I suppose that he, to whom he forgave most" (v. 43). Even a hard-hearted Pharisee could see this. Jesus gave him "A" for his answer but not for his attitude.

Up to this point Jesus had not looked at the woman. Now He turned toward *(pros,* suggesting "face," v. 44) her. He faced the woman, and told the Pharisee (Simon) to do the same. Then He addressed Simon, not the woman. Though Jesus was his invited guest, Simon had omitted certain gestures of hospitality. To get the full impact of Jesus' words let us translate them literally. "I entered of you into the house [I was your invited guest], water to me upon [my] feet you did not give. But [by contrast] she with tears wet my feet and with her hair wiped [them]. A kiss to me you did not give. But she since I entered has not ceased kissing affectionately my feet [she showered His feet with loving kisses]. With oil my head you did not anoint. But she with costly ointment anointed my feet" (vv. 44-46). Simon did not even use plain oil on His head, the highest part of the body, but she used precious ointment on His feet, the lowest part of His body.

How could words have made the contrast any greater? G. Campbell Morgan expresses it for us. "Simon, you said, if I were a prophet I could see her. Can *you* see her, Simon? I have put you side by side, and by comparison you are as coarse as sackcloth, and she is as fine as finely spun silk!" *(in loco).*

And then Jesus drew His lesson from the story. "Her sins, which are many, are forgiven" (v. 47). "Are forgiven" *(apheōntai)* is a perfect passive form. They were forgiven in the past and stand forgiven. Her sins had been forgiven before she came into Simon's house. That is why she came, to show her love for her Saviour. She was not forgiven because she loved. Because of His grace toward her in forgiving her many sins, she "loved much." That forgiveness precedes love is seen in the phrase, "but to whom little is forgiven, the same loveth little." This does not mean that Simon had been forgiven a little, and so, loved little. It simply completes the lesson of the parable, and confirms Simon's own words (v. 43). We can only hope that Simon learned the lesson, not only in word but in experience.

Even though Jesus had forgiven the woman previously, Simon's attitude may have caused her to wonder. So to reassure her Jesus said, "Thy sins are forgiven" (same verb as in v. 47). They still stand forgiven. Those who were reclining about the table, probably more Pharisees, mused within themselves, "Who is this that forgiveth sins also?" (v. 49). To them only God could do this. So in their judgment Jesus was claiming deity.

Jesus ignored their thoughts, even though He doubtless knew them. Instead, He gave His full attention to reassuring the woman. "Thy faith hath saved [perfect] thee; go in peace" (v. 50). Lack of faith left the Pharisees still in their sins. Truly, harlots entered the kingdom before them! Not because they were harlots, but because they repented and believed. Amen!

Luke 8:1-3

The Glory of Christian Womanhood

This is one of the most beautiful stories in Luke's Gospel. It is a lovely gem set in the midst of our Lord's busy ministry. Like a careful and skilled jeweler it demonstrates Luke's sense of accuracy and detail. Furthermore, it shows his high respect for noble womanhood. In this we see the delicate sense and touch of a dedicated physician.

Using his customary phrase "and it came to pass [soon] afterward," Luke introduces Jesus' second tour of Galilee. This time He was accompanied by the Twelve (v. 1). It is a vivid picture of a busy ministry. "He was making his way [imperfect] through cities and villages, heralding and evangelizing [declaring good news] the kingdom of God" (author's translation).

Besides the Twelve Jesus was accompanied by "certain women, which had been healed [perfect, suggesting that the healings had taken place some time before this] of evil spirits and infirmities" (sicknesses, v. 2). Each woman had some special reason for being devoted to Jesus.

With careful detail Luke identifies three of these women. The first is "Mary called Magdalene." Mary is a common name, so she was singled out as the one "of Magdala." The location of Magdala is not known. This is the Greek form of the Hebrew *Migdol,* watch-tower, and could have been any one of a number of places. Plummer suggests that probably it was a place known as Mejdel, near the center of the western shore of the Sea of Galilee.

However, the most important designation is that she it is "out of whom went seven devils" (demons). It is this statement which has led many to identify her with the sinful woman of Luke 7:37. But is such identification justified? The only basis is the proximity of this mention of her to the sinful woman. And that is really no basis at all. If it were true, why did not Luke say so? And if he wished to hide her identity, why mention her immediately thereafter? And does being possessed by seven demons necessarily imply immorality? Plummer is right when he says that a woman of such demoniacal tendencies would hardly be able to follow the trade of prostitution. It is far more reasonable to understand the seven demons as some terrible physical or mental malady. This certainly could explain her great love for Jesus (cf. John 19:25; 20:1ff.).

The second woman was "Joanna the wife of Chuza Herod's steward" (v. 3). Little is known of her. She is mentioned again with Mary Magdalene in Luke 24:10. The Herod mentioned is probably Antipas. Godet believes that Chuza is the nobleman *(basilikos)* of John 4:46-53 who believed with all his house. If this be true, it explains why he would permit his wife to follow Jesus about Galilee. As a "steward" of Herod he probably was the manager of his household and estates. This would indicate that Joanna was a woman of station and of means.

The third woman was Susanna. Nothing else is known of her. But there were "many others." They remain in blessed anonymity.

But the sparkle in this gem is "which ministered unto him of their substance." They "kept on ministering [imperfect] out of the things belonging to them."

Prior to His public ministry Jesus supported Himself and, probably, His household, as a carpenter. But, thereafter, He had nowhere to lay His head. Except for the occasional hospitality of friends, how did He live? Here is the answer. He was supported by friends. And it is significant that the only specific mention of such tells of a faithful group of women. In the Gospels no woman is ever mentioned who was hostile to Jesus.

Jesus had ministered to these women out of His *substance*. Now they minister to Him and the Twelve out of theirs. Robertson notes that "this is the first women's missionary society for the support of missionaries of the Gospel." And their descendants have been legion! This is indeed the glory of Christian womanhood.

Luke 8:4-18

The Parable of the Soils

One of Jesus' favorite methods of teaching was the parable. It was something akin to the use of illustrations in preaching. The word "parable" *(parabolē)* means a casting alongside. It is to cast a natural truth alongside a spiritual truth for the purpose of teaching the latter. Someone called it an earthly story with a heavenly meaning. Or, a handle by which to pick up a truth and carry it. In a sense a parable both conceals and reveals. It conceals truth from those who will not receive it; it reveals it to those who will.

A study of the Synoptic Gospels (Matthew, Mark, Luke) shows that at this point in His ministry Jesus began to make a greater use of parables in teaching. The growing hostility of the Pharisees made this necessary. He did not deliberately *conceal* truth from them. But this method was necessary to enable Him to *reveal* truth to His disciples. The callous minds of the Pharisees would fail to grasp the truth, a truth which they would have twisted to their own nefarious ends. But those of sensitive and willing minds would grasp and retain the truth which was taught (v. 10). Even today people retain more than any other the truth which Jesus taught in parables.

Matthew and Mark together give ten parables taught at this time (Matt. 13:3-53; Mark 4:3-34). Luke gives only two. But he does give the one which seems to be regarded by all three as the principal one, namely, the parable of the sower or soils.

Somewhere along the shore of the Sea of Galilee (Matt. 13:1) crowds came to Jesus. And He taught them "a parable" (v. 4). Although Luke records two, he focuses on the main one. Since Matthew and Mark relate several, they say "in parables."

It was a common sight in Palestine. A sower went out to sow his seed (v. 5). Two methods might be used in sowing. Sometimes a sack of seed was placed on a donkey, with holes cut in both ends of the sack. As the donkey walked over the field, the seed fell to the ground. Another method was for the farmer to scatter the grain broadcast by hand. This was probably the method used here.

The grain fell on different kinds of soil. Some fell "alongside the way," or, a hard path left in the field for travellers. It fell so near the path that it was trodden down. Since it was uncovered birds ate it. Other seed fell upon "the rock," or "rocky places" (v. 6; Matt. 13:5). Palestine was underlaid by limestone rock. Where the soil was thin the warm rock would cause the grain to sprout rapidly (Matt. 13:5). But the plants had little root and consequently little moisture, so that they soon "withered away" (aorist). Still other grain fell on soil infested with thorn roots (v. 7). The thorns grew alongside the grain, so that they choked it. Hence the yield of grain would be small. But some grain fell "into" *(eis)* rich soil (v. 8). And its yield was "an hundredfold." This may seem like an unusually large crop. But Herodotus reports yields in the plain of Babylon two and three times as great.

The parable was finished. But its importance is seen in Jesus' loud admonition (suggesting the size of the crowd), "He that hath ears to hear, let him hear."

The disciples asked Jesus to explain the parable (v. 9). Perhaps they saw dimly the meaning but wanted greater light upon it. It might be well at this point to consider the method of interpreting parables. A parable is not a fable. Fables might or might not be true to life. But a parable was true to life. Furthermore, a parable usually illustrates one truth, even though subordinate truths are involved. Failure to recognize the *one truth* element can lead to all kinds of extravagant and misleading meanings. Jesus Himself called the parable at hand the parable of the sower (cf. Matt. 13:18). But the emphasis of His interpretation is upon the *soils.* The same kind of seed fell upon different kinds of soils with varying results. So in that light we call this the parable of the soils. This is in keeping with its central thought.

So Jesus explained the parable. "The seed is the word of God" (v. 11), or the word coming from God. In the Christian sense, therefore, the seed is the gospel. He does not identify the sower. In all likelihood he is anyone who proclaims the gospel. As one does so the word falls into different kinds of lives as depicted by the different soils. The wayside soil is the *hard hearted* (v. 12). He hears the gospel. But before it can sprout and take root, the devil comes and takes it away. Jesus did not say that an impersonal principle of evil does this. It is the devil, the slanderer, a person. This the devil does lest they should believe it and be saved. Alas, how many hear the gospel but do not believe it unto salvation!

"Those on the rock" (v. 13), or shallow soil, are those who hear and receive the word with joy. But they have no root. They are *superficial believers,* not true believers, who fall away. Having no real experience of regeneration, they wilt under temptation or trial. "Fall away" means to stand off from. They stand off from God rather than follow Him (cf. Heb. 3:12). How many people seemingly make professions of faith in Christ, but soon drop out of sight! Perseverance is an evidence of true faith. Falling away or standing aside is proof of no faith. In Hebrews 3:12 the word "unbelief" *(apistia)* means "no faith." It does not mean to *unbelieve* something which has been believed. It means that one never had faith.

Those falling among thorns are *fruitless Christians* (v. 14). In verse 12 the time element is nil. In verse 13 it is of short duration. In verse 14 it is of indefinite but longer duration. This suggests that the seed take root in deep soil. But "when they have heard, go forth, and are choked...." Perhaps the best translation would be "going on their way under the influence of cares, etc." (Plummer). Cares, riches, and life's pleasures so entangle them that they are choked or strangled. And like wheat growing among thorns they get little spiritual nourishment, the result being puny plants and no harvest. Such are Christians, but are fruitless Christians. The multitude of such believers is a tragedy and a scandal to the name of Christ.

Happily some seed fell on "good ground." Literally, "beautiful and noble land." In "an honest [noble] and good [beautiful] heart," having heard the word they "keep it" [hold it fast]. The devil does not snatch it away, the sun does not wither it, and the thorns do not choke it. But they bear fruit "in patience," in rugged endurance or perseverance despite the trials. This is the *deeply spiritual life* which produces first the shoot, then the blade, and then a full head of grain. It takes time and rugged endurance to produce the fruits of a Christian life. Nothing less than this is worthy of the name.

Then Jesus illustrated the final point of this parable with another parable (vv. 16-17). The man who has had a true experience with Christ should not seek to hide it. Instead, he should let it be seen. Light is meant to shine.

Therefore, Jesus' hearers should beware [*blepete*] how they hear

(v. 18). The one who has a genuine experience with Christ will receive more. But the one whose experience is superficial will lose even "that which he seemeth to have."

What kind of soil are you? The failure will not be in the gospel or seed but in the person or soil. This is the lesson of the parable of the soils.

Luke 8:19-21

The New Relationship

Even though Jesus was born of a virgin, He was born into a family relationship. He had a mother, a foster-father, four half-brothers, and at least two half-sisters (cf. Matt. 13:55-56). Some, holding to the perpetual virginity of Mary, insist that these brothers and sisters were either cousins or else children of Joseph by a former marriage. But there is no valid reason for denying that after Jesus was born Joseph and Mary had children by natural births (cf. Matt. 1:24-25; Luke 2:7). Luke's use of "firstborn" surely means that there were other children born to Mary.

And we may well imagine that the relationships in this family were normal ones up until Jesus left Nazareth to enter His ministry. But it is equally evident that this relationship underwent a change thereafter. John 2:4 suggests that Jesus gave Mary a gentle reminder of this fact.

Sometime during Jesus' "Busy Day" He apparently was teaching in a house. At this time Mary and her other sons came to see Jesus (v. 19). Why they came is not stated. Some hold that due to the pressure of His work they feared for His well-being. So they wanted to take Him home. But this is pure conjecture. The tone of Luke's account (cf. Matt. 12:46-50; Mark 3:31-35) does not merit such a position. The fact that in Mark 3:30 some called Jesus insane does not mean that His family shared this opinion. In all likelihood they merely came to see Jesus and for no other reason.

At any rate they were unable to approach Him because of the crowds. But some told Him of their presence. "Thy mother and thy brethren stand without, desiring to see thee" (v. 20). Did they have a prior privilege over the needy masses?

When Jesus heard of their presence He said, "My mother and my brethren are they which hear the word of God, and do it" (v. 21). The Christian relationship is more than one of human parentage. John the Baptist had already declared this truth (Luke 3:8). And now Jesus places it on an even higher plane. Plummer comments, "Family ties are at best temporal; spiritual ties are eternal."

In His words Jesus was not inconsiderate of family ties. But when He entered into His ministry He deprived Himself of the joys of family life that He might effect a more wonderful relationship, that of leading men to become sons of God. And "as many as received him, to them gave he power to become sons of God, even to them that believe on his name" (John 1:12).

Luke 8:22-56

The Power of Jesus

It had been an unusually "Busy Day" for Jesus. Mark 4:35 (RV) says, "And on that day, when even was come, he saith unto them, Let us go over unto the other side" of the lake. Luke 8:22 simply says, "Now it came to pass on a certain day, that he went to a ship with his disciples: and saith unto them, Let us go over unto the other side of the lake. And they launched forth." Thus both Evangelists (cf. Matt. 8:18, 23-34; 9:18-26) introduce a series of events which show forth Jesus' power over nature, demons, disease, and death.

Jesus' Power over Nature (8:23-39)

This is seen in Jesus' stilling a storm on the lake of Galilee. He was utterly exhausted after a hard day of ministry. The crowds took much out of Jesus, emotionally and physically, as everyone who follows His calling knows. Here as nowhere else we see the humanity of our Lord. He had given and given until His body and spirit demanded rest. So as the disciples sailed the boat Jesus fell asleep (v. 23). This is the only mention of Him sleeping. Mark 4:38 adds the detail that He slept on a cushion in the stern of the boat.

Suddenly a storm "came down" (*katebē,* aorist) on the lake. Matthew calls it a "tempest" (*seismos,* our word "earthquake," 8:24). It was like a mighty earthquake as the lake pitched, shook, and rolled. From the waves the boat "was filling" (imperfect) with water, so that the little band was in dire peril.

Apparently the disciples had exhausted their skill at seafaring to no avail. So excitedly they awoke Jesus, saying, "Master, master, we are perishing" (v. 24, present). The twice-used word "Master" is *epistata* (cf. 5:5). The crew called, "Captain, Captain, we are perishing" or "are being destroyed" (this follows Morgan's translation). Jesus, arising, rebuked the wind and raging sea. He spoke to them as though they would understand. And both "ceased immediately, and immediately there became a calm" (both verbs aorists). One moment there was a boiling cauldron; the next there was a placid lake. It was a miracle. Otherwise the wind and sea would have subsided gradually.

Then Jesus rebuked His disciples with a question. "Where is your faith?" (v. 25). Matthew reads, "Why are ye fearful, O ye of little faith?" (8:26). Mark adds, "Have ye not yet faith?" (4:40 RV). Why did they fear as long as Jesus was in the boat? Did they not know that He would not perish in a storm at sea? God would not permit the Christ so to die. This gives meaning to Jesus' question, especially as recorded in Mark and Luke. "Where is your faith?" (Luke). "Have ye not yet faith?" (Mark). Did they not yet believe that He was the Christ?

But are we any better? We see storms raging over the earth, and are fearful of being destroyed—and God with us. But God is not dead or in danger of dying. So long as Jesus is in our *boat* we need have no fear. Even so, in their extremity they did call on Jesus. Have we done as much?

It was too much for the Twelve. They could only marvel at the miracle. "What manner of man is this? for he commandeth even the winds and water, and they obey him."

What manner of man, indeed! These men were familiar with the destructive powers of a storm at sea. Yet these powers obeyed Him as their Master *(epistata)*. It is no wonder that "they being afraid wondered." Whereas a moment before they were afraid of the destructive powers of nature, now they were afraid in the presence of a supernatural power which in a second, and at a word, could chain such powers, yea, change them into a calm, obedient sea. If we stand in awe before the almost unbelievable powers of nature, even nuclear power, how much more so should we stand in reverential worship before nature's God.

Jesus' Power over Demons (8:26-39)

The boat arrived on the eastern shore of the lake "at the country of the Gadarenes" (v. 26). The best texts read "Gerasenes" (cf. Mark 5:1). But "Gadarenes" is correct in Matthew 8:28. For a long time interpreters had difficulty with this seeming conflict. But Thompson many years ago discovered the ruins of a city called Khersa (Gerasa). Even though it is some miles from the sea, it is in the district of the city of Gadara. So both readings are correct. It was in the "region" *(chōra)* of Gerasa.

Arriving in the area Jesus was met by a man "having a demon" (cf. vv. 27, 30). Matthew mentions two such men. There is no problem here, since Mark and Luke evidently focus on the one man who was the more demonized (Legion, Mark 5:9). The man had been in this condition a long time, during which he went naked and dwelt in a cemetery. He was of a violent nature, as seen in the fact that he was repeatedly bound (imperfect) with chains and ropes (v. 29). This was done during his quiet moments in order to restrain him when he became violent. But in his seizures he broke the bonds.

When the man saw Jesus, he (the demon) cried out (v. 28). Then the man fell down before Jesus, as the demon with a great voice asked, "What have I to do with thee, Jesus, thou Son of God most high? I beseech thee, torment me not" (cf. Luke 4:34). What did the demon have in common with the Son of God? It could be only that He had come to destroy or punish the demon.

In response, Jesus asked the man his name (v. 30). Note the interplay between the man and the demon which possessed him. Jesus ignored the plea of the demon in order to deal with its unfortunate victim. He replied, "Legion." That was the name by which he was known, for many demons had entered into him. A Roman "legion" was made up of six thousand soldiers. This does not mean that the man was possessed by that many demons. For the word had come to mean a great number or a host. In any event the man was in a pitiable condition, which in part explains why Jesus asked the man his name. It was for His disciples' benefit, not His, that they might see the power of the act which He was about to perform.

Knowing that Jesus was about to cast them out of the man, the demons ("they") *kept begging* (imperfect) Him not to send them into the "deep" (abyss, v. 31). "Abyss" was something without a bottom, like "the bottomless pit." Revelation 9:1-2 uses it of the abode of demons (cf. Rev. 11:7; 17:8; 20:1, 3). This was Gentile country, which explains the nearby presence of a herd of swine (v. 32). Mark says that there were about two thousand (5:13). So the demons asked to be sent into them. And Jesus permitted it. Some see a difficulty in Jesus' granting the wish of demons. But to do so suited His purpose. Did He do so that the man might have visible proof of his being freed from them? Or for the disciples' benefit?

Whatever was His reason, the herd itself was driven wild (v. 33). The swine rushed down a steep place into the lake, and were "choked," or strangled. Those who imagine a difficulty in that

Jesus was involved in the destruction of the swine stumble over a grain of sand, and miss the spiritual lesson involved. Which is more important, a hog or a man?

The keepers of the swine ran into the city to report what had happened. Evidently they told everyone whom they met on the way (cf. "in the country," v. 34). The people rushed out to see about it (v. 35). They found a quiet man instead of a quiet herd. For the former wild man now was sitting at Jesus' feet, clothed, and in his right mind. And they were afraid. Whereas formerly they were afraid of the man, now they were afraid of the strange thing which had happened (vv. 35-36).

And then a very odd thing happened. People had come from throughout the neighboring region (v. 37). They asked Jesus to leave their area, because they were filled with great fear. Why did they want Jesus to leave? A popular reason is that they valued their property more than they did a man. However, nothing is said about the owners of the swine. It was the people in general who made this request. The answer is found in their fear. These were Gentile, pagan people. They had a dread of the unseen world. In Jesus' act they saw a supernatural power at work. So in fear they asked Him to leave. And leave He did. They missed the greatest of blessings because they feared Him who came to grant men freedom from fear.

As Jesus was about to disembark the healed man *kept praying* (imperfect) Jesus to take him along (v. 38). So great was his joy that he wanted to be with Jesus. But the Lord told him instead that he should remain as a witness to His great work in him (v. 39). He was to return to his own home. But the man did more. He proclaimed or preached over and over again (present tense) the message of Jesus' power over demons. He had a great story to tell, and he told it faithfully and powerfully. What a challenge to everyone who has been liberated from Satan's power!

Jesus' Power over Disease (8:40-48)

Jesus had been asked to leave the region of the Gerasenes (Decapolis), but He was welcomed back to Galilee (Capernaum?) by great crowds (v. 40). Suddenly through the crowd came a man with a great need (v. 41). He was Jairus, a ruler of the synagogue. He fell down before Jesus and kept begging, or begged profusely, that Jesus would come to his house. He had an only daughter about twelve years of age (v. 42). And she *was dying* (imperfect). As Jesus started for the house the people kept pressing about Him. He was in a regular jam of people.

In the crowd was a woman who had had an issue of blood (hemorrhage) for twelve years (v. 43). Mark, in characteristic layman's fashion, says that she had suffered many things from many physicians, had spent all of her money, but instead of getting better she grew worse (5:26). But Luke, with a physician's touch, points out that she "could not be healed of any." The best manuscripts of Luke do not have the statement about the physicians. She simply had an incurable disease.

The Talmud lists at least eleven different cures for her disease, some medical and others pure superstition. Probably she had tried them all, and had gone to accredited physicians also. But to no avail. In her condition she was considered to be ceremonially unclean. But when she heard of Jesus' power to heal, in desperation she dared the wrath of custom in order to get to Him (v. 44). In the crowd she came up behind Him, touched the border (tassel, cf. Num. 15:37-41) of His outer garment, and her issue of blood "stopped at once" (aorist). She had faith, a superstitious faith to be sure, that if she but touched His robe she would be healed. And her faith was honored.

Jesus asked, "Who touched me?" (v. 45). The people about Him denied doing so. But Peter reminded Him that everybody was pressing in upon Him. So evidently all of them had touched Him.

But Jesus had reference to a special touch (v. 46). "For I perceive that virtue [power] is gone out of me." Literally, "had gone forth from me." It went from Him when the woman touched Him. Many were merely jostling Jesus. But this woman's touch was one of faith. Not all who crowd about Jesus receive cleansing power from Him – only those who touch Him in faith.

When the woman knew that her act was known, she came trembling and fell before Jesus (v. 47). Her secret act she declared before the people, telling why she had done it, and how she had been miraculously and immediately healed. When all others had failed her, she found in Jesus all that she needed. What a sermon she preached!

Then Jesus said, "Daughter, thy faith hath made thee whole" (v. 48 RV). "Hath made whole" *(sesōken,* perfect tense of completeness) could also mean "hath saved." Either, perhaps both, may apply here. Not the superstitious faith of touching the tassel, but the faith which caused her to do it. That she was both well and saved is seen in Jesus' final words to her. "Go in [*eis*] peace." Not just "go in peace," but "go into peace." Thus Jesus showed not only His power over disease but His power over sin also.

Jesus' Power over Death (8:49-56)

Luke now resumes the story about Jairus' daughter (v. 49). Jesus' words to the woman were interrupted by the arrival of one from Jairus' home. His daughter was dead. The perfect tense *(tethnēken)* leaves no doubt about it. She was not in a coma, but dead. Such final words. There was no more hope. So why trouble the Teacher further? The fear of despair filled the heart of the father.

But Jesus said, "Stop being afraid" (v. 50). Then from the negative Jesus changed to the positive. "Only believe, and she shall be made whole." This gave the father something to which to hold. So when they arrived at the home Jesus found the house filled with mourners, both personal and professional. But He permitted only the parents and Peter, James and John to enter the child's room with Him (v. 51). To the mourners He said, "Stop weeping; she is not dead, but sleepeth" (v. 52). Some hold that this means that she was not really dead. But verse 49 speaks to the contrary. To hold such a position is to twist the meaning of Jesus' words. She was dead, but she would not remain so.

The mourners laughed scornfully, especially those who *mourned* for hire, for they knew that she was dead. This within itself should answer the critics. So Jesus put them all out of the house. Then He took the child by her hand, called to her that all might see her response to Him, and said, "Maid, arise" (v. 54). At His command her "spirit" *(pneuma,* spirit, breath) *returned* (aorist, v. 55). It did so immediately. This could mean that life re-entered her in that she began breathing again. Both make sense and were true. If we think in terms of *breathing,* this emphasizes the fact of death and of life returning.

To complete the picture Jesus ordered that she be fed. Doubtless her illness had left her weak. Unlike Peter's mother-in-law who was healed of a fever, her strength did not return miraculously. Jesus by divine power over death restored her to life. But He would permit her to be strengthened by natural means.

Nothing is said of the parents' joy, even though we can be sure that it knew no bounds. The significant thing was their amazement, literally, standing outside themselves (v. 56). This was a natural reaction. As death brings on a state of shock, even so this miracle left them in a similar state.

And then Jesus strangely told them not to tell what He had done. Some question the genuineness of this clause. Were they not to tell it at all? What about those who had come for the funeral? Did Jesus simply want them not to spread the news abroad to prevent the people from becoming overly excited? How could such be kept a secret with so many people about?

Plummer makes an interesting suggestion. "It was given more probably for the parents' sake, to keep them from letting the effect of this great blessing evaporate in vainglorious gossip. To thank God for it at home would be far more profitable than talking about it abroad." Even if this be true, we may be sure that this couple and their daughter never forgot Him whose power over death had driven away the lowering clouds of grief to let the sun of faith and joy bathe their home once more.

Luke 9:1-10a

The Mission of the Twelve

The Great Galilean ministry was rapidly drawing to a close. For this reason Jesus called together the Twelve and "gave them power [*dunamin,* note 'dynamite'] and authority [*exousian*] over all devils [demons], and to cure diseases" (v. 1). Then He "sent them forth" *(apesteilen* from *apostellō,* root word for apostle) for the continuing purpose of preaching the kingdom of God and healing the sick (v. 2), to minister to men's souls and bodies. "To preach" and "to heal" are present infinitives of purpose. The word "cure" *(therapeuein,* note our *therapeutics,* v. 1) basically means to heal by medical practice. But in verse 2 "heal" *(iasthai)* means to heal miraculously. However, as seen here these words often are used interchangeably. Jesus did not make the Twelve "M.D.'s." He gave them power and authority to heal by miracle.

This was to be a hurried trip. So they were to travel light (v. 3). They were to take "neither staff [walking staff or stick], nor wallet, nor bread, nor money; neither have two coats [*chitōn,* under garment]" (v. 3 RV). Mark 6:8 says "a staff only." Evidently Luke means that they were not to take an extra walking staff. They were to make no special preparation, but were to go as they were. These instructions were for this journey or tour only, and are not applicable generally.[1]

Along the way they were to find lodging with friendly people (v. 4). But if a home or a city refused to welcome them, apparently hostile to Jesus and His work, when they left they were to shake the very dust of that city from their feet (v. 5). This was a typical expression of condemnation. Pharisees did this when they re-entered Judea from pagan territory. Such an action on the part of the apostles would be a testimony against such

1 Matthew 10:5-42 records more detailed instructions covering from this point to the end of the age. See my *An Exposition of The Gospel of Matthew* (Baker, 1965), chap. 10.

hostility to Jesus. Verse 6 reads literally, "And *departing* they kept on going through [imperfect] the villages *evangelizing* and *healing* every where" (author's italics are present participles). This is a vivid description of the progressive and continuous spread of their ministry.

While the apostles were on their mission Jesus went elsewhere to teach and preach in cities of Galilee (Matt. 11:1). Apparently during this time word came to Him as to the attitude of Herod Antipas concerning Him (vv. 7-9). Herod heard "all that was coming to pass," or about the ministry of Jesus. Three reports had come to him: that John the Baptist was risen from the dead; that Elijah had appeared; that one of the prophets of old had come to life again. Evidently Herod believed the first of these. For Mark reads that he said that John was risen from the dead, and that "therefore do these powers work in him" (6:14). "Powers" probably means evil powers. Herod's superstitious and godless mind would so interpret Jesus' work.

And well might this evil ruler be troubled. "He was perplexed" (v. 7, imperfect, a continuing experience). He was at a loss to explain it. Literally, "he was unable to find a way out." For he said, "John have I beheaded: but who is this, of whom I hear such things?" (v. 9). See Mark 6:14-29 for a more detailed treatment of this.

Herod Antipas had a brother Philip, a private citizen, who lived in Rome. His wife was Herodias. On one of Herod's visits to Rome he had led her to leave her husband to marry him. She was only too glad to exchange being the wife of a private citizen to become the wife of a tetrarch. John the Baptist denounced this unholy marriage, and Herod arrested him. The tetrarch recognized John as a prophet, and was hesitant to punish him further. But Herodias "set herself against him; and desired to kill him" (Mark 6:19 RV). Literally, "she had it in for him." By one ruse or another Antipas protected John. But finally at a banquet in a drunken state he ordered him beheaded. Josephus says that Herod did this because he "thought it best, by putting him to death, to prevent any mischief he might cause, and not bring himself into difficulties, by sparing a man who might make him repent of it when it should be too late." In plain words, Herod feared that John might cause a revolution. In a dungeon? Obviously Josephus has stated Herod's public and political excuse for John's imprisonment and death. But Mark, followed by Matthew, tells the true story. And Luke takes note of it (cf. also 3:19-

20). Since he had given details earlier, he merely mentions Herod's state of mind at this point.

Then Luke adds a word not found in the other Gospels. "And he desired [kept on seeking, imperfect] to see Jesus" (v. 9). John the Baptist he had known by sight. If he could see Jesus he would know for certain whether or not He were John risen from the dead. But a more ominous note is involved. He had beheaded John. If he could get his hands on Jesus, he would do the same to Him. And thus he would be rid of the whole thing.

Finally, the apostles returned from their tour (v. 10a). They reported in detail all that they had done. "Told" renders a verb meaning to carry a narrative through to the end. It must have been a glorious account. The pupils had tried their hand on their own, but in Jesus' power and authority. They were a joyful but tired group. Furthermore, ominous clouds were beginning to hover over Jesus and His little band. So He brought His Galilean ministry to a close. Henceforth, with brief intervals, He pursued His work elsewhere.

V
The Period of Withdrawals

Luke 9:10b-17

The Feeding of the Multitude

It is now just one year before the crucifixion. John tells us that it was shortly before the Passover (6:4). So it was in the spring of A.D. 29.

The Galilean ministry was over. Therefore, for six months (Passover to Tabernacles) Jesus spent the time in a series of withdrawals from Galilee into surrounding areas. There were five reasons for these withdrawals. Jesus wanted to get out of the territory of conniving Herod Antipas; to avoid the fanatical crowds; to escape the hostility of the Jewish rulers; to rest; and to instruct the Twelve. The end was rapidly approaching, and they were not prepared for it.

These withdrawals carried Jesus east of the lake of Galilee, to Syrophoenicia, back to the eastern shore of the lake, and into the region of Caesarea Philippi. Luke records only two: the first and the fourth.

Jesus and the Twelve crossed the lake to a deserted area near Bethsaida Julias (v. 10b). Luke says "Bethsaida." There was a Bethsaida on the western shore. But Matthew, Mark, and John[1] all agree that Jesus crossed the lake. So the place was near Bethsaida Julias. However, He could not get away from the crowds, for they followed Him, probably going by land around the northern end of the lake. "And receiving them he kept on speaking [imperfect] to them concerning the kingdom of God, and the ones having need of healing he kept on healing" (imperfect, v. 11).

Sometime after mid-afternoon the Twelve came to Jesus with a problem (v. 12). Night was coming on, and the people needed lodging and food. When Luke said that "the day began to wear away" he used an infinitive "to wear away" which means to bow or bend down. The sun was hastening toward the horizon. Perhaps

---

[1] This is the only event recorded by all four Gospels prior to Passion Week.

the people had not eaten since early morning. Naturally they were hungry.

The Twelve recognized that fact. And they wanted something done about it. So what did they do? They did not ask Jesus what to do. Instead, they ordered Him to do something. "Send away [imperative] the multitude." Send them into the towns and surrounding country that they may "get victuals." The people must be fed, but let them feed themselves.

They were like so many of us today when we face a problem. We do not ask the Lord; we tell Him. We recognize people's spiritual needs, but we want them to satisfy them elsewhere. Just do anything, only do not look to us for sustenance.

But Jesus says to us as He said to them, "Give *ye* them to eat" (v. 13) (author's italics). Literally, "Give [imperative] to them to eat you." "You," written out and coming at the end of the sentence, gives it emphasis. This was Jesus' plan in contrast to theirs. They said, "Send away." Jesus said, "Give to them." They said, "They." Jesus said, "You."

Then the Twelve raised a very practical problem. They had but five barley cakes and two small fishes. John says that they even found these with a little boy (6:9). There were five thousand men present, besides women and children (v. 14; cf. Matt. 14:21). How many people? No one knows. But there must have been considerably more than five thousand.

So the only way to feed so many was to purchase food. And the Twelve did not have enough money to do so. The trouble with them, like us, is that they reckoned only in their power, not that of Jesus. They saw the problem through themselves, and it was beyond them. What they needed was to see the problem through the Lord. And that is quite a different matter.

It was at this point of the Twelve's frustration that Jesus took charge. He ordered that the people should sit down in groups of fifty (v. 14). Mark 6:40 says "hundreds and fifties." Literally, he said that they sat down "garden beds garden beds." On the green grass the highly colored clothes looked like beautiful beds of flowers. Note that Jesus used organization in order not to miss anyone. Organization has a place in Christian work.

When the people were seated Jesus, looking up to heaven, blessed the food, broke it (aorist), and kept on giving (imperfect) it to the disciples, who, in turn, gave it to the people (vv. 15-16). In the aorist tense one can almost hear the quick snapping of the food being broken. Likewise, the imperfect tense pictures the process of distributing it.

All the people ate, and were filled (v. 17). And there remained enough uneaten food, broken pieces but not scraps, to fill twelve baskets or *kophinoi*. These were wicker baskets used by the Jews for carrying things. Plummer notes that they were used by the Jews for carrying food in order to avoid buying it from Gentiles. This custom is reflected in Juvenal's description of "Jews whose furniture is a basket *(cophinus)* and some hay" (for a bed).

Various efforts have been made to explain away this miracle: the disciples found a military cache of food in a cave; Jesus and the Twelve divided their lunch and this set off a chain reaction among the people. It takes more faith to believe these than to believe that the Lord, who made the food in the first place, multiplied it miraculously in keeping with His benevolent will and purpose.

Certainly the people who saw it accepted it as a miracle. For John says that it so excited them that they sought to make Jesus their political Messiah in a revolution (6:14-15). While their reaction was wrong, certainly they were in a better position to judge the event than those who are removed from it by almost two thousand years.

John notes that on the following day in Capernaum the people came to Jesus seeking more food. When He interpreted this miracle in terms of spiritual food, the crowds left Him. This marked the turning point in His popularity in Galilee. In this sense the feeding of the five thousand marks a focal point in Jesus' ministry. This explains the fact that it is recorded by all four Evangelists.

Luke 9:18-27

The Identity and Mission of Christ

Several months transpired between this event and the preceding one. Jesus and the Twelve have gone to the region of Caesarea Philippi (Mark 8:27). The mountains (Mt. Hermon) would provide a blessed relief from the summer heat. This region was in Herod Philip's territory, away from Herod Antipas and the Pharisees, and was an isolated spot in which Jesus might concentrate on teaching the Twelve.

Luke takes up the story at the point where Jesus "was alone praying" (v. 18). While Matthew and Mark also record this event, only Luke mentions that Jesus was praying. As stated previously, he places great stress on His prayer life. The disciples were nearby.

This was an important moment for Jesus. A little over six months remained before the crucifixion. For several months He had been majoring on teaching the Twelve. It was so important that they should fully comprehend His person and mission. So now examination time had arrived. Therefore, Jesus asked, "Whom do the people say that I am?" (v. 18). The Galilean crowds had largely forsaken Him when they learned that He would be neither a political nor a bread Messiah. Jesus was aware of this. So this question was more of a lead question looking toward a greater one.

Note that the disciples' answer was but a repetition of the popular gossip as to Jesus' identity (cf. Luke 9:7-8). The people were saying that He was John the Baptist, Elijah, or one of the prophets of old who had come back to life. These opinions reflected many thoughts: Herod Antipas' concept of Jesus; the belief that Elijah would return before the Messiah came (cf. Matt. 17:10; Mal. 4:5-6); and the popular reaction to Jesus' wonderful teaching and works.

And then the real question. "But whom say ye that I am?" (v. 20). Literally, "But you [plural], who me do you say to be?" The first "you" is written at the beginning, which gives it a double emphasis. It was not of primary importance what others thought. The vital point was what the Twelve thought about Jesus. If their thinking was right, they could preach the gospel to others. But if not, then what? We may well imagine that Jesus had been praying for them before the examination was given. He waited for the answer. And then it came.

Immediately "answering" (aorist participle), Peter said, "The Christ of God" (v. 20). Mark reads, "Thou art the Christ" (8:29), and Matthew adds "the Son of the living God" (16:16).[1] Jesus had questioned the Twelve. Peter, ever the forward one, had answered for all (cf. John 6:67-69). They did not yet fully understand the nature of Jesus' Messiahship. But that much they did know. He is "the Christ [Messiah, Anointed One] of God."

And then Jesus said what at first thought seems to be a very strange thing. He told them not to tell anyone that He was the Christ (v. 21). We are so accustomed to being urged to do this that such a prohibition seems unusual indeed. However, if we could put ourselves in the thought environment of the time, it would not be strange. The word "Christ" means but one thing to us — the Anointed One of God for our spiritual salvation. But to Jesus' contemporaries the term "Christ" had a highly nationalistic connotation (cf. John 6:15). Even the Twelve were not entirely immune to this concept. Had they gone forth to preach the Christ at that time, they would have presented, to say the least, a warped picture of His person and work. Even to say publicly that He was the Christ would have brought the wrong reaction from their hearers. Jesus, for this reason, never called Himself Christ before them. He did so to the Samaritan woman, but this was in a private conversation (John 4:26). He led the Twelve so to identify Him at this time in order that He might begin plainly to teach them as to the meaning of the title with reference to Him.

"From that time forth began Jesus" to reveal this meaning (Matt. 16:21). According to Luke He said, "The Son of man must suffer many things, and be rejected of the elders and chief priests and scribes [Pharisees and Sadducees], and be slain, and be raised the third day" (v. 22). Note the word "must." It renders a word *(dei)* which speaks of a moral, spiritual, and logical necessity. In the Greek text this word is followed by four infinitives. He *must* suffer. He *must* be rejected after trial (meaning of word for "rejected"). He *must* be slain. He *must* rise again on the third

---

1 For a full discussion of Matthew's longer report see my *An Exposition of The Gospel of Matthew,* pp. 213ff.

day. All these things are morally, spiritually, and logically necessary if the Christ is to accomplish His mission of redemption. This is by divine decree as is shown in the prophets. But note that even now Jesus used the term "Son of man." This was His favorite designation of Himself. But, even so, it was His purpose to apply these experiences to "the Christ of God" whom they had just confessed Him to be. The Christ *must* be the Suffering Servant.

The fact that Jesus began at this time to set forth plainly such teaching does not mean that it was a new concept. For an examination of His teachings reveals that often He had alluded to such (cf. John 2:19, 21-22). But now the end is rapidly approaching So He began to teach these things plainly, in order that the Twelve would be prepared for them when they took place.

Luke does not record Peter's protest to this teaching (cf. Matt. 16:22 f.). It was so foreign to the popular concept of the Messiah! And the apostles were the products of their age. False concepts die a hard death.

However, Luke implies Peter's protest. For beginning with verse 23 Jesus applies His words even to the Twelve. They rejected the idea of a crucified Messiah. But Jesus presses the point. Even they, if they will to come after Him, must be willing to deny themselves as though they did not exist (Christ is all that matters), and daily to take up a cross. They were quite familiar with the meaning of taking up a cross. For crucifixion was a common occurrence. And the victim was required to bear his own cross to the place of execution. To bear a cross is not simply to endure some sorrow or hardship. It is to die. So any man who wills to follow Christ must be prepared every day to die for Him.

In paradox Jesus pressed home His lesson. He speaks of losing one's life by saving it; of saving it only by losing it for His sake (v. 24). The Twelve protested that Jesus should avoid the cross in order to save His life. But that would be to lose it insofar as the purpose of His being was concerned. The only way to save His life was to lose it. And the same is true of those who would follow Him.

Actually Jesus used a play upon the word "life" *(psuchē)*. It may be rendered either "life," or "soul." So there is involved both the animal principle of life and also the greater spiritual meaning of life. If one saves the former he may lose the latter. If he is unwilling to pay the price (cf. athlete or student) for achievement, he may lose the joy of achievement. But one who sacrifices in order to pay the price will enjoy the satisfaction of the realization of his goal. There can be no question but that Jesus demands the supreme sacrifice, if necessary, in order for us to be His disciples.

In fact, Jesus asks, What good will it do a man to gain the whole world, and lose or forfeit "himself"? (v. 25). "Himself" may be considered as *psuchē* or "life." But here "life" is thought of in the highest sense of spiritual being. In contrast with "life" as the world reckons it, there is "himself," or the full self as "life" in the kingdom of God. To lose or forfeit the latter in quest of the former is a bad bargain indeed. For those who are ashamed of Christ and His words in this life, He will be ashamed of them in heaven (v. 26).

And then Jesus uttered words which have caused considerable trouble in interpretation. "But I tell you of a truth, there be some standing here, which shall not taste death, till they see the kingdom of God" (v. 27).

What did Jesus mean? Some relate verses 26-27 and see a reference to the second coming of Christ and the final judgment. And since none of those present lived until that time, they say that Jesus was in error as to the time of the events. But Jesus distinctly said that it was not in His knowledge to date His return (Mark 13:32).

Whatever event we choose, it must be one which some of the Twelve, not all, lived to see. It should be kept in mind that Jesus was using apocalyptic language, in which any great intervention of God in history would be regarded as a coming of the kingdom of God. Several such events have been suggested. Among them are the Transfiguration, the crucifixion and resurrection, Pentecost, and the destruction of Jerusalem. The first is ruled out since all of the Twelve were alive when it occurred. Judas died before the other events. But Jesus' language seems to imply that more than one would taste death prior to the event of which He spoke.

In this light, it is more probable that He spoke of the destruction of Jerusalem. Many of them died before that time. Certainly John, and perhaps others, lived beyond that event. The destruction of Jerusalem marked the end of the Jewish State. Thereafter, Judaism declined and exercised little influence. The Christian movement was liberated from any association with it. Thereafter, it went forth in possession of the field, to spread abroad, not regarded by the world as a branch of Judaism but as the full and final revelation of God. In this sense those who lived beyond A.D. 70 truly saw "the kingdom of God."

Luke 9:28-36

The Transfiguration of Jesus

The transfiguration of Jesus occurred about a week after Peter's confession of Jesus as "the Christ of God." Matthew and Mark say "after six days" (17:1; 9:2), while Luke uses the more general term "about eight days" (9:28). At this time Jesus, leaving the other nine behind, took Peter, John, and James up into the mountain to pray. This was the second time that these three were taken into an intimate experience with the Lord (cf. 8:51).

The mountain involved evidently was Mt. Hermon, which would be in the general vicinity of Caesarea Philippi. An early tradition places this event on Mt. Tabor in Galilee. However, the fact that a village was on this mountain at this time makes this an unlikely place. Jesus was seeking seclusion, a point which favors Mt. Hermon. This mountain rises to a height of ninety-two hundred feet, and dominates the entire land of Palestine. On a clear day it may be seen from as far away as the Dead Sea. And from its lofty peak one may get a panoramic view of the land. It is still called *Jebel-esh Sheikh,* "the great mountain."

In keeping with his emphasis upon Jesus' prayer life, Luke alone mentions that "as he was praying" He was transfigured (v. 29). This fact introduces the question as to the purpose of this event. Was it for Jesus' benefit or for some other reason? Many, holding to the former view, insist that Jesus was discouraged. The Twelve had recognized Him as the Christ. But they had rejected the idea of a crucified Christ. Their rejection was the wilderness temptation to avoid the cross all over again. So, according to some, the transfiguration, including the heavenly visitors, was designed to encourage Jesus to continue on the way which led to the cross. But the record fails to reveal that Jesus ever entertained any other idea. Therefore, this can hardly be the reason for the event.

We may well imagine that Jesus at this point was discouraged. So little time remained before Calvary, and the Twelve had no comprehension whatever of the true role of the Christ. G.

Campbell Morgan sees a note of estrangement between Jesus and the Twelve during these eight days. The fact that Jesus "began" to teach and Peter "began" to rebuke Jesus with respect to the cross suggests that this exchange of ideas continued during this time (cf. Matt. 16:21-22, "began," imperfect). In this light, therefore, it seems more likely that the transfiguration was for the benefit of the Twelve, not of Jesus. In fact, this suggests the significance of Jesus' praying. He had taught the Twelve in plain words, and they were so enamored of the political-military concept of the Christ that they failed to understand. So we may well imagine that He was praying that God would give to them a demonstration of His deity and purpose that they would understand. Such density of mind and spirit called for such an experience as is seen in the transfiguration.

And Jesus' prayer was answered. For as He was praying "the appearance of his face became different" (Robertson). ("Became," *egeneto,* aorist, suggests the suddenness of the change, v. 29). At the same time His raiment became white and dazzling, or "white radiant." Matthew and Mark say that He "was transfigured" *(metemorphōthē)*. But because among the Gentiles this word suggested the metamorphosis of heathen deities, Luke simply says that "the appearance of his face became different."

The added thought of Matthew ("before them," 17:2) adds credence to the position that this event was for the primary benefit of the Twelve. It is entirely possible that this change in Jesus' appearance had taken place at other times when alone He prayed in perfect communion with the Father. But here it occurred "before them."

What is the significance of this dazzling change in Jesus? It is quite evident that this was not due to a light from without shining upon Jesus. The entire tone suggests that the light came from within Him. It was His deity from within flashing forth in resplendent glory. The deity, which had been like a wick turned down low, suddenly was turned up to its brilliant brightness. Jesus was more than a superman sent to give worldly deliverance. He was God Himself in human form to bring spiritual redemption to a lost world. All the while the Twelve had been in the presence of God, and they knew it not. But now in a demonstration never before seen by human eyes they had the evidence.

Suddenly a second phenomenon appeared. "And, behold, there talked [imperfect] with him two men, Moses and Elias" (v. 30). The imperfect tense pictures a continuing conversation. These two visitors appeared in heavenly glory to converse with the Lord of glory! Why Moses and Elijah? To the Jews they were representatives of the Law and the Prophets respectively.

So the Law and the Prophets "spoke of his decease which he should accomplish at Jerusalem" (v. 31). Literally, "They were speaking of his exodus" or Jesus' departure out of this world. This involved the crucifixion, resurrection, and ascension. The Twelve thought that Jesus' words concerning this represented a new idea. But here were the Law and the Prophets testifying to it (cf. Luke 24:44-46). So it was not a new thought at all, but the true meaning of that which the Jews had read all of their lives.

Here, then, were two heavenly demonstrations – the deity of Christ and the testimony of the Law and the Prophets. The three apostles were impressed. One wonders how they could fail to understand. But we must not judge them too hastily. They were enslaved by the old concept. And both error and mistaken custom die hard.

At least Luke is kinder to them than are the other two Evangelists. For the latter simply record Peter's suggestion as to what to do on this occasion. But Luke says that they were heavy with sleep (v. 32). Apparently they had been sleeping while Jesus was praying, and they awoke to see this glorious scene. Literally, "they were fully awake" (v. 31). Such an event would certainly drive away sleep. Matthew and Mark make it clear that they awoke to see and hear all that transpired (Matt. 17:3; Mark 9:4).

Even as the heavenly visitors were departing Peter injected himself into the scene. Not even such an experience as this could silence him. For to Jesus he said, "Master [*Epistata,* note Luke's word; Matthew uses *Kurios,* Lord; Mark, *Rabbi,* Teacher], it is good for us to be here: and let us make three tabernacles; one for thee, and one for Moses, and one for Elias" (v. 33). The Feast of Tabernacles was approaching. So he proposed that they should celebrate it on Mt. Hermon instead of in Jerusalem.

Luke adds that Peter spoke, "not knowing what he said" (v. 33). Tertullian held this to mean that he spoke in a heavenly ecstasy, as one caught up into another world. But it is more likely that the words have a very earthly meaning. Peter did not realize the involvements in what he was saying. Mark plainly says that out of fear he did not know what to answer (9:6). And he probably received this thought from Peter himself. Evidently he thought that he should say something. And in his fearful state he said the wrong thing.

Plummer suggests that Peter wanted to make this present glory permanent. Perhaps so. Jesus had been talking about a cross. Peter had been talking about Messianic glory. So in effect he said, "Lord, this is what I have been talking about. Not a gory cross, but this glorious moment."

However, there is more involved in Peter's error. He proposed three tabernacles, not one or six, but three: one for Jesus, one for Moses, and one for Elijah. In this sense he placed them on an equality with Jesus. He was not yet able to forsake the old order for a complete espousal of the new.

This explains the significance of the cloud which overshadowed them (v. 34). Clouds form quickly about the summit of Mt. Hermon. But this was no ordinary cloud. It was the Shekinah Glory of the presence of God. The apostles so recognized it, for "they feared as they entered into the cloud" along with Jesus. Out of the cloud there came a voice, saying, "This is my beloved Son: hear him" (v. 35; cf. 3:22). The best manuscripts read, "My son, my chosen." The form of "chosen" means that the choice is complete and final.

The apostles had been arguing with Jesus about this role as the Suffering Servant. God says that He is His Son, His chosen One, and that there will be no other. They are to hear and heed Him. They are to break with the popular concept of the Messiah. No longer are they to remain enslaved to the old order. Neither are they to regard Jesus as only a great Prophet. They are to hear and heed Him only. This is an exhortation both timely and timeless in nature. It is sorely needed today.

When the voice "came" Jesus was found alone (v. 36). Literally, "on the coming as to the voice" (Robertson). Moses and Elijah were gone. Jesus alone remained. This is not only a statement of fact but a recognition of a truth. "Jesus . . . alone." He and He alone was left with them. So this very fact compounded the meaning of God's word to them.

Luke closes the scene by noting that the apostles "held their peace" (v. 36). They told no one about what they had seen. Both Matthew and Mark tell that this was in compliance with Jesus' own word (Matt. 17:9; Mark 9:9). They were not yet ready to declare it with full understanding. Neither were people ready to hear it. Not until after Jesus' "exodus" would this be possible. Then His followers were to proclaim it to the ends of the earth and unto the end of the age.

Luke 9:37-45

The Dilemma of the Disciples

The Transfiguration probably took place at night. The next day when Jesus descended from the mountain He was met by a crowd of people (v. 37). Out of the crowd a man cried to Him for help (v. 38). His only son was grievously possessed of a demon. He was subject to sudden attacks of epilepsy, the symptoms of which are clearly described in verse 39.[1] "Suddenly" *(exaiphnēs)* is used by medical writers to describe such seizures. It was a pitiful sight.

But not so pitiful as the dilemma of the nine disciples. "And I besought thy disciples to cast him out; and they could not" (v. 40). Previously they had cast out demons. But now they were helpless. Why? Plummer suggests that these were not the apostles. But a natural reading seems to indicate otherwise. Had something happened to them to leave them in such a helpless state?

Perhaps Mark 9:29 gives us a clue. Here Jesus says, "This kind can come forth by nothing, but by prayer" ("and fasting" not in best manuscripts). Jesus and the other three apostles had been praying in the mountain. What had the other nine been doing in the meantime? Jesus' words suggest that they were not praying. Were they so filled with jealousy over Jesus' selection of the other three to be with Him that they had spent their time in criticism of His seeming favoritism? If so, unknown to them power had fled from them. Who can tell the damage done by jealousy, criticism, and lack of prayer to sap the spiritual power of God's people?

Note Jesus' rebuke of the helpless apostles. "O faithless and perverse [twisted, divided] generation, how long shall I be with you, and suffer you?" or "bear with you" (v. 41). Goodspeed trans-

[1] Aretaeus, a physician who may have been a contemporary of Luke, notes in treating epilepsy that this disease possibly could be produced by diabolical agency.

lates this "put up with you." While Jesus was undergoing such a heavenly experience, Satan was at work among His followers. Plummer notes that while the three apostles were blinded by heavenly light, the other nine were blinded by darkness.

In response to Jesus' word the lad approached Him. Even as he was coming he was thrown to the ground by a seizure (v. 42). "Threw down" is a verb sometimes used of boxers knocking down an opponent. But Jesus rebuked the unclean spirit, healed the child immediately, and gave him to his father. What a contrast between the powerless disciples and the powerful Christ! It is no wonder that the people were amazed at the mighty power of God (v. 43).

But even as they were wondering Jesus spoke solemn words to the Twelve. Literally, "put you yourselves into your ears these sayings." "You" is written out, and so is emphatic. "You" in contrast to the wondering multitudes. In effect He said, "Do not be misled by this praise of my works. I still shall be delivered into the hands of men."

"But they understood not this saying, and it was hid from them, that they perceived it not: and they feared to ask him of that saying" (v. 45). Does "they" refer to all of the apostles, or to the nine only? It is difficult to believe that the three had forgotten so soon. It makes sense to relate this to the nine who had not heard Jesus' previous declaration. And the three apparently did not tell them. They remembered Jesus' command of silence.

What a subdued group these nine apostles were. They had failed so utterly in a moment of opportunity. Now they were afraid to ask Jesus a question as to His words. Failure produces fear. Sin separates us from the loving fellowship of God. This is a tragic scene indeed, following so closely upon Jesus' moment of glory.

Luke 9:46-50

The Standard of Greatness

Following the last retirement Jesus returned to Capernaum (Mark 9:33). He was probably in the home of Simon Peter. While there the Twelve disputed among themselves as to which of them should be "greatest" (v. 46). This dispute may have been going on during the return to Galilee. Perhaps it grew out of the selection of Peter, James, and John to go with Jesus into the mountain. The events of recent days seemed to indicate a definite change in Jesus' ministry. Could it be that He was about to set up His kingdom? If so, which disciple would occupy the principal place? Had the three apostles so soon forgotten about the cross that they were involved in such a dispute concerning personal glory?

Apparently the dispute became so intense that Jesus finally intervened. For knowing of the dispute in their hearts, He took a child (Peter's?), and set him in the midst of the group alongside Himself (v. 47). Then He spoke to the Twelve. "Whosoever shall receive this child in my name receiveth me: and whosoever receiveth me receiveth him that sent me: for he that is least among you all, the same shall be great" (v. 48). The word for "receive" used in this verse means more than mere reception. It involves the further thought of warmth and affection.

How like Jesus to take a simple child to illustrate a great truth. The disciples were thinking of sitting alongside Jesus on thrones of glory. He took this little child, probably playing and unconcerned with worldly ambition, and placed him by His side. The disciples thought in terms of ruling great masses of people. Jesus spoke of ministering to one little child. In effect Jesus was saying, "If you forget glory to serve in my name those whom the world considers unimportant, you will achieve kingdom greatness."

Working with little children is a totally unselfish task. For it involves not what you can get from them, but what you can give to them. Yet the rewards of such humble service are greater beyond comparison than those of exercising authority over masses of men. To see a little child develop into his potential under one's guiding hand is all the reward his teacher could desire. It requires more grace and skill to guide a little child than to serve as chairman of the "Board" in the church. The world may call such a person "least," but Jesus calls him "great."

It would appear that the Twelve were embarrassed by this gentle but decided rebuke of their selfishness. For John suddenly tried to change the subject. "Master [*Epistata*], we saw one casting out devils [demons] in thy name; and we forbad him, because he followeth not with us" (v. 49). The nine had failed to do this so recently. But the Twelve sought to prevent another from doing it. Did they want a monopoly in this ministry? It is so easy to claim sectarian privilege to the exclusion of others. Does any one group of Jesus' followers have all the access to God's truth and power?

Jesus replied, "Stop forbidding him: for *he who is not against you, he is for you*" (best text, v. 50). The italicized words are a proverb. Even though the man was not of the inner circle, he did it in Jesus' name. Paul said that even though men preached Christ out of varying motives, as long as they preached Christ he rejoiced (Phil. 1:14-18). John Wesley said that if another's heart was as his heart, he would join hands with him in doing the Lord's work.

True kingdom greatness lies not only in rendering humble service, but also in Christian understanding of others who do the same.

VI
The Judean Ministry

Luke 9:51-56

The Tragedy of Mistaken Zeal

At this point we enter a section of Jesus' ministry which is reported only by Luke (9:51—18:14). Matthew and Mark record Jesus' final visit to Jerusalem through Perea. John shows that He had made two visits to Jerusalem prior to the feeding of the five thousand (cf. 2:13; 5:1). He also gives Jesus' visits to that city for the feasts of Tabernacles and Dedication (cf. 7:10; 10:22). The former of these came shortly after Jesus' return from Caesarea Philippi. Luke implies this visit although he does not record it (9:51). None of the Synoptic Gospels place Jesus in Jerusalem until His final visit. We are indebted to John for accounts of four previous visits, which, incidentally, explain Jewish opposition to Jesus in Galilee. Luke's account of the Judean and Perean ministries blends into both John's and the other two Synoptic records.

Luke begins this section peculiar to him by noting that "the time was come that he [Jesus] should be received up" or the Ascension (v. 51). He was preparing for His *exodus*. Actually it was about six months prior to the crucifixion. This was Luke's way of noting that Jesus shifted His ministry from Galilee to Judea. Before the end the Judean people outside Jerusalem must also have His witness. So Jesus "stedfastly set his face to go to Jerusalem." This expresses His fixed purpose in the face of danger. For months He had avoided Judea. He would not tempt either God or man. But the time had now arrived when He must go to this hostile area. His hour was rapidly approaching, and He would not avoid it.

John 7:2-9 notes that Jesus' unbelieving half-brothers had challenged Him to accompany them to Jerusalem for the feast of Tabernacles. However, He refused, but later went not publicly but in secret. He did not travel in a caravan. Neither did He take the usual route southward through Perea. Instead He went with His disciples through Samaria.

This within itself would have been a *secret* route for Jews.

For centuries the Jews and Samaritans had been enemies. Because of this Samaritans were hostile to Jews who travelled through their country toward Judea. Strangely they did not seem to care if Jews travelled northward through Samaria (cf. John 4).

The hostility of the Samaritans probably explains a new tactic employed by Jesus. He sent messengers ahead to prepare for His coming into a certain village (v. 52). But because He was going by Mt. Gerizim, their place of worship, to worship in Jerusalem the Samaritans did not receive or welcome Him (v. 53). So when the messengers returned with the news that Jesus was not welcome in that village, James and John, the sons of thunder, said, "Lord, are you willing we should bid fire to come down from heaven and to destroy them completely?" (v. 54, author's translation). The infinitive "to destroy," or "consume," is an effective aorist, hence, "to destroy completely." They had a zeal for Christ, but it was a mistaken one.

Jesus said as much when He turned and rebuked them, and went to another village. "Another" *(heteron)* means another of a different kind, so a friendly village that would welcome Him. The best manuscripts omit "and said, Ye know not what manner of spirit ye are of" (v. 55 KJV) and, "For the Son of man is not come to destroy men's lives, but to save them" (v. 56 KJV). But the spirit expressed in both cases is true to Jesus' actions. Their spirit was an evil one. His was of God. John 4 shows how Jesus had overcome the hostile Samaritan spirit with love, and thereby had saved many souls.

This brief passage teaches at least three great lessons. Note the resolute purpose of Jesus to fulfil God's will for His life, even though it led to a cross. Think of the great opportunity for spiritual blessings which the village lost through prejudice. But perhaps the greatest truth set forth is the tragedy of mistaken zeal. We might say that James and John had a zeal for Christ, but not according to knowledge. They missed the whole purpose of His being. They would destroy, but Jesus came to save. These mistaken apostles would employ the power of heaven to express vengeance, not love.

In the first century there was a party called the Zealots. They were a revolutionary group bent upon liberating the Jews from Roman rule. Their fanaticism played a leading role in precipitating the war with Rome (A.D. 66-70) which ended with the destruction of Jerusalem and the Jewish nation. Zeal is a noble quality, but it must have a proper motive and direction. Or else it may defeat the very cause which it espouses.

Luke 9:57-62

The Prior Claim of Christ

As Jesus and the Twelve were journeying on their way they met three men who aspired to being Jesus' followers. One would think that the Lord would have welcomed such. But in each case He made demands beyond the conditions set forth by these volunteers. Barclay calls these incidents "The Honesty of Jesus." In a sense these represent those who are not willing to pay the price involved in being Jesus' disciples.

First, there was the one possessed by a shallow enthusiasm. Matthew calls him "a scribe" (8:19). He said, "I will follow thee whithersoever thou goest" (v. 57). Some hold this to mean on this particular journey. But the natural meaning seems to involve more.

But Jesus replied, "Foxes have holes, and birds of the air have nests; but the Son of man hath not where to lay his head" (v. 58). Note that Jesus did not invite this man to follow Him. He volunteered. But he did so without counting the cost.

Was Jesus stressing His poverty? More likely He had another thought in mind. Foxes and birds are vagabond in nature. But even a fox has a hole in which to sleep. And at certain seasons of the year birds have nests to which they may return. But Jesus possessed no permanent home. He was constantly on the move. Would this man be willing to leave the comforts of home in order to accompany Jesus? Since nothing more is said of him, we may assume that his enthusiasm cooled at Jesus' words.

Second, there was the man with a prior obligation. To him Jesus said, "Follow me" (v. 59). He replied, "Suffer me first to go and bury my father." Filial duty is a noble thing (cf. Gen. 25:9). The only trouble is that his father probably was not dead. Tobit 4:3 records such a case. The man said that he must wait until his father was dead and buried before he could follow Jesus in His nomadic life. He may even have used his father as an excuse for not answering Jesus' call. Many who are called hesitate because of family obligations. But those who have followed Jesus despite the problem have found that He somehow provided a way.

In Jesus' reply He used a play on words. "Let the dead bury their dead: but go thou and preach the kingdom of God" (v. 60). What He meant was to let the spiritually dead perform this family task when necessary. But this man should answer the call. "Thou" is written out and appears first in the clause. So it has a double emphasis. "Thou" in contrast with the spiritually dead. Whether the man responded to Jesus' call is not stated. We can only hope that he did.

Third, there was the man who was wedded to the past. "Lord, I will follow thee, but let me first go bid them farewell which are at home at my house" (v. 61). Plummer says that he wanted to enjoy his home just one more time. Robertson sees him as wanting to set his house in order, and at some later time to follow Jesus. Certainly it meant more than merely to say "goodbye."

In reply Jesus used a commonly used proverbial saying. "No man, having put his hand to the plough, and looking back, is fit for the kingdom of God" (v. 62). Certainly a plowman must look ahead if he is to plow a straight furrow. The word "fit" means "suitable" or "well placed." Service in the kingdom demands undivided attention. He who is unwilling to give it will not make a suitable servant of God.

In calling His followers Jesus never courted the half-hearted. He demands all that there is of a man. His claim upon us takes priority over all others'. Bruce describes these men respectively as being hindered by "inconsiderate impulse," "conflicting duties," and "a divided mind." Neither of these possessed the qualities necessary for successful discipleship.

Luke 10:1-24

The Mission of the Seventy

In Galilee Jesus had sent the Twelve on a preaching mission (Luke 9:1-6). Now in Judea He appointed seventy other disciples for a similar mission (10:1). Some see this as confusion on Luke's part, stating that this is really the mission in Galilee. But the fact that he had already taken note of the former event would speak to the contrary. There is no reason why Jesus did not send out both groups. The fact that He is now beginning a Judean ministry makes it seem natural that He would repeat in Judea what He had already done in Galilee.

Why did Jesus choose seventy disciples for this mission? The number "seventy" is found often in Jewish life. Moses appointed seventy elders to assist him in governing Israel (Num. 11:16, 24). The Sanhedrin, following this pattern, consisted of seventy members plus a president who corresponded to Moses. Plummer notes that the seventy were sent out at about the time of the feast of Tabernacles. During this feast seventy bullocks were sacrificed. The Talmud says that these seventy bullocks correspond to the seventy nations of the world (cf. Gen. 10). Whether any of these things figured in Jesus' choice of this number cannot be affirmed. It may be simply that seventy were necessary for the task at hand, even as twelve had been sufficient in Galilee.

At any rate Jesus appointed "other seventy" or "seventy others." "Other" renders *heterous,* others of a different kind. This within itself is intended to distinguish them from the Twelve in Luke 9. They were sent forth "two by two." Such an arrangement provided both courage and companionship to the witnesses (cf. Mark 6:7; Acts 13:2; 15:27, 39-40). The testimony of two witnesses would serve to give credence to the message (cf. John 8:17). And they were to go before Jesus into the cities and villages into which He was about to come. In a sense they were forerunners for Jesus to prepare the way for His coming.

Here as in Samaria (John 4:35) and Galilee (Matt. 9:37-38) the harvest is great, but the laborers are few (v. 2). Jesus sees the multitudes as ripened grain just waiting to be harvested. The tragedy, then as now, is that there are so few harvesters. There never are enough. For this reason Jesus urges His followers to pray the Lord of the harvest that He would thrust forth laborers into the harvest. Despite the great need, there is always an unwillingness in the human heart. And prayer to God is the only means at our disposal by which to overcome this hesitancy. In recent years some Christian groups have even put on recruiting campaigns to secure enough men to fill the needs of the ministry. Jesus did not counsel such. Instead, we are to pray that God will supply the laborers. The lack of laborers is in direct proportion to our lack in praying to God to this end.

Before Jesus sent the seventy forth He gave them certain instructions. They are similar to those given to the Twelve (cf. Matt. 10:16). He first warned them of the danger which awaited them. They go as lambs among wolves (v. 3). These "wolves" hounded Jesus wherever He went. And His servants could expect no better treatment. It requires great courage to follow Jesus. As the Twelve could expect to receive a cross, so the seventy could anticipate the sharp teeth of opposition.

Furthermore, Jesus emphasized the urgency of their task (v. 4). They were to carry no money bag or extra luggage. Neither were they to "salute" any man along the way. Oriental greetings were extended and tedious. They were not to stop and palaver, but were to hasten on their way.

They were to depend upon those to whom they ministered for food and lodging. Upon those homes which welcomed them they were to pronounce the oriental blessing of peace (v. 5). But where they met hostility they were to withhold such a blessing (v. 6). Where they were welcomed they were to abide and to eat and drink that which was offered. This should not be regarded as charity but as their due in the Master's work. "For the laborer is worthy of his hire." Jesus forbids them to go from house to house, that is, for hospitality. Such social life would be a waste of their time on this mission.

They were to minister in every city which received them (vv. 8-9). But in those cities which refused them they were to shake the dust of such a city from their feet (vv. 10-11). This was a strong oriental gesture of condemnation. And at the judgment it will be more tolerable for the wicked city of Sodom than for that city (v. 12). For the reaction of a home or city to the seventy, whether good or bad, would be a reaction to Jesus Himself (v. 16).

The rebellion of hostile cities suggested the rebellion of cities of Galilee which had not repented at the ministry of Jesus (vv. 13-16). Their fate will be worse than that of Tyre, Sidon, and Sodom, Old Testament cities of great wickedness. For had they received the ministry of Jesus they would have been brought low in repentance. Jesus singled out Capernaum, a city of great privilege, for a special condemnation. It will be thrust down to Hades. Hades was the abode of the dead. So Jesus is speaking not of a final judgment for these cities but of the judgment of history. Inhabitants of these cities who rejected Jesus will be judged in the final judgment. But cities and nations are judged in the context of history. All that remains of the once great city of Capernaum are a few ruins. Truly she was thrust down to death.

The seventy went forth. And they returned overflowing with joy (v. 17). Jesus had not specifically told them to cast out demons. But "even the devils [demons] are subject unto us through thy name." It was even better than they had hoped. Note that they achieved this not in their own power but in Jesus' name or by His authority and power.

Jesus also rejoiced with them. "I beheld Satan as lightning fall from heaven" (v. 18). In their victory over demons He saw the foretaste of that day when Satan's power would be completely broken. It will be a long struggle, but victory is certain.

Verse 19 should not be regarded as grounds for taking undue risks in proving one's faith. Jesus refused such in not leaping from the pinnacle of the temple. This was simply His way of expressing in extreme oriental fashion the protection which God provides for His servants. In view of Genesis 3:15 "tread upon serpents," etc., is simply another promise of victory over Satan.

Of interest are the two uses of "power" in verse 19. The first one is *exousia,* authority, or the power resident in one's very nature (cf. Matt. 28:18). The second is *dunamis,* a power expressed through another. The former is the stronger word. It is the *exousia* of Christ triumphing over the *dunamis* of Satan. This victory is stressed in the strong triple negative seen in "nothing [*ouden*] shall by any means [*ou mē*] hurt you."

But even their power over demons is not the seventy's greatest reason to rejoice. That reason is that their names are written in heaven (v. 20). "Are written" is a perfect passive tense. The passive voice shows that their names were written in heaven not by their works. It was the work of God and by His grace. The perfect tense shows that their names are written never to be erased. What God does, He does not undo.

The report of the seventy caused Jesus to rejoice (v. 21). Luke says that "in that very hour [*en autēi tēi hōrai*] Jesus exulted in the Holy Spirit" (best manuscripts). Nowhere else is this statement made about Jesus. It was something akin to His being led of the Holy Spirit in the wilderness (4:1). And over what did He rejoice? He praised God because He had revealed the glory of the kingdom to "babes," while it was hidden "from the wise and prudent." The "wise and prudent" evidently refers to the scribes and Pharisees who had closed their minds and hearts to Jesus' teaching. But the "babes," or those untrained in the Rabbinical schools, had received His revelation. It is tragic to see that the religious schools, rather than opening minds to the truth, had closed them to it.

Jesus is the full revelation of the Father. There is perfect understanding between them. And Jesus reveals the Father to those who receive His revelation (v. 22).

This statement in Luke (cf. Matt. 11:25f.) sounds as though it were in the Gospel of John. It is a gem of truth which within itself serves to authenticate the Gospel of John which by some is rejected as a theological treatise devoid of historical accuracy. But the more we know of John the more this Gospel reflects the thought environment of the first century.

Jesus closed this incident by pronouncing a blessing upon the seventy (vv. 23-24). Prophets and kings had desired to see and hear the things which they had seen and heard, but did not live to do so. The seventy had been appointed and sent forth by Jesus. They had done His bidding. And all rejoiced in the result. Blessed beyond measure are those in any age who have this experience.

Luke 10:25-37

The Parable of the Good Samaritan

This is one of the best known and loved of all the parables of Jesus. And only Luke records it.

Somewhere in Judea Jesus was seated in a group. Present was a "lawyer," or one who was especially skilled in the interpretation of Jewish religious law. He stood up and asked Jesus a question "trying to tempt him" (v. 25). Depending upon his attitude he either wanted to test Jesus as a teacher or else to ensnare Him so as to discredit Him. Perhaps both thoughts were in his mind.

"Teacher, what shall I do to inherit eternal life?" The tense of the verb "do" (aorist participle) means "by doing what single deed shall I inherit eternal life?" He evidently was thinking of some great charitable or heroic act. His question shows that he did not understand either the nature of eternal life or how he might acquire it (cf. Acts 16:30). But his concept was in keeping with the Jewish religious teaching, salvation by works.

It was natural that Jesus would refer this legal expert to his own law. So He aked, "What is written in the law? how readest thou?" (v. 26). And the lawyer replied, "Thou shalt love the Lord thy God with all thy heart, and with all thy soul, and with all thy strength, and with all thy mind; and thy neighbor as thyself" (v. 27; cf. Mark 12:30-31). The former part of this statement is from the *Shema* (Deut. 6:4-5); the latter is from Leviticus 19:18. These were considered as a summation of all of the law. A man is to love God with the totality of his powers, and he is to love his neighbor as he loves himself.

Jesus commended the lawyer for his answer. He then added, "This do, and thou shalt live" (v. 28). "Do" is a present imperative. "This keep on doing forever, and thou shalt live." In effect Jesus said that if he would keep perfectly the Ten Commandments he would have eternal life. The first four of these commandments deal with man's relation to God; the last six deal with man's relation to man.

As we think of salvation by grace through faith this may sound like strange teaching. But it is what Jesus said. The man asked, "What shall *I* do to inherit eternal life?" (author's italics). So Jesus told him. If he depended upon himself for salvation then he must keep perfectly the commandments without one slip. Of course, no man, save Jesus, can do this; hence the need of a Saviour. But Jesus was simply answering the man's own question.

Evidently the lawyer caught the point. We must give him credit for honesty. Still he wanted to justify himself. So he sought to split hairs by asking, "And who is my neighbor?" (v. 29). According to Jewish custom he had a point. For while ney agreed that one should love his neighbor, they excluded both Gentiles and Samaritans from this category. A neighbor was a *nigh-dweller,* but they made exceptions along racial lines. This attitude is reflected in the parable which followed.

In the parable of the Good Samaritan it should be noted that Jesus was not answering the question about eternal life, but the one as to "who is my neighbor?" So this should not be construed as teaching about how to be saved, but as to the identity of one's neighbor.

It is possible that Jesus was on the road leading from Jericho to Bethany (cf. vv. 38-42). So He related what could have been a true story about this "red and bloody way." We are not necessarily to identify the characters in the parable as real people, but the event was a common one.

A certain man was travelling down the road from Jerusalem to Jericho (v. 30). We may understand him to be a Jew. This area was infested with robbers. A band of such fell upon this man. Not only did they take his money but his clothing. Furthermore, in the process as he probably resisted them, they beat him unmercifully and left him half dead. Then they slipped back into the hills, leaving their helpless victim lying in the middle of the road.

By a coincidence a priest came along. He saw the poor man. But instead of helping him, "he passed by on the other side" (v. 31). This verb is most expressive. It is a double compound word: *anti,* over against, *para,* alongside, *erchomai,* come. The priest came alongside the man, and then to avoid ceremonial pollution by touching the wounded man he crossed over to the side of the road in order to continue on his way. A Levite did exactly the same thing (same verb, v. 32). Ceremonialism meant more to them than humanity.

And then the story takes a surprising turn. "But a certain Samaritan . . . came where he was" (v. 33). He "came down upon him." The Jews did not regard Samaritans as neighbors. So Jesus chose the most unlikely man possible as the hero of the story—a despised and hated Samaritan who felt the same way toward a Jew. It should be noted that Luke in presenting Jesus as the universal Saviour, with one exception (9:52ff.) presents the Samaritans in a good light (cf. 17:16). If you would bring this parable up to date, substitute for the Samaritan someone upon whom you look with contempt and who returns the compliment.

Instead of despising this helpless Jew the Samaritan had compassion upon him. Rather than passing by over against him, he came to him *(proselthōn, pros,* face to face, *erchomai,* come, same basic verb as in verses 31-32 but with a different preposition, v. 34). And he did more than to say that he was sorry for the man. He "bound up his wounds, pouring in oil and wine." Luke the physician noted this medical detail. Oil (soothing oil) and wine (antiseptic alcohol) were remedies for the wounded. Hippocrates prescribed for ulcers: "Bind with soft wool, and sprinkle with wine and oil."

After rendering first-aid the Samaritan placed the man on his donkey, brought him to an inn, and "took care of him." He might have felt that he had done his duty when he deposited him at the inn. But not so. He remained with him, inconvenienced himself by delaying his journey, and cared for him through the night. But that was not all. The man must have a time of convalescence. He had been robbed, so he had no money. Therefore, the Samaritan, before continuing his journey, left two pence *(dēnaria,* about thirty-four cents, but with greater purchasing power than today) with the innkeeper (v. 35). He told him to take care of the man, and upon his return he would reimburse him any further expense that he might have. He did all that he could for a man who despised his race, and whose race in turn was despised by his own people.

What a lesson for today! Racial prejudice is dissolved in person-to-person relationships. A man in need, regardless of his race or his attitude, is my personal responsibility. Human need and human response are the two bases upon which to rest human understanding. One cannot help but wonder if Jesus meant to imply that this Samaritan was a Christian. For only the Spirit of God can so change a man that in Christ man-made barriers are broken down.

Jesus concluded by applying the lesson (vv. 36-37). The lawyer had asked, "Who is my neighbor?" So Jesus asked him which of the three had shown a neighborly spirit to the poor man. The answer was obvious. But the Jewish lawyer gagged on the word "Samaritan." Instead of using that word, he said, "He that showed mercy on him."

"Go, and do thou likewise."

"Thou" is written out and comes before "do" or "keep on doing." So it is emphatic. "You" in contrast to the priest and Levite; "you," like the Samaritan, should do the same.

Who can estimate the power of this parable? It has built hospitals and inspired men to meet human need. If practiced today it would be the death knell to race prejudices and everything which produces man's inhumanity to man.

Luke 10:38-42

The Haven in Bethany

On one of their journeys Jesus and the Twelve "entered into a certain village" (v. 38). Luke for some reason does not name it. Some suppose that to have done so would have subjected the people involved to persecution by the Jews. This is hardly likely since he mentions them by name. From John we know that they were well known in the area. This very fact may explain Luke's omission of the name of the village. It was unnecessary to do so.

But from John 11-12 we know that the village was Bethany, located about two and one-half miles southeast of Jerusalem, just over the crest of the Mount of Olives. Neither does Luke mention why Jesus came to Bethany so near to Jerusalem. The entire tone of the story suggests that Jesus was no stranger to the home in which He visited. Perhaps it was a haven for Him where among friends He could escape the pressure of His ministry. During His previous visits to Jerusalem no mention is made of His spending a night within the city. In all likelihood He spent them elsewhere, and this home may have been such a place.

At any rate "a certain woman named Martha received him into her house" (v. 38). The word "received" is a warm word meaning to welcome as a guest. Martha had a sister named Mary (v. 39). Since Martha is named first, evidently she was the elder. Some manuscripts read "into the house of her." Even the best reading "the house" suggests that it belonged to Martha. Some suppose that she may have been a widow or else the wife of Simon the leper (Mark 14:3; John 12:2). But these ideas are pure conjecture. Even though John tells us that these sisters had a brother named Lazarus, Luke makes no mention of him. Of interest is the fact that in an old cemetery at Bethany have been found the names Martha, Eleazar (Lazarus), and Simon.

Immediately we are introduced to a difference in these two sisters' natures. For when Jesus arrived we see Mary seated at Jesus' feet listening to His word or teaching. This statement shows that she sat beside Jesus and in front of Him, the position of a pupil before the teacher. Luke says that she "also sat at Jesus' feet." Why the "also"? Does it imply that Martha was accustomed to doing the same?

However, at this time "Martha was cumbered about much serving" (v. 40). "Cumbered" means to be drawn about in different directions, and so, distracted. It was probably late in the afternoon when Jesus arrived in Bethany. So Martha, instead of visiting with Jesus, was busy in the kitchen. So important a guest called for an elaborate meal. But all the while Mary sat at Jesus' feet.

Finally, Martha's distraction reached the boiling point. She burst in upon Jesus. The verb form denotes an explosive act. "Lord, dost thou not care that my sister hath left me to serve alone? bid her therefore that she help me" (v. 40). The verb for "help" is a double compound verb *sunantilabētai (sun,* with, *anti,* over against, *lambanō,* take hold). In modern parlance she said, "Tell her that she carry her end of the load with me." The very manner in which Martha spoke indicates that she knew Jesus well. He was no chance visitor, but one who enjoyed the intimacy of the family circle.

And Jesus took her *scolding* in the same manner. One can almost see a twinkle in His eye as He twice used her name. "Martha, Martha, thou art careful and troubled about many things," or, many dishes for the meal. "Careful" means to be divided in mind or to be distracted. "Troubled" means outward expression of this distraction. She was inwardly distracted and gave an outward expression to it. Then Jesus continued, "But one thing is needful" (v. 42). There is a variety of readings found in old manuscripts: "But one thing is needful"; "There is need of few things"; "There is need of few things or one." They all emphasize that Jesus said that a simple meal was all that was necessary, instead of the elaborate one planned by Martha. The "one thing" is not a spiritual thing as over against material things. It is in contrast to the "many things" on Martha's menu. In effect Jesus mildly rebuked Martha for spending so much time in the kitchen that she had no time for visiting with Him or listening to His word.

By contrast He said, "Mary hath chosen that good part, which shall not be taken away from her" (v. 42). Over against the many dishes of Martha, Mary had chosen the good dish, fellowship with Jesus. Certainly the "good part," or portion, is not salvation, for Martha had that also.

It is strange how one event in a person's life can mark him. From this story has come the attitude that Martha was nothing more than a good cook, while Mary was a spiritual person. How often when asked to render some spiritual service, a woman says, "But I am a Martha, not a Mary."

To be sure Mary had a spiritual nature. But the "also" suggests that Martha, too, possessed such a nature. What we often fail to see is that it never seemed to occur to Mary that Jesus might be hungry after a long day's journey. Martha recognized that while a man does not live by bread alone he must have bread. The worst that we can do is to censure Martha for her explosive outburst. But the entire atmosphere, including Jesus' reply, suggests that it was a friendly kind of fussiness.

Perhaps it was this one-sided picture of Martha which, along with other purposes, led John to relate the incident of the raising of Lazarus. Here Mary appears somewhat helpless in a crisis. But Martha, ever the practical one, was composed. Indeed, this event shows that Martha was a woman of great faith. For though her brother was dead, and as far as she could tell at the moment Jesus had failed to come to her aid, she still could say, "Yea, Lord: I believe that thou art the Christ, the Son of God, which should come into the world" (John 11:27).

Martha was a good cook. But she was also a woman with a great faith. There is no incompatibility between being practical and spiritual at the same time.

Luke 11:1-13

The Model Prayer

Once again we see Luke's emphasis on the prayer life of Jesus. For "he was praying in a certain place" (v. 1). When He finished one of His disciples asked Him to teach them to pray, even as John had taught his disciples to pray. And Jesus responded by giving the Model Prayer. "When ye pray, say..." (v. 2).

Matthew records a similar prayer in the Sermon on the Mount (6:9-13). Did Jesus give both prayers, or has Luke or Matthew confused the time of the giving of just one prayer? There are those who hold to this position. However, there is no reason why Jesus did not teach this lesson in prayer on two different occasions. Throughout this section of Luke we find many teachings which had already occurred in Galilee. But in Judea Jesus had a different audience. So it is not surprising to find Him repeating words which He had uttered previously in Galilee.

Some see a problem in that the apostles seem to have forgotten the earlier lesson. But Luke does not say that it was one of them who made this request. It was "one of his disciples," or learners. It could have been any disciple. Whoever it was, it was one who was familiar with the teachings of John the Baptist, and most likely a Judean disciple.

So Jesus gave him, and others, a pattern or model by which to pray. It is not a ritual to be repeated, but a guide in praying. At first glance the prayer is both God-ward and man-ward. The first section relates to God, His name, kingdom, and will. The second section deals with man's needs as they are related to God.

First, let us look at the God-ward side of the prayer. It is to be directed to God as Father, the Father who is in heaven, or the heavenly Father (v. 2). In this thought alone we are reminded that this prayer is not given to mankind in general, but to Jesus' followers. For only the Christian can in truth call God "Father." God is fatherly in nature toward all men; He longs to be every man's Father; but He is Father only to those who are children of God through faith in His Son, Jesus Christ (John 1:12; Rom. 8:14-17). The word "Father" as used by Jesus is strictly a Christian name.

In prayer we are to approach the Father reverently. "Hallowed be thy name" (v. 2). Plummer translates this, "Let it be acknowledged to be holy, treated as holy, venerated." For in His name is revealed all of God's nature, attributes, and His relation to us. A person's name stands for himself. If you profane his name you treat him with contempt. We can expect to be heard of God only when we regard Him in His true Self. Someone has said that reverence is the ante-room which leads into the audience chamber of the King.

"Thy kingdom come" (v. 2). In a sense this is the first petition in the prayer. The Christian's first concern, therefore, should be the coming of the kingdom of God. And, of course, one cannot truly pray for it to come unless he is willing to work to that end. It should be his first concern, even before daily bread. The "kingdom" *(basileia)* of God is really the "sovereignty" of God. Satan claims to be the sovereign of the world. So the prayer is for his overthrow whereby the sovereignty of God will be recognized on earth as it is in heaven. This means that His will shall be done absolutely on this earth. It is a tremendous prayer and a glorious prospect. But, of course, God's will must first be done in your heart.

Second, the prayer turns to the man-ward side. "Give us day by day our daily bread" (v. 3). "Give" is a present tense. So, "continually give according to the day," or "day by day." "Daily" *(epiousion)* means "the coming day." It is a prayer that each day we shall receive bread for tomorrow. This does not prohibit the accumulation of food or other necessities. But it does mean that we shall live lives of faith that God will provide.

But man does not live by bread alone. He must have spiritual provision also. Therefore, "forgive us our sins" (v. 4). Matthew reads "debts," the same idea expressed by Luke in the following segment of the prayer. But there is a difference in emphasis. In Matthew the plea for forgiveness is based on our willingness to forgive. But in Luke our forgiveness of things due to us is an example of what we ask of God.

Furthermore, we are to pray that we shall not be brought into temptation (v. 4). God does not *lead* us into such. The idea is that instead of being brought into temptation, we shall be spared such a trial. We are so weak that our greatest hope is to avoid being tempted. The phrase "but deliver us from evil" is not found in the best manuscripts of Luke, but it is genuine in Matthew. However, the idea is present here as in Matthew. The "evil" could mean "the evil one," or Satan. Do not let us fall into his clutches.

Looking back over this prayer it is indeed a model. For in embryo it contains all for which the Christian should pray. It is the call of a child to his Father, a worshipper to his God, a subject to his King, a slave to his Master, a beggar to his Benefactor, a sinner to his Saviour, and a follower to his Guide.

Following this pattern for prayer Jesus proceeded to give assurance that God answers prayer. Even a man will grant your request, if not out of love, at least in answer to your persistence in asking (vv. 5-8). How much more will our loving Father grant the persistent prayers of His children (vv. 9-10). Even an earthly father will not give his son less than he asks (vv. 11-12). "If ye then, being evil, know how to give good gifts unto your children: how much more shall your heavenly Father give the Holy Spirit to them that ask him?" (v. 13). In contrast to the material gifts of earthly fathers, Jesus mentions the Holy Spirit as the best gift, the *summum bonum,* which God bestows.

Truly, then, we should pray, "Lord, teach us to pray."

Luke 11:14-36

The Sin of Blasphemy

This section is filled with events and teachings recorded elsewhere as having occurred in Galilee. But there is no reason why they could not have taken place in Judea also. The enemies of Jesus followed Him here as in Galilee. And the hearers were different, so had not heard this teaching before.

Jesus cast out a demon who had made its victim dumb (v. 14). The crowd marvelled. But there were those present who were unaffected by this miracle. They said, "He casteth out devils through Beelzebub the chief of devils" (v. 15). Luke does not identify these critics, but we may suppose them to have been Pharisees. They had made this same accusation in Galilee to no avail. But they tried again before different people.

"Beelzebub" (Greek, *Beezeboul*) is a term related to the Canaanite god, Baal. While there is some question as to the meaning of the word, it probably means "lord of flies." II Kings 1:1-3, 6, 16 speaks of Baal-Zebub, the fly god of Ekron. This designation probably came from the fact that flies abounded in Palestine during the growing season when this nature god was said to be in the ascendancy. To show their contempt for him the Jews applied his name to Satan, the prince of demons.

Quite obviously this charge against Jesus' work was the blasphemous accusation in Galilee repeated in Judea. Others of Jesus' critics "kept on seeking" (imperfect) a "sign from heaven." This was Satan's temptation all over again for Jesus to give some demonstration of heavenly power such as his demand that Jesus jump from the pinnacle of the temple. The healing of the dumb man was to them an earthly sign. So they dared Him to perform a greater work.

In reply Jesus showed how unreasonable was the charge that He worked by the power of Satan. His act in casting out the demon was not *by,* but *against* Satan. So if Satan worked through Him he worked against himself. Such a divided house, or kingdom of evil, was doomed to fall (vv. 17-18). The Pharisees' pupils claimed to cast out demons by the power of God. So, while not admitting that they did so, Jesus used this claim to refute His critics. Let their disciples judge as to Jesus' source of power (v. 19). Since they claimed divine power, why should they deny the same power to Jesus? So if He cast out demons by God's power, then "no doubt the kingdom of God is come upon you" (v. 20). This proves that Christ is stronger than Satan, therefore He does not need his help. For in order to cast out Satan's demon He had to overcome Satan's power (vv. 21-22). It is of interest to note that on this occasion Jesus said nothing of the sin against the Holy Spirit (cf. Matt. 12:31ff.). Were Luke merely reporting the event in Galilee it is difficult to understand why he would omit so vital a matter (but note Luke 12:10).

In one terse sentence Jesus turned the tables on His critics. "The one not being with me is against me, and the one not gathering with me scatters" (v. 23). Jesus had shown that He worked by the power of God, and His critics opposed Him. So instead of His being in league with Satan, they were. And instead of working with Him to gather God's harvest, they were scattering it. This was an adroit statement of affairs indeed.

Jesus proceeded to prove His charge by referring to the Pharisees' work in claiming to rid men of unclean spirits (v. 24). A dispossessed demon wanders in the desert, seeking rest, or a cessation from wandering. The wild desert was thought to be the abode of evil spirits. But it was also believed that they found rest only as they inhabited people. So failing to find rest the demon decided to return to his "house," the person in whom he had dwelt. Note that he called him "my house." Illegitimately Satan claims the bodies of men.

And then came the climax (vv. 25-26). He found the man's body "swept and garnished." Both of these words are perfect tenses, suggesting completeness. He was completely swept clean and decorated. But the implication is that he was also *empty*. The Pharisees had removed all evil, and had decorated the man's life with empty rites and ceremonies. But they had not given the man any vital spiritual experience to replace his evil possession. He was a perfect set-up for further evil. So the evil spirit gathered seven more of his kind, and they all took up their abode in the poor man. He was worse off than before the Pharisees had taken hold of him. Having tried their *better* life and failed, he would be less susceptible to the genuine life which Jesus offered to him.

It is a devastating condemnation of the work of an empty religion.

Jesus' utter defeat of His critics brought an exclamation of joy from a woman in the crowd (v. 27). She blessed the womb which bore Him and the breasts of Jesus' mother whence He had received succor in infancy. But Jesus replied that true blessedness was to those who heard and kept, or guarded the word of God (v. 28). Here again was an indirect condemnation of His critics who had seen the power of God at work, but had denied it.

With this Jesus spoke to the crowds which had gathered about Him. He called the present generation an evil one (vv. 29-30). They kept on seeking a sign of His deity. But no sign "shall be given" other than the sign of Jonah. This suggests a future sign. Repeatedly Jesus' enemies asked for a sign. But Jesus never worked a miracle on demand. He always pointed to the sign of Jonah as a type of the resurrection (cf. Matt. 12:39ff.). As Jonah was in the belly of the fish for three days, so would Jesus be in the tomb. But as Jonah came forth from the fish's stomach alive, even so Jesus would come out of the tomb alive. This "sign" *shall be given*. It is yet in the future. Yet the record shows that even then the Pharisees and Sadducees did not believe it.

Furthermore, the queen of Sheba will witness against that generation in the final judgment (v. 31). For she journeyed to Jerusalem to hear the wisdom of Solomon. But a greater than Solomon was among them, and they refused to hear Him. From the sign of the resurrection Jesus turned to His preaching which His enemies rejected. The Ninevites "repented at [*eis,* as the result of] the preaching of Jonas" (v. 32). But this generation did not repent at the preaching of Jesus, a greater than Jonah. So both the queen of Sheba's and the Ninevites' response will be the basis of a condemnatory judgment (*katakrinō,* to judge down) of Jesus' contemporaries.

What Jesus said about His generation applies to all subsequent ones. Added to His wisdom, preaching, and resurrection is the record of history. No one has influenced history as has Jesus. The greater the light sinned against, the greater the condemnation. He that hath ears to hear, let him hear!

Jesus had put His light on a lampstand where all might see (v. 33). But man must see if the light is to suffice. The light of the body is the eye (v. 34). If one has good vision he will see, and his life will be full of light. But if one's eye is evil, or has a distorted vision, the body is filled with darkness. So Jesus warns

His hearers to be certain that their vision is not out of focus (v. 35). It cannot be focused on heaven and earth at the same time. A true vision, or one focused on spiritual things, fills the entire life with the light of Christ, even as a burning lamp drives darkness from a room (v. 36). Plummer comments, "Complete illumination is illumination indeed, and those who possess it have no need of a sign from heaven in order to recognize the truth."

The reality of the Christian revelation is not seen by outward spectacle, but by the inward dwelling of Christ through the Holy Spirit. But, alas, our generation still looks for "signs."

Luke 11:37-54

The Condemnation Continued

Apparently the foregoing incident took place in the early part of the day, because as Jesus spoke a Pharisee invited Him "to dine with him" (v. 37). "Dine" is a verb derived from the word for *breakfast (ariston)*. It was not the very early meal of the day, but one eaten after the return from morning prayers in the synagogue. So Jesus entered his home and reclined on a sofa. He did this without washing His hands. The Pharisee noticed this (v. 38).

This washing had nothing to do with body cleanliness. It was the ceremonial washing which the Pharisees did before each meal and sometimes at intervals during the meal. Involved in this were both superstition and racial prejudice. The Jews thought that demons got on the hands with the purpose of entering the body through the mouth. Therefore, they dipped their hands in water before eating in order to wash off the demons. Furthermore, the utensils may have been touched by a Gentile. Therefore, after handling each utensil they sought to wash the pollution from their hands. An incident similar to this one occurred in Galilee where the Pharisees criticized Jesus' disciples for not washing their hands before a meal (Matt. 15:1-2).

Evidently Jesus' host looked with disdain upon His failure to observe this ceremony, a fact that was known to the Lord. So He used this occasion to speak His condemnation of Pharisaic formalism and hypocrisy. That which fell from Jesus' lips here was repeated in greater detail on Tuesday of Passion Week (Matt. 23).

Jesus began in a general way by noting that the Pharisees were very careful about outward cleanliness, but inside they were filled with *plunder* and *wickedness* (v. 39). In contrast to these evils He exhorted them to be charitable. This would denote an inward cleanliness, which would mean that all things were clean to them (v. 41). Giving alms would not make them clean, but would indicate a clean spirit. Jesus then pronounced a series of woes upon the Pharisees for their deeds which denoted their evil spirits.

"But woe unto you, Pharisees!" (v. 42). For they tithed every herb, but passed by "judgment," or a discernment between right and wrong, and the "love of God" *(agapēn)*. The love of God is not expressed through them to others. This is Luke's only use of *agapē,* the highest form of love. They were stern in observing the law of the tithe. But they were void of positive good. Thus they drove men from God rather than to draw them to Him. Jesus did not condemn them for tithing. Rather He approved the tithe. But He censured them for neglecting these more spiritual matters. It is possible for one to be rigidly legalistic, yet to obscure the true values in religion.

"Woe unto you, Pharisees!" (v. 43). For they "loved" *(agapate)* the chief seat in the synagogue. This was the semi-circular bench which faced the congregation. Furthermore, they loved to be greeted in public. Both of these things fed their egotism and sense of importance. They took pride rather than a humble spirit to church. They were addicted to the recognition of men, even if their whole attitude was repulsive to God. This disease is too common today to require further comment.

"Woe unto you, scribes and Pharisees, hypocrites!" (v. 44). Note that Jesus added the words "scribes" and "hypocrites." The scribes, or lawyers, usually were Pharisees. "Hypocrites" means "play actors." All of their religious formalism was merely a theatrical performance for the view and applause of men. Jesus likened such to hidden "graves," or tombs. For a Jew to touch a tomb made him unclean and so unfit for worship for seven days (Num. 19:16). People associated with these people thinking that they were so good and clean. But unknown to them they were full of dead men's bones and decaying flesh. Such people unknowingly became contaminated with the vices of the make-believe religionists. What a picture of a dead religion bereft of all semblance of life!

This last word struck home to the scribes, or lawyers (v. 45). A hit dog hollers. So the lawyers complained. To them Jesus had gone to meddling. It would have been well for them had they remained still. For their complaint turned Jesus' wrath upon them.

"Woe unto you also, ye lawyers!" (v. 46). In their interpretations of the law they devised grievous legalistic burdens which they required the people to bear. But they did not touch these burdens even with one finger. This could mean that they gave the people no power with which to live up to their meticulous rules. More likely it refers to their evasive tactics by which they got around obeying their own rules. It is so easy to preach to others, yet so hard to practice what we preach.

"Woe unto you!" (v. 47). The lawyers built tombs to the prophets whom their forebears had slain. Some of these may still be seen in the valley just east of Jerusalem. Outwardly they pretended to disapprove of what their fathers had done (v. 48). But actually their attitude showed them to be of the same stripe. Their very opposition to Jesus and their plotting to kill Him were evidences of this fact. Had they lived in the days of the prophets, they would have killed them even as they sought Jesus' death. All of the honor which they paid to the prophets of old could not hide their present murderous spirit (v. 49). For this reason Jesus' own generation is held responsible for all of the martyrs' blood shed throughout the Old Testament (vv. 50-51). "The blood of Abel" was the first to be shed (Gen. 4:10). "The blood of Zacharias" (II Chron. 24:22) was the last to be shed. Robertson notes that the murder of Uriah by Jehoiakim (Jer. 26:23) was later. But Genesis was the first book in the Jewish canon and II Chronicles was the last; thus all of the blood in the Old Testament. In a sense Jesus anticipates His own death which will be the crowning act of all such evil deeds. It is for this reason that that generation will suffer for all.

"Woe unto you, lawyers!" (v. 52). They had taken away the key of knowledge of salvation. They were supposed to teach the people. Instead they had kept them in spiritual ignorance. They barred the path to Christ to those who were trying to come to Him. And by their opposition to Him they themselves would not come to Him. This was His crowning accusation against them. They were experts in the Scriptures. Yet the Scriptures witnessed to the Christ. But they, by their multitude of rote rules, failed to recognize Him for themselves or for others. It is a great privilege but also a tremendous responsibility to be charged with teaching the Word of God.

We are not surprised at the reaction of the scribes and Pharisees (vv. 53-54). They were in a rage because Jesus had held their hypocrisy up to ridicule. Literally, "they had it in for him" (*enechein,* "urged vehemently"). It is the verb used to express Herodias' attitude toward John the Baptist (Mark 6:19). So they plied Him with questions with but one thing in mind. Like vicious animals they were "laying wait for him, and seeking to catch something out of his mouth." "That they might accuse him" is not in the best manuscripts. But the truth is present anyway. They had no interest in learning from Jesus. But they held on to His every word with demonic purpose. And this was the greatest condemnation of all.

Their kind lives on in those who listen to a preacher for no reason but to criticize him, who study the Bible only to argue about it and against it. The preacher is responsible for what he preaches; the congregation is responsible for how it hears. Both will meet the sermon at the judgment. God grant that the Lord's word in that day will not be "woe" but "blessed."

Luke 12:1-12

The Leaven of the Pharisees

Jesus' attack upon the Pharisees did not go unheeded. Evidently word spread abroad about it. For a great crowd gathered to listen. And we may well imagine that they were delighted with the spectacle. For though the people feared the Pharisees, they did not love them. They were quite aware of the very things which Jesus had said about them. The words "innumerable multitude" translate "myriads." Robertson renders it "many thousands."

Chapter 12 really contains a series of teachings directed to first one and then another group. But Jesus began by talking to His disciples, but in the hearing of the crowd. Quite naturally He began by warning them against the "leaven" or teachings and practices of the Pharisees, which He describes as "hypocrisy" (v. 1). At the beginning of the fourth withdrawal He had issued a similar warning, only then He included the Sadducees also (Matt. 16:6). They had just joined the Pharisees against Him. Now in Judea, suiting His words to the occasion, He repeats this warning about the Pharisees.

Hypocrisy gives one expression outwardly, but it possesses another attitude inwardly. But evil will out (v. 2). That which is spoken in darkness will be revealed in the light. And words whispered in the ear in a secret place will be proclaimed upon the housetops (v. 3). We, therefore, should be careful about our words, deeds, and attitudes.

Then Jesus addressed His disciples as "friends" in contrast to the enmity of the Pharisees. Out of fear of the Pharisees the disciples might be tempted to play the hypocrite. But Jesus reminds them that they can do no more than kill their bodies (v. 4). They should shun hypocrisy in the fear of God. It is better to have the body killed than for one to be cast into "hell" *(Gehenna,* v. 5). This was the Vale of Hinnom southeast of Jerusalem. Here had stood the fire god Molech, into whose red-hot arms were thrown little children as a sacrifice to him. Josiah had abolished this practice (II Kings 23:10). In Jesus' day this valley was the garbage dump of the city. Into it were thrown the dead bodies of animals and of executed criminals whose bodies were unclaimed. Maggots worked ceaselessly in the garbage. To consume it fires burned day and night. At night wild dogs snarled and gnashed their teeth as they ate edible portions of the garbage.

Jesus used this revolting picture to depict the horrors of hell. With one exception (James 3:6) only Jesus used this word *(gehenna)* to refer to a place of punishment. And He is the very essence of love and mercy. This fact alone refutes the denials of some with respect to the reality of hell. If hell is not real fire, as some insist, then it is worse than fire. For the reality is always greater than the symbol.

It should be noted in passing that Jesus was not warning His disciples about the danger of losing their salvation. He stated the general principle that it was better to lose one's life in being faithful to Him than to follow the way of the Pharisees and wind up in hell.

In being faithful to Him despite persecution the disciples have the assurance that they are not left to stand alone (vv. 6-7). Even little birds are remembered of God. God knows the very number of hairs on each disciple's head. Surely, then, He is aware of their trials. If God does not forget sparrows, they need have no fear that He will forget His children.

And their faithfulness to Jesus on earth will find a like faithfulness on His part in heaven or at the judgment (v. 8). If they confess before men that He is the Lord Christ, He will confess in the presence of the angels that they are His faithful disciples. By the same token, denial of Him before men here will mean His denial of them there (v. 9).

Before closing this segment of His teaching Jesus harks back to the charge of the Pharisees that He cast out demons by the power of Satan (v. 10). "Whosoever shall speak a word against the Son of man, it shall be forgiven him: but unto him that blasphemeth against the Holy Ghost [Spirit] it shall not be forgiven." To blaspheme is to speak insultingly against one. Jesus had cast out the demon in the power of the Holy Spirit. The Pharisees attributed it to the power of Satan, the evil spirit. Thus they insulted the Holy Spirit. It is the Holy Spirit who convicts of sin. To reject Him is to remove oneself from His convicting work. Thus one loses his awareness of sin and the need for a Saviour. God's grace is still available and sufficient, but the person loses the ability to respond to its offer through faith.

What is the nature of this sin? It is not simply profaning the name of God or deity, murder, adultery, or any other of the so-called scarlet sins. Neither is it a sin of impulse. It is a sin of deliberate knowledge, coming at the climax of a long series of refusals of the convicting work of the Holy Spirit. The Pharisees had the same knowledge of Jesus' miracles as others had, but with so different a result. Others saw it and "wondered." They saw it and blasphemed (Luke 11:14-15). The Pharisees had repeatedly refused to believe in Jesus. They had lost the power to discern between good and evil. To them good was evil and evil was good. An obviously good work was said to be the work of Satan. So hardened of heart were they that they had lost the ability to respond to the work of the Holy Spirit through Jesus.

Who can commit this sin? Certainly not the Christian, who is already saved by Christ through the Holy Spirit's power. Some hold that this sin is rejecting Jesus until the point of death. Certainly such a person finds no forgiveness thereafter. But even in life one can reach the point where he cannot respond. So he has no forgiveness. The problem is not in God's attitude, but his. The person who thinks that he has committed this sin has not done so. His very consciousness of sin shows that he is still sensitive to the conviction of the Holy Spirit. The person who boldly and adamantly insists that he has no sin should beware. There are those who insist that it was possible to commit this sin only while Jesus was on earth doing His wondrous works. But is He not also doing them now? To spurn salvation, a good work of Christ by the Holy Spirit, is dangerously near regarding it as an evil work, and, therefore, of Satan. The safest course is for one to receive Christ as his Saviour. For such already is passed from death into life.

From this word about the Pharisees Jesus turned once again to His disciples (vv. 11-12). They will be persecuted, even brought before courts in synagogues, which had the authority either to excommunicate or to scourge them; or even before civil courts. But they were not to worry about preparing a defense. For the Holy Spirit will teach them what to say.

Unfortunately some quote this verse (12) as Scriptural grounds for lack of sermon preparation. *The Holy Spirit will fill your mouth.* The writer has found that too often when he is unprepared in mind and heart, his mouth is filled with wind and noise. But the Holy Spirit should not be charged with such. It is the work of another kind of spirit, the spirit of laziness.

Specifically this promise was for the period before the body of Christian faith had been hammered into logical form. Even so, it is an abiding promise to those who dare to do for Christ. We must use our intellects. But beyond our own ability the Holy Spirit supplies our lack.

Luke 12:13-34

The Sin of Covetousness

Jesus' teaching was interrupted by a member of His audience. A man said, "Master, speak to my brother, that he divide the inheritance with me" (v. 13). Apparently their father had died, leaving his estate to the two brothers. According to Deuteronomy 21:17 the elder should receive two-thirds and the younger one-third. Evidently it was the latter who brought the complaint to Jesus. Either the elder did not want to divide it at all, or else the younger wanted an equal share. He did not ask for arbitration, but for a decision against his brother. Family squabbles over the estate were common then as they are now.

But Jesus did not propose to be drawn into this family quarrel. His reply, "Man," implies sternness on His part. "Who made me a judge or a divider over you?" (v. 14). This was not in accord with Jesus' mission.

In this question Jesus stated a principle which has a wide application for His followers through the ages. Too often the church is asked to step into disputes between people, groups, or even races. What should its role be in such cases? Should it become an umpire in disputed social problems? Should it sponsor crusades or become bodily involved in such? Or should its role be to declare principles of righteousness to both sides of an issue? It is quite clear that Jesus adopted this last position. He refused to become embroiled in a dispute as the champion of either side. For in such no one party has a monopoly on the right.

Jesus did not suggest a division of the inheritance. Rather He spoke to both disputants. "He said unto *them, Take heed,* and *beware* [guard yourselves] of [from all] covetousness: for a man's life consisteth not in the abundance of the things which he possesseth" (v. 15). Note that the italicized words are all plurals. Jesus spoke to both brothers. The trouble with both was the sin of covetousness or the desire for more. Rather than to become involved in their struggle, He preached to both sinners. The true life is not gauged by material abundance. No matter how much or how little property was involved, it was shutting them off from the higher values of life.

To illustrate His point Jesus spoke the parable of the rich fool (vv. 16-21). There was a certain man who was already rich. His land produced a bumper crop. But instead of being happy, it only added to his problem. How to use his prosperity caused him to reason within himself. "Thought" (imperfect) suggests a continued reasoning.

His first problem was storage room; his second problem was how to use his goods. The first problem he solved by tearing down his old barns to build new and larger ones. There was nothing wrong with this. But he stumbled over the second problem.

"And I will say to my soul, Soul, thou hast much goods laid up for many years; take thine ease, eat, drink, and be merry" (v. 19).

Jesus called such a man a "fool." The Greek word is *aphrōn.* It is formed with the alpha privative and *phrēn,* sense. It means one with no sense. Why did the Lord so designate him?

First, his life centered in himself. Note the personal pronouns in verses 17-19 (English; KJV). "I" is used six times; "my" appears four times; "thine" is found once. In one statement he referred to himself eleven times. Someone has noted that the middle letter of *sin* is "i." And the bigger the "I" the greater the "sIn." In truth sin is selfishness.

Second, he thought to feed his soul on things. He lived for personal pleasure, and he thought that life consisted of the abundance of things. In 1840 the average American had seventy-two wants and sixteen needs. In 1940 he had four hundred and eighty-four wants and ninety-four needs. In 1840 there were six thousand articles manufactured in the United States. In 1940 the figure was three hundred and sixty-five thousand. These figures in 1966 doubtless have been heightened immeasurably over 1940. The widespread unrest today is ample evidence that things cannot satisfy the longings of the soul.

Third, in seeking the answer to his problem of wealth he reasoned with himself alone. He sought no advice from God or from anyone else. Consequently, his answer was selfish indulgence. He gave no thought to the possibility of helping others or of using his abundance to the glory of God. Instead of using things he took his ease. He ate, drank, and was merry. Instead of following the Christian gospel, he followed pagan Epicurean philosophy —and that of the lowest sort.

He did not ask God's advice. But he received God's condemnation. The King James Version softens God's word into *"Thou* fool." But God simply said, "Fool, this night thy soul shall be required of thee: then whose shall those things be, which thou hast provided" (v. 20). Literally, "This night they [things] are demanding thy soul of thee." He worshipped *things,* and they led him to his doom.

The phrase, "whose shall those things be," suggests the dispute between the two brothers. The man did not use his wealth properly. At his death he merely left it to be fought over by his heirs. Alas, how often is this the case. And there is no greater estrangement within a family than this. Instead of using his wealth to bless others, he left it to be a curse to his family. And so is everyone who lays up treasures for himself but is not rich toward God (v. 21).

From preaching to these brothers and the crowd Jesus turned to teaching His disciples. He urged them to stop being anxious about food and clothing (v. 22). This does not mean that we should have no concern about such things, but that we should not be overly anxious about them. Literally, "stop being anxious for your soul." The *psuchē* is the source of physical life and enjoyment. But it can also refer to one's higher nature (v. 22). The lesson is drawn upon the fate of the rich fool. Therefore, "the soul is more than meat, and the body than raiment" (v. 23). These things cannot satisfy man's greatest needs. The true values of life are based upon faith in God. He feeds the ravens who do not struggle for things. And man is of greater value than these (v. 24). Likewise the lilies of the field (vv. 27-28). No man by worry can add a single span to his age ("stature" used in this sense in the papyri, v. 25). In fact, worry can even shorten life. So if worry will not add to life, it certainly will not enrich it (v. 26).

Therefore, "you [emphatic] stop seeking" food and drink as the end of life, neither live in worried suspense (v. 29). These are the things which pagan nations of the world (in contrast to "you") are seeking (v. 30). Those who worship the heavenly Father should realize that He is conscious of and will supply their needs. This is not an excuse for laziness; it is a call to faith as over against anxiety. Setting aside all useless anxiety God's people are to keep on seeking His kingdom, knowing that all these necessities, not necessarily luxury, will be supplied. "Seeking" the kingdom probably refers to endeavoring to bring the kingdom in the hearts of men. How the kingdom lags as we chase after material things!

So few are really seeking the kingdom that Jesus referred to them as the "little flock" (v. 32). Even so, they are not to despair. For it is God's good pleasure to give success to their efforts. In the meantime they are to place little value on material things (v. 33). They are to be used in pursuing their heavenly purpose. In so doing they may have little treasure on earth, but their treasure will be great in heaven.

"For where your treasure is, there will your heart be also" (v. 34). It is just as true that where your heart is, there will your treasure be also. Covetousness is a sin of the heart. A heart that is wholly dedicated to God will truly be guarded against covetousness.

Luke 12:35-59

The Need for Watchfulness

Jesus' teaching concerning the witnessing to the kingdom on the part of His followers naturally pointed to the time of the Lord's return at the end of the age. At such time there will be a reckoning. Two thoughts run throughout this section: the duty of the Christian to be watchful or to be found faithful in the responsibility placed upon him by Jesus; and the need for the unsaved to receive Jesus as Saviour. Jesus began with a general call to watchfulness (vv. 35-40). "Let your loins be girded about, and your lights burning" (v. 35). The long garments worn by the Jews were a hindrance to them in their work. So in order to have freedom of activity they drew them up and fastened them with a girdle. This also was done for travel if haste were necessary. But the figure of work applies more naturally here. Since the scene is laid at night a lighted house would suggest that the servants were not in bed but were busy about their tasks. Some see this as an indirect reference to the parable of the Ten Virgins (Matt. 25:1-13). But the thoughts are different in the two incidents. The five virgins with oil in their lamps were prepared to be received in the bridegroom's feast, the other five were not. But in Luke the people involved are servants in the house of their lord or owner. The only thought common to the two accounts is preparedness, but the preparation is different.

A further difference is in the "lord" (v. 36). In the parable of the Ten Virgins the man is the bridegroom. But here it appears that he is one who had attended the wedding feast, but not the bridegroom. We must not press every point, however. The key thought is that the servants should be watching for their owner's return in order to receive him. "Ye yourselves" (KJV) expresses the emphasis involved in the word *humeis* written out at the beginning of the sentence. It sets Jesus' followers over against those who are more concerned with material things than with the kingdom of God.

After this general introduction Jesus in two parables contrasts these two groups (vv. 37-48). In this contrast it is quite evident that one's faithfulness, or lack of it, discloses a man's character which expresses his relationship to Christ.

First, He dealt with the faithful servants. "Blessed are those servants [slaves, *douloi*]" who are found faithful to him. When the lord comes he will cause his slaves to recline at the table, and he will serve them (v. 37). This is quite a reversal of custom. But beyond this Jesus was looking to the blessings which will be enjoyed by His servants or friends at His return. One here is reminded of His washing of the disciples' feet at the final Passover meal.

The uncertainty of the time of Jesus' return calls for constant watchfulness (vv. 38-40). If a householder knew what time a thief would appear (note the change in the figure), he would be on the alert to prevent his breaking into his house. In certain schools of thought the image of the thief is made to teach a secret coming of Jesus before His final appearance. But this is to misconstrue the meaning. Certainly we would not press this to mean that we should be on the alert to prevent Jesus from coming. The one thought here is uncertainty as to the time of the event. If we knew the date that knowledge would tend to lessen watchfulness until that date approached. The point is to encourage watchfulness through the ages. Jesus emphasizes this when He adds, literally, "And you keep on becoming prepared, because in the hour you think not the Son of man comes" (v. 40).

These words were spoken to the Twelve. But others were present also. We are not surprised, therefore, that Peter interrupted Jesus with a question. Literally, "Lord, to us [Twelve] this parable you are speaking, or also to all [the crowd]?" (v. 41).

Jesus answered him with another question. "Who then is that faithful [trustworthy] and wise steward?" (v. 42). Here He changes from "servant" (slave) to "steward" *(oikonomos)*. The latter was a *slave* who was made a *house manager,* the meaning of *oikonomos*. He was given charge of the owner's goods and other slaves. He was to feed the other slaves, along with his other duties. So Jesus says that the trustworthy slave is the one who discharges his responsibility in keeping with his privilege. The obvious meaning is that both Peter, the other apostles, and anyone who serves the Lord faithfully are such "faithful and wise steward[s]." When the Lord comes he will receive a promotion or reward commensurate to his service (cf. Matt. 25:21).

Second, Jesus now dealt with the unfaithful servant. "But and if that servant say in his heart, My lord delayeth his coming..." (v. 45). Instead of feeding the other servants he beats them, begins to eat and drink until he is drunk. This is a pitiful picture of sinful living on the part of those who deny the return of the Lord and His final judgment. But Jesus plainly affirms both of these facts (v. 46).

"The lord will come in a day when he looketh not for him... and will cut him in sunder, and will appoint him his portion with the unbelievers." "Cut him in sunder" renders a verb meaning to cut in two *(dichotomēsei,* note our word "dichotomy"). Bruce takes this to refer to Peter and the other apostles. Thus he softens it to mean some severe punishment. But Robertson and Plummer take it literally to cut or saw the body in two. The latter seems to be the case. Jesus is not talking about the apostles but about an untrustworthy servant. The reference is not to a saved person, but to one who by his attitude shows that he is not a true servant. He is an unsaved person.

That this is the case is seen in verses 48-49. Here Jesus speaks of degrees of punishment as in hell. The entire passage turns on the contrast between the apostles and others like them (faithful servants) and those who were wedded to material things with no concern for Christ (unfaithful servants). One is not a Christian by being faithful in kingdom work; one is faithful in kingdom work because he is a Christian. And the opposite is true of the unfaithful servant. It may be argued that both are servants of their lord, or owner. True. And all men belong to God by right of creation. But only those who give the consent of their wills are servants indeed. The very attitude of the unfaithful servant shows that he was not one in his heart. His was forced servitude, not willing service.

So the unfaithful servant corresponds to one who proves by his attitude that he is not really a Christian. Now in that light Jesus spoke of degrees of punishment for such. The servant who wilfully sinned against knowledge will be beaten with many stripes (v. 47). The one who sinned, but in ignorance, will be beaten with few stripes. The greater privilege called for a corresponding punishment. This suggests that the Pharisees and others like them will receive greater punishment for rejecting Jesus than the masses of uninformed people. But both will be punished in hell. Bringing the figure up to date, the person who hears the gospel yet rejects Christ will receive a greater punishment than the one who did not hear it. Both reject Christ and are lost. But their degrees of punishment in hell will be different.

The fate of the heathen who never hears the gospel poses a problem for many. But Jesus clearly teaches that he is lost. He does not live up to the light that he has. Paul in Romans 1-3 shows that both Jew and Gentile are lost: the Jew because he does not live up to God's law; the Gentile because he does not live up to the law of God written in his conscience and heart. Both will be lost, but their degrees of punishment will be in accord to their understanding of God's will and purpose for them.

Someone asked Charles H. Spurgeon if the heathen would be saved if we do not preach the gospel to him. He replied, "My great concern is are we saved if we do not preach the gospel to him." Not everyone who says, "Lord, Lord" shall be saved, but those who receive Him into their hearts.

The division between peoples Jesus describes in verse 49. "I am come to send fire on the earth; and what will I, if it be already kindled?" This is a difficult verse to translate. Plummer says that Christ came to set the world on fire, and the conflagration had already begun. Bruce sees this fire as a burning enthusiasm in believers which will incite the antagonism of unbelievers. Perhaps this is what Jesus meant. At least it fits the larger context. Those who are enthusiastic in declaring the gospel of the kingdom will arouse the enmity of those opposed to it.

In this regard Jesus Himself has a baptism awaiting Him (v. 50). Here He speaks of the cross and all that it involves. This is His part in establishing the kingdom, as the part of His followers is to declare that gospel of the kingdom. The urge of the cross is upon Jesus as He speaks. Plummer notes that the prospect of His suffering was a perpetual Gethsemane. He is "straitened till it be accomplished." The word "straitened" renders the same word used by Paul in Philippians 1:23 in which he expresses his condition as being torn between living and dying. Was Jesus speaking of His natural human desire to live and His divine desire to die for the sins of the world? At any rate He faces forthrightly the baptism which awaits Him.

Then Jesus returned to the idea of division among men (vv. 51-53). While all who come to Him in faith will have peace, that very fact will produce a division between these and those who reject Him. This division will even be within family circles. And history, both ancient and modern, records this to be so. The Jews thought that the Messiah would usher in an era of peace and prosperity. But Jesus denies such a role. Instead, loyalty to

Him will mean tribulation. The era which comes through His work will result in strong loyalty to Him or strong opposition to Him. The record shows that in the resulting persecution of His followers Christians were betrayed by members of their own families. Tragic to be sure. But Christ demands supreme loyalty. There can be no compromise, even if it means to choose Him over the closest of human relationships.

At length Jesus had spoken to His disciples. Now in conclusion He turned once again to the crowd about Him. He charged them with being worldly wise but heavenly ignorant. They are adept at predicting the weather (vv. 54-55). A cloud coming from the west, from over the Mediterranean, means that rain is on the way. When the south wind blows it means scorching heat. Yet they are unable to discern the spiritual things which were taking place about them (v. 56). They were in the midst of a revolution and did not know it. Even without His teachings Jesus said that they were able of themselves to discern the right (v. 57). So they are without excuse for their rebellious behavior.

These words of Jesus are most meaningful in the present day. With all of our scientific knowledge we seem to be incapable of recognizing or coping with the revolution in human relations which rages through the earth. As we win the battle with outer space we are losing that of inner space. The more we know about the material universe the less we seem to acknowledge and obey the laws of the spiritual universe.

With a parable Jesus closed the lesson (vv. 58-59). On the way to the magistrate it is better to reach a settlement with your adversary than to wait until after a judgment has been handed down. This could reflect the problem between the two brothers over the inheritance. But a greater principle seems to be involved. There is a judgment ahead for those who reject Christ. Before that time comes it would be wise to make a settlement with Him by receiving Him into the heart. Else one will be beyond grace, and the law will take its course.

This warning Jesus gives to each individual. "I say to you" (singular, v. 59). Judgment and punishment will not be *en masse,* but individually. And a *settlement* with Christ must be on an individual basis. Watchfulness, therefore, is not only necessary for the Christian. It is expected of the non-Christian also.

Truly, then, the words of Jesus take on added meaning in that light. "Be ye therefore ready also: for the Son of man cometh at an hour when ye think not" (v. 40).

Luke 13:1-9

The Demand for Repentance

In His preceding discourse Jesus had spoken of judgment. This may have prompted some in His audience to come forward with a report on a horrible current event. They told of "the Galilaeans, whose blood Pilate had mingled with their sacrifices" (v. 1).

There is no other record of this event. But it fits well into the character of the Roman governor. Josephus lists a number of his atrocities. Such common occurrences may explain why this particular one was not recorded elsewhere. Perhaps certain Galileans were in Jerusalem for the feast of Tabernacles. Either they were known insurrectionists, or else they had become involved in some such event in Jerusalem. Pilate's soldiers found them in the temple engaged in making sacrifices. They slew them there so that their own blood was mixed with that of their sacrifices.

Certainly such a thing would be most objectionable to the Jews. Those who told Jesus about it seem to imply, however, that it was an act of judgment upon the victims. If they expected Jesus to react violently to this news, they were disappointed. For instead of doing so He turned it into an object lesson on the need for repentance.

Note His answer. "Suppose ye that these Galilaeans were sinners above all the Galilaeans, because they suffered such things?" (v. 2). Not all Galileans were active insurrectionists, to be sure, if this were the cause of Pilate's act. But such rebellion was in their hearts. However, Jesus went beyond this overt act to the problem of sin in the heart. And all men are guilty at this point. No man could point the finger of accusation at another.

Jesus answered His own question. "No!" The strong negative *ouchi* standing alone lends emphasis to it. "I say to you, But if you do not repent [keep on repenting, present], all likewise will perish," or be destroyed (v. 3). Perhaps two ideas are involved in this. If the Jewish people do not change their rebellious minds and attitudes their entire nation will likewise be destroyed. This actually happened about forty years later (A.D. 70). But even on an individual basis, failure to repent will result in the loss of their souls.

To this event Jesus added another. The tower of Siloam had fallen on eighteen people, killing all of them (v. 4). This incident also is recorded nowhere else, but it must have been recent and fresh in the minds of His hearers. Now, asked Jesus, were they greater "debtors" (note the change from "sinners" in verse 3, but the meaning is the same) than all others dwelling in Jerusalem? Jesus brought the lesson closer to home. Not just Galileans, but Jerusalem dwellers. Judeans might agree that Galileans were all great sinners. But this event was another matter. The one involved an act of the Romans; the other was an accident. But did not current Jewish thought say that in such cases men were punished for given sins?

Jesus brushed all this aside to apply the lesson as in the former case (v. 5). The need was not to try to explain this accident. Rather it was repentance lest they also should perish, or be lost. This applies to individuals, of course; but the primary lesson in both instances points to the nation of Israel. In verse 5 "repent" is an aorist tense. The Jewish nation must repent at once if it is to escape destruction.

This is seen in the parable which Jesus drew from this dialogue. A man planted a fig tree in his vineyard. In time he came seeking its fruit but found none (v. 6). He told his vinedresser of the experience. For three years he had sought fruit, but the tree had not borne any. So he ordered him to cut it down. Literally, "Cut it out" of the vineyard. It simply occupies space and makes the ground unproductive (v. 7).

Some see the "three years" as referring to the time of Jesus' ministry. It is a suggestive thought. But the greater meaning of the parable suggests that the "three years" involve the span of time in which God had come seeking fruit from the nation of Israel (cf. Isa. 5). She had entered into a covenant relation with Jehovah to be a priest-nation to the pagan nations of the world (cf. Exod. 19). But through the centuries she had lost this sense of mission. Now God is at the point of ending this covenant relationship. The permanency of the covenant depended upon Israel's faithfulness in it. She had not been so. Therefore, she had forfeited her right to such.

But the vinedresser pleads that the tree be given another chance ("this year also"). Perhaps through added cultivation and fertilization it will become fruitful (v. 8). If after this added opportunity it bears no fruit, then it may be cut down (v. 9).

Obviously this reference is to the Jewish nation. Up to this time it has failed to bring forth spiritual fruit. But it has one more chance in its attitude toward Jesus. If it repents at once and receives Him then it will become fruitful, and will continue. If not, then God will remove it from His vineyard. Jesus did not give the final outcome since it was still in the future. But history records that as a nation the Jews did not repent, even though many individual Jews did. They continued in the vineyard, and bore much fruit. But it was in the relationship as Christians. The nation itself was "cut down" in A.D. 70.

That which happened to the Galileans (v. 1) and the dwellers in Jerusalem (v. 4) was as nothing as compared to the Jewish nation and Jerusalem at the close of the Jewish war with Rome. The highway of history is littered with the debris of individuals, groups, and nations which refused to heed this warning of Jesus. Each of them stands as a sad memorial to teach us the need for repentance. For except we repent, we shall all likewise perish.

Luke 13:10-21

The Contrast of Values

According to the Gospel record Jesus had long since ceased to teach in the synagogues in Galilee. Due to the increasing hostility of the Pharisees He may have been barred from doing so. Or more likely it had been His own choice due to this hostility and to His desire to reach more people. But in His ministry in Judea He did on one occasion return to the synagogue for teaching (v. 10). It is the last mention of His doing so.

On this particular occasion it was on a Sabbath day. Present was a woman who for eighteen years had been "bowed together" (v. 11). This was a medical term for curvature of the spine. Evidently she was a well known case. Seeing her, Jesus called her and said, "Woman, thou art loosed from thine infirmity" (v. 12). The perfect tense means that she was loosed permanently. Then He laid His hands on her, and "immediately she was made straight" (v. 13, aorist). And "she kept on glorifying God" (imperfect).

One would think that this would have caused great rejoicing. A poor woman loosed from an infirmity of eighteen years' duration. But the ruler of the synagogue saw it otherwise (v. 14). He was indignant about the whole affair. For Jesus had done this on the Sabbath. It was the Galilean Sabbath controversy all over again. No one had spoken to him. But due to his position the ruler evidently thought that he should protest such an action. Lacking the courage to challenge Jesus, he spoke to the people. He reminded them that there were six working days. If they wanted healing they should seek it on one of those days, not on the Sabbath. To him the institution was more important than men.

Of course, Jesus knew that the censure was directed at Him. Unlike the ruler, He had no fear. So He answered him directly. He flung at him the word "hypocrites" (v. 15). He used the plural, so His answer was general. Such men as he took animals to water on the Sabbath day. Should not this woman, therefore, a daughter of Abraham, be healed on the Sabbath? (v. 16).

He was a hypocrite indeed. For he censured Jesus while pretending to censure the people. He pretended that the woman had come to the synagogue seeking healing. This was not true. She simply came to worship. Furthermore, he placed institutional values above human values. People to whom he was supposed to minister could remain in the hands of Satan as long as his precious man-made laws were kept intact.

It is so easy to lose the sense of values with respect to people in a highly organized society. People lose their identity and become statistics or a name on a card. This may be true even in religion. But Jesus says that people come first. In healing the woman He did not violate God's law of the Sabbath, only man's impersonal application of it. In fact, He put the Sabbath in a right relationship to persons. The Sabbath was made for man, not man for the Sabbath.

Jesus' answer put His adversaries to shame (v. 17). They were not ashamed of their act or attitude, only of the fact that Jesus had embarrassed them before the people. And their shame was compounded as the people rejoiced over Jesus' wondrous works.

But Jesus was not through teaching. To His adversaries the kingdom of God consisted of outward splendor, rote rules, and a show of worldly greatness. But unto what did Jesus liken it? It was as a grain of mustard seed (v. 18). A small seed, yet it produced a plant which sometimes grew to a height of twelve feet, so much so that birds might lodge in its branches. In spite of the opposition to it the kingdom of God would grow from an insignificant beginning to tremendous proportions.

Furthermore, the kingdom is like leaven put into three measures of meal (vv. 20-21). Though it is very small, it grows and spreads until it permeates the whole. It would so permeate society that a woman would be considered of greater value than an institution.

Some interpreters see leaven always as a symbol of evil. So they say that as the kingdom grows, in its outward form it will be permeated by evil. Others even see the birds in the same way. But such is to miss the meaning of Jesus' words. Leaven does not always refer to evil. In Leviticus 23:17 the law required that bread baked with leaven should be used as wave offerings offered unto the Lord. Should we offer to the Lord that which is mixed with evil? We should not seek to force these words of Jesus into a preconceived mold.

In these two parables He simply said that externally the kingdom would grow to great proportions, and internally it would permeate all of society.

In this section Jesus is dealing with a contrast in values. The value of an institution is contrasted with the value of a human being. The value of Judaism is contrasted with the value of the kingdom of God. And in each case the latter infinitely exceeds the former. We should never place an institution above a person. Neither should we emphasize mere bigness as over against spiritual dynamics. To do either is to follow the gauge of the world rather than the gauge of the kingdom of God.

With these words Jesus brought this Judean ministry to a close. John tells us that at this point He went to Jerusalem for the feast of Dedication (10:22-39). From there He went to Perea beyond Jordan (10:40-42). The account in Luke 13:22 probably begins what may be called the Perean Ministry.

VII
The Perean Ministry

Luke 13:22-30

The Last and the First

It is now a little over three months before Jesus made His final visit to Jerusalem. The time is probably late A.D. 29 or early A.D. 30. Jesus will spend some time in Perea, after which He will journey to Bethany near Jerusalem (John 11) before going back to Galilee (Luke 17:11) whence He will make the journey through Perea on His way back to Jerusalem. Luke sums up this activity in 13:22. Then he proceeds to relate specific events which took place during this time.

On one occasion someone asked Jesus a question. "Lord, are there few that be saved?" (v. 23). Literally, "the ones from time to time being saved" (present passive participle). This was a debated question among the rabbis as to the number of the elect.

Jesus directed His answer to the group. "He said unto them, Strive to enter in at the strait [narrow] gate" (v. 24). "Strive" renders the word *agōnizomai* from which comes our word "agonize." It was used originally of athletes contending for the prize of victory. Plummer translates it "strain every nerve." The present tense calls for a continuous striving, and emphasizes the earnestness of those who strive. Jesus pictured the way of salvation as a narrow gate. He knew nothing about many ways of salvation. In fact, He warns against such. For many "will seek" (much weaker word than "strive") to enter and will not *be able* to do so. "Be able" renders the word to have strength. They will not have enough strength to force open the door into the kingdom after it has been closed.

The time will come when the master of the house will close the door (v. 25). This suggests the passing of opportunity. Those without, finding the door closed, will plead, "Lord, Lord, open unto us; and he will answer and say unto you, I know you not whence you are." Continued pleading will not avail. "We have eaten and drunk in thy presence, and thou hast taught in our streets" (v. 26). But instead of granting them entrance, this claim will react against them. They had enjoyed His fellowship and heard Him teach. But they had not heeded His teaching. It is one thing to live in a Christian environment; it is another thing to be a Christian. One should beware how he treats his exposure to Christ's presence and teachings. Every such spurned opportunity will rise up to accuse the lost at the judgment.

So with a curt dismissal the Lord will say, "Depart from me, all ye workers of iniquity" (v. 27). They may or may not have been outwardly evil. But their rejection of Christ is the greatest sin.

In verse 28 Jesus has in mind the horrors of Gehenna or hell as He speaks of "weeping and gnashing of teeth." And all the more as they shall see "Abraham, and Isaac, and Jacob, and all the prophets, in the kingdom of God, and you yourselves thrust out" (v. 28). This, of course, is a picture of heaven in contrast with hell. The Jews claimed to be children of Abraham, and so automatically in the kingdom of God. The Pharisees claimed to be the official interpreters of the prophets. Yet these Old Testament worthies are in the kingdom, but they are not. This suggests that one of the greatest sufferings in hell will be the realization of a lost opportunity.

The picture is made even more impressive by verse 29. For many shall come from the four quarters of the earth to recline at this heavenly banquet. This, of course, refers to Gentiles who will be in the kingdom of God through their faith in Jesus Christ, while the unbelieving Jews will be outside that kingdom because of their rejection of Him.

"And, behold, there are last which shall be first, and there are first which shall be last" (v. 30). This is the crux of the entire matter. To the Jews, Gentiles were "last," or outside the scope of God's mercy. The Jews were "first" or the primary object of His love. But their conceptions are reversed in the final analysis. "Behold" suggests the element of surprise. The Jews, *seeking* through various means of rite, ceremony, and legalism, but all the while rejecting the "strait gate" of Jesus, are left out. The Gentiles, in dead earnest coming to Christ in faith, are included in the kingdom. The first last, and the last first. Truly no one should presume upon the grace of God apart from Christ. Neither should one despair of the grace of God when it is freely offered to all who come to Him in faith. In this teaching of Jesus there is a warning to the self-righteous, and a promise to the greatest of sinners.

Luke 13:31-35

The Lament over Jerusalem

"In that very hour" while Jesus was speaking certain Pharisees came to Him with a warning about Herod Antipas (v. 31). Literally they said, "Get out immediately [aorist], and keep on going [present] away from here: because Herod keeps on willing to kill you."

In Perea Jesus was in Herod's territory, probably near where John the Baptist had been arrested. He was not far from Herod's castle at Machaerus in which John had been imprisoned.

Whether or not Herod actually was trying to kill Jesus we cannot say. This was merely the report of the Pharisees. The tetrarch may have had such designs but was fearful of Jesus' popularity with the people. Or it may be that he merely wanted to frighten Him out of his territory. He not only feared Jesus personally, but he may also have been concerned lest Jesus might be the cause of an uprising in his territory.

Some see the Pharisees as messengers of Herod. But it is more likely that they acted on their own initiative. Why did they warn Jesus? Was it a friendly warning? In all likelihood it was not. Some see their act as an effort to get Jesus into Judea where they might seize Him.

In any case He did not panic (v. 32). He showed His contempt for Herod by calling him a "fox." He recognized him as a cunning person who posed little danger for Himself. Rather than to flee from such a person He would continue His work on schedule. He was moving toward a goal. "I shall be perfected" renders a present tense with a future effect. This verb *(teleioō)* means to carry something out to its intended end. His destiny lay not in Perea but in Jerusalem. "For it cannot be that a prophet perish out of Jerusalem" (v. 33). If Jesus were to fear anyone it would not be Herod Antipas. It would be the Sadducees and Pharisees whose power centered in Jerusalem. Prophets had perished outside Jerusalem, but they were the exception not the rule. John the Baptist himself was beheaded in Perea. But Jesus knew that His "end" was to be in Jerusalem. This within itself was an indictment of these very Pharisees who feigned friendship for Jesus.

Mention of Jerusalem brought forth an outburst of emotion on Jesus' part. "O Jerusalem, Jerusalem, which killest the prophets, and stonest them that are sent unto thee; how oft would I have gathered thy children together, as a hen doth gather her brood under her wings, and ye would not!" (v. 34). Matthew records a similar lament (23:37 f.). Some hold these laments to be one but recorded in different places. However, the contexts in both Matthew and Luke make it natural that Jesus uttered both laments at different times.

In giving this lament Luke takes note of previous visits of Jesus to Jerusalem as recorded in John. On these occasions He had witnessed to the city only to be refused by the leaders of the people. The figure here is that of a hen gathering her chicks under her wings for protection against an approaching storm. Jesus had endeavored to do the same for Jerusalem. He knew the rebellion that was in her heart against Rome. It will finally produce the storm of the Jewish War. If Jerusalem would forsake her worldly ambition for His spiritual salvation she would be spared the blood bath of A.D. 70. But she was unwilling to receive Him. She was looking not for a spiritual Messiah but for a political, military one. And that *looking* would spell her doom.

"Behold, your house is left unto you" (v. 35). "Desolate" is not in the best manuscripts. Jerusalem and the Jewish nation had chosen to seek salvation apart from God's plan. They would go it alone. The choice was theirs, not God's. But He would not violate man's right to choose. When men reject God's overture of grace, He has no choice but to leave them unto themselves with no help from Him.

Jesus concluded this lament by saying, "Ye shall not see me, until the time come when ye shall say, Blessed is he that cometh in the name of the Lord" (v. 35). To what was He referring? In Matthew 23:39 these same words most likely refer to Jesus' second coming. For already His Royal Entry was in the past. But here it makes better sense to refer the meaning to Jesus' entrance into Jerusalem on Palm Sunday. Certainly on that occasion Jerusalem would see Him, which was before the second coming. Indeed this former event will be Jesus' final challenge to the city either to receive or to reject Him.

The city will reject Him. And when that is final, God Himself will reject Jerusalem. Truly, then, her house will be left unto her. History records the terrible outcome of her refusal of the Christ.

Luke 14:1-24

The Distortion of Values

In this section Jesus exposes the Pharisees' distorted sense of values. With consummate skill He causes them to look into God's mirror to show them how foreign are their standards from those of the kingdom of God. Then He crowns the whole with a parable which shows their attitude toward the kingdom with its tragic results for them.

First, there is the distorted value of institutions over men. On a Sabbath day Jesus was the guest of a leading Pharisee for a meal (v. 1). Robertson suggests that it was a breakfast. Feasting on the Sabbath was common among the Jews, although they ate cold food prepared on the previous day. This show of friendliness on the part of the Pharisee and his friends evidently was a sham. For "they watched him." "Watched" means that they were looking at Him on the sly. With side glances they sought to gain some ground for criticizing Jesus' actions.

True to form, others than guests were present. Among them was a man with dropsy (v. 2). Seeing the man, Jesus asked the lawyers and Pharisees, "Is it lawful to heal on the Sabbath day, or not?" (v. 3). With this one question He turned the tables on His critics. They had thought to put Him in a dilemma. Now they were in one. Certainly the experts in the law could have answered the question. But what could they say? If they said, "Yes," that would be contrary to their teachings. If they said, "No," the people would resent that. Either way they answered they would be in trouble. So "they held their peace" (v. 4). They sought refuge in silence. Therefore Jesus simply healed the man and sent him on his way.[1]

Then He exposed their hypocrisy (v. 5). Any one of them on the Sabbath would pull an ass or an ox out of a well into which it had fallen. Some strong manuscripts read "son" instead of

---

[1] Of seven healing miracles on the Sabbath, Luke reports five (4:31, 38; 6:6; 13:14; 14:4; cf. John 5:10; 9:14).

"ass." The figure of speech is stronger if we allow the word "ass" to stand. Palestine was filled with unprotected wells, cisterns, and holes. So this could have been a common experience.

Jesus did not condemn this act of mercy. But He did condemn their attitude toward men with regard to their law of the Sabbath. The Pharisees were concerned about the welfare of their property, but were totally indifferent to the needs of a man. Their laws of the Sabbath must come before human kindness. Institutions before people. These distorted values were in direct opposition to kingdom values. The Sabbath was to be a blessing and not a burden. And man is of infinite value above that of animals or property.

Still the lawyers and Pharisees could not answer (v. 6). They were not able to continue the argument. For they did not want to admit that they valued their law and property more than they valued a man. But their attitude spoke louder than words.

Second, there is the distorted value of pride over humility. The healing of the man probably took place before the meal. When they were called to eat every man sought the chief reclining places (v. 7). The Talmud says that on a couch holding three persons the center place was of highest honor, the left side was second, and the right side third. Everyone wanted a center place.

Seeing this, Jesus drew a lesson from it. When one is invited to a wedding feast he should not out of pride seek the chief reclining place (v. 8). Instead out of humility he should seek the lowest place (v. 10).

Even on a practical basis this is good advice. Suppose that you seek the place of greatest honor. Should someone more deserving come, you may be asked to take the place of second honor. Even in this honored place you would be shamed before the group (v. 9). It would be far better to take the lowest place. Then if the host asks you to take a higher place you would be honored before the guests. Thus shame is the reward of pride as one moves *down* from the center reclining place to the one on the left. By contrast honor is the reward of humility as one is asked to move *up* from the right to the left side. The two men wound up in the same place of honor, but with what a difference.

Certainly one should not take the lowest place hoping to be moved up. This would be mock humility or hypocrisy. For humility to be pleasing to God and man it must be genuine.

The point of this example is summed up in verse 11. Whosoever exalts himself shall be brought low. Whosoever humbles himself shall be exalted. Self-seekers are an abomination to both God and man. Those who are willing to play second fiddle make beautiful music indeed in the symphony of life.

Third, there is the distorted value of selfishness over true hospitality. Looking over the group of invited guests, Jesus noticed that it included only the Pharisees' friends, relatives, and rich neighbors (v. 12). It was obvious that he had invited them with a view to receiving like invitations from them in return. His was a selfish hospitality. He had an angle by which to benefit himself. He expected to get back the cost of the meal in invitations to dine elsewhere. The "rich neighbors" suggest that he may have expected even more. His hospitality could become a paying proposition.

But Jesus said that if he would show true hospitality he should invite poor unfortunates from whom he could expect no return (v. 13). He would be blessed in doing it. He would receive their gratitude. This would be quite a change from the boredom suffered by those who engage in an endless round of dinners within one's set, which have little purpose beyond staying in the social whirl. But beyond the sense of satisfaction which comes from an unselfish deed, there would be the far greater spiritual reward in heaven "at the resurrection of the just" (v. 14).

This last phrase suggested to one guest, probably a Pharisee, the kingdom of God. So he said, "Blessed is he that shall eat bread in the kingdom of God" (v. 15). Among the rabbis a banquet was a common figure for the joy of heaven. This man assumed that he would be present at such a meal.

But evidently Jesus cooled his ardor as He spoke a parable to him. A certain man gave a great supper, and invited many guests (v. 16). It is implied that they all accepted the invitation. A common practice was to invite the guests in advance; when the meal was ready servants were sent to tell them to come to the feast (v. 17). But when the servants did so, the invited ones all made excuses as to why they could not come. One had bought some land, and must go to see it (v. 18). Another had purchased five yoke of oxen, and must go to try them out (v. 19). Buying land without seeing it, or oxen without proving them? On the surface their excuses were too flimsy. At least one man had a shadow of an excuse. He had married a wife, and therefore could not come! (v. 20).

The truth of the matter is that none of them had a reason, only an excuse. They had agreed to come, but now they had other interests. They simply did not want to attend the supper, regardless of the trouble and expense the host had been put to in order to prepare it.

Naturally when the host heard this he was angry. So he sent his servants into the streets and lanes of the city to invite the poor, maimed, halt, and blind (v. 21). They literally scoured the city for the unfortunates. But still there was room (v. 22). Then the lord sent them outside the city to the highways and fenced fields to compel, or urge, passersby to come (v. 23). His banquet hall would be filled, but none of those who were originally invited would taste of his meal (v. 24).

Now the meaning of this is quite clear. God has prepared a heavenly feast in His kingdom. The Jews regarded themselves as having a priority on this privilege. God had chosen Israel as His peculiar people (cf. Exod. 19). And she had accepted the bidding. Now in Christ the feast is ready. But the Jews as a people refused to come to it on the terms of God's invitation. This was especially true of the Pharisees and Sadducees, the religious and social elite. They were so involved in their system of religion and their pursuit of worldly glory that they were not interested in the kingdom as proclaimed by Jesus and His disciples.

Therefore, the invitation is given to those Jews (inside the city) who were considered as being social outcasts. And they gladly accepted the invitation. Furthermore, those outside the city, the Gentiles, are invited and urged to come. They too will come. But those who considered themselves the privileged ones shall not "taste of my supper."

Distorted values indeed! For they sold their birthright, even their souls, for a mess of material pottage.

Luke 14:25-35

The Cost of Discipleship

Had Jesus followed worldly standards He would have courted the multitudes. But the very opposite was true. He was interested in quality, not quantity.

In Perea He enjoyed the same popularity that He had known in Galilee prior to His refusal to become a political and bread Messiah. So on one occasion "many multitudes" were going along with Him (imperfect, v. 25). Suddenly He "turned" (aorist), and said unto them, "If any man come to me, and hate not his father, and mother, and wife, and children, and brethren, and sisters, yea, and his own life also, he cannot be my disciple" (v. 26).

This was a strong challenge indeed. The orientals are fond of strong language. Actually, the word "hateth" *(misei)* carries the idea of choice. Jesus said that if one would be His disciple he must be prepared to choose Him over every one of life's closest relationships. What is more, he must choose Jesus over life itself if such a choice is necessary. No Christian should court martyrdom. But he should not shrink from it if that is the price which he must pay in order to be faithful to Jesus. No one can be His disciple who is not prepared to die daily for Him (v. 27).

The crowds followed Jesus thinking that they would find a life of ease. Instead He made the greatest of demands upon them. One of the greatest perils to the Christian cause today is its popularity. It is so fashionable to be a member of the church. The vast number of inactive church members shows how few have counted the cost of following Jesus.

But He challenges men to count the cost before assuming the role of a disciple (vv. 28-32). To do otherwise is to invite shame, failure, and defeat. Verse 32 does not mean that Jesus will compromise His demands. This is simply a part of the parable, and should not be pressed. The point of these parables is that one should count the cost before proposing to be His disciple. There is no need of attempting it unless one is willing to pay the price. Anything less is not true discipleship.

"So likewise, whosoever he be of you that forsaketh not all that he hath, he cannot be my disciple" (v. 33). Literally, you must be willing to say *goodbye* to all your belongings for His sake. This does not mean to take the pauper's oath. It speaks more of dedication of all that one has to the cause of Christ. You cannot serve God *and* mammon. But you can serve God *with* mammon.

"Salt is good," said Jesus (v. 34). Why this statement at this point? This is His illustration of the self-sacrifice about which He has been talking. To do its work salt must be applied to the object of its work. In a sense it loses itself in the process. Jesus called Christians the salt of the earth (Matt. 5:13). Salt gives zest, or taste, to life. It preserves as it prevents corruption. And it possesses curative powers. All of these relations the Christian is to have to life.

But savorless salt is worthless. It is fit for neither land nor manure (v. 35). And since it is useless it is simply cast out. Even so, spurious disciples are also worthless. It is no wonder that Jesus sought to cull the crowd.

"He that hath ears to hear, let him hear" (v. 35).

Luke 15:1-10

The Friend of Sinners

Luke 15 is one of the best known and most beloved chapters in the life of Jesus. After posing a setting it is composed of three parables: the lost sheep; the lost coin; and the lost son. In the first two we see God's attitude toward sinners. In the third we see the Pharisees' attitude toward them. We shall treat them in this fashion, with the third being given separate consideration.

On an occasion publicans and sinners drew near to Jesus for the purpose of hearing Him (v. 1). They were grouped together as one despised class of people, the bottom rung of the ladder of society. Seeing this the Pharisees and scribes murmured, saying, "This man receiveth sinners, and eateth with them" (v. 2). The Greek is most picturesque. The publicans and sinners "kept on drawing near" and the Pharisees "kept on murmuring." To the latter class such was an immoral act on Jesus' part. For their charge implies that He was one of them (cf. Luke 7:34).

Jesus answered their charge with two parables (vv. 3, 8). He spoke directly to the Pharisees and scribes in the parable of the lost sheep. "What man of you, having an hundred sheep, if he loses one of them, doth not leave the ninety and nine in the wilderness [their usual pasturage, not a place of danger], and go after that which is lost, until he find it?" (v. 4). Having found it he brings it home, rejoicing. Furthermore, he calls on his friends to rejoice with him because he has found the lost sheep (vv. 5-6). And then the lesson. "I say unto you, that likewise joy shall be in heaven over one sinner that repenteth, more than over ninety and nine just persons, which need no repentance" (v. 7).

Now what is the meaning of this parable? Certainly it does not mean that a person may be saved, lost again, and must be reclaimed. This is altogether foreign to the lesson. The point is to show God's attitude toward a lost man as over against those who claim to be self-righteous. The Pharisees correspond to the ninety-nine sheep. They claimed to be in God's flock. They needed no repentance. And they looked with scorn on the publicans and sinners who, in their judgment, were not the objects of God's love.

But they were wrong, said Jesus. That one lost sheep was so precious that God risked all to find it and bring it back to Himself. He took the Pharisees at their word as being without need for repentance. And heaven rejoices more over one publican or sinner who in repentance and faith comes to Jesus than over the whole lot of these spiritually proud Pharisees. His words were a powerful blow to their smug complacency. They may despise publicans and sinners, but God loves them. And Jesus came to seek and to save the lost.

The parable of the lost coin places added emphasis upon God's love for the lost. A woman had ten pieces of silver, but lost one (v. 8). How diligently she seeks it. She lights a lamp, sweeps the house, and keeps on searching until she finds it. Then, like the shepherd, she calls in her neighbors to rejoice with her (v. 9). For she had found that which was lost. And then the same lesson. Only here Jesus made no mention of the unrepentant Pharisees. They are no longer in the picture. It is now rejoicing in heaven over one sinner that repenteth (v. 10).

Just one repentant sinner. Yet he sets the bells of heaven ringing with joy. If one sinner is so precious to God why should not Jesus receive them and eat with them? Indeed, why should not we, if in so doing we can be used of God to find that which is lost?

Luke 15:11-32

The Lost Lesson

The parable of the prodigal son has been called the best short story in literature. But, strange to say, its primary lesson has been lost in the maze of much preaching. The fact that it is popularly called *the parable of the prodigal son* testifies to this truth. For the prodigal son, while he plays an important role, is merely the background against which the picture is painted. Barclay calls this "The Story of the Loving Father." This is nearer to the purpose of the parable. But again this is not the primary lesson that Jesus was teaching. This lesson is central in the parables of the lost sheep and the lost coins.

To determine Jesus' real purpose in the present parable we must go back to the beginning of the chapter and see the attitude of the Pharisees and scribes toward publicans and sinners. This focuses attention not on the younger son or father but on the elder brother. The primary lesson in the parable, therefore, is to show in a real life situation the attitude of the self-righteous Pharisees toward publicans and sinners. The contrast between the attitude of the elder brother and that of the father is an exact parallel to the attitude of the Pharisees and that of God toward publicans and sinners.

A certain man had two sons (v. 11). The younger son was rebellious against the discipline of the home. He wanted to be free and to try life on his own. So one day he said, "Father, give me the portion of goods that falleth to me" (v. 12). Jewish law at the father's death allotted one-third of the estate to the younger son and two-thirds to the elder (Deut. 21:17). But this son wanted his share even while the father lived. The father did not refuse. He did not violate his son's personality. So he divided his estate between "them." Note that the elder son got his share also. The father wisely did not play favorites.

Soon thereafter the younger son took all of his goods, and departed into a far country (v. 13). He left nothing behind to indicate that he might return. He thought that he was sufficient unto himself, so he burned his bridges behind him. What need had he of his father and home as long as he had his inheritance?

One is not surprised that this headstrong youth "wasted his substance in riotous living" (v. 13). This means that he went the whole route in sinful indulgence. Evidently he was quite a popular person among his fellow-sinners as long as his money held out. But then one day he was strangely alone. For he had spent all (v. 14). Furthermore, at precisely that very moment there "arose" *(egeneto,* aorist) a mighty famine in all the land *(kata tēn chōran)* to which he had gone. And he began to be in want.

So great was his need that he hired out to a citizen to feed swine (v. 15). This would imply that the "far country" was a Gentile area. The depths to which he had fallen may be seen in his occupation. A Jew feeding swine! To the Jewish mind he could sink no lower. A great, profligate sinner. And now a feeder of hogs!

But this was not the end. So hungry was he that he even wanted to eat the "husks" which he fed to the hogs. "Husks" *(keratiōn)* are the pods of the carob or locust tree which is still seen in Palestine. Inside it is a gelatinous substance with a sweet taste. It was used to feed swine, and was also eaten by poor people. It is called Saint John's Bread, since it was erroneously thought to be the food which John the Baptist ate in the wilderness.

Even though the man "kept desiring" this food "no one kept giving to him" (v. 16, imperfects). He was not allowed to eat even the food of hogs.

Now at this point let us seek to identify this younger brother. Who was he? Some hold that he was a Christian who had lost his salvation. He was in the father's house, and left it to plunge into sin. However, this cannot be the case. The context is Jewish, not Christian. Does he correspond to the Gentile world? The tone of the story suggests that he was a Jew. He was a Jew who had left his father's house to plunge into the depths of sin. He was, therefore, a *sinner.* He had sunk so low that he worked for a Gentile (publican?). And if that was not enough, he fed hogs and would even have eaten with them. Evidently, therefore, in painting this portrait Jesus had in mind the "publicans and sinners" who were so despised by the Pharisees. It is a portrait painted by One who was indeed an Artist with words.

Now the Artist begins to touch up the portrait. For this miserable man "came to himself" (v. 17). Literally, "But unto himself coming." Note the emphatic position of "unto himself." More than merely being in a "far country," he had been away from "himself." His greatest travel had been spiritual, not geographical. Robertson notes that he had been "out of his head, and now began to see things as they really were." All sin is a form of insanity. So he came "unto himself," or back to his right senses.

Jesus is saying that even a publican or a sinner is capable of repentance. No man sinks so low but that there is hope for him. There is something even in the worst of sinners which still reminds him of what God intends that he should be. The memory of his father's house brought this man "unto himself."

"How many hired servants of my father's have bread and to spare, and I perish [am perishing] with hunger!" (v. 17). The "many" suggests the luxury of the home which he had left. So he determined to return to his father's house (vv. 18-19). Furthermore, he would confess his sins and unworthiness as a son. He would ask not to be restored to sonship, but merely to become a "hired servant." Now a hired servant was not only less than a son but less than a slave. A slave at least had security. But a hired servant could be dismissed from his position. So this symbol of publicans and sinners did not ask for the best but for the least in the father's house. Whatever he received would be by grace rather than merit. Here is true repentance indeed!

Now Jesus shifted the focal point of the story from the son to the father. While the son was yet quite a distance from his home his father saw him coming (v. 20). This suggests that the father had been constantly looking and yearning for his son's return. The son presented quite a different spectacle from his appearance when he had left. He went away well dressed, rich, and self-confident. Now he returns ragged, penniless, and beaten. But the father did not see this. He only saw his son. Instead of chastening him he had compassion on him. Note the eagerness of the father to welcome his son home. "Running [aorist participle] he fell [aorist] upon his neck, and kissed him much [aorist]," or "kissed him again and again."

The son made his confession up to a point (v. 21). He said that he was unworthy of sonship. But he was cut short before he could say, "Make me as one of thy hired servants." His confession was interrupted by the forgiving father. To his slaves he said, "Bring forth [quickly, in best manuscripts] the best robe, and put it on him; and put [give] a ring on his hand, and shoes on his feet: and bring hither the fatted calf, and kill it; and let us eat, and be merry; for this *my son* was dead, and is alive again; he was lost, and is found. And they began to be merry" (vv. 22-24, author's italics). The verbs "bring forth," "put," and "give" are all aorists expressing the father's happy excitement.

Each of the items which the father gave to the son is significant. The robe stands for honor, the ring for authority, and the shoes for sonship. Children of the family wore shoes; slaves did not. So the son was fully restored to sonship, not because he deserved it but because of the father's forgiving love.

It is hardly necessary to point out that in the father Jesus painted a portrait of the heavenly Father. His attitude toward a lost sinner is adequately drawn. Not only does His love go out to the sinner in his sin, but He is eager to forgive and to confer full sonship upon those who repent and turn to Him. The making merry corresponds to the joy in heaven over one sinner that repents (cf. vv. 7, 10). And in this portrait Jesus also justified His own act in receiving and eating with publicans and sinners.

But all that has gone before is only background for that which follows. For suddenly the picture changes. The villain of the story comes on the scene.

"Now his elder son was in the field: and as he came and drew nigh to the house, he heard music and dancing" (v. 25). From a slave he learned the cause of such merriment (vv. 26-27). His long-lost brother had returned, and his father was giving him a feast. Instead of joining in the celebration he was angry, and "did not will to enter." Literally, "he flew into a rage." The father came out and "kept begging" (imperfect) him to come in. Instead he accused his father of being unfair to him. "Lo, these many years do I serve [keep on serving] thee, neither transgressed I at any time thy commandment: and yet thou never gavest me a kid, that I might make merry with my friends [he did not admit that he had received his share of his father's goods, v. 12]: but as soon as this thy son [he did not call him his brother] was come, which hath devoured thy living with harlots, thou hast killed for him the fatted calf" (vv. 29-30).

And whose portrait did Jesus paint this time? Why, that of the Pharisees, of course. Everything in this picture points to them. Their claim to self-righteousness, their claim of salvation by merit, and their attitude toward publicans and sinners are all here. They were angry that these despised ones were enjoying a heavenly feast. Yet they refused to enter even though the Father through Christ kept on begging them to do so.

One cannot escape the contrast between the father's joy over the return of his repentant son and his heavy heart over the self-righteous one. "Son, thou art ever with me, and all that I have is thine" (v. 31). He was with him in body, but so far away in spirit. All that the father had was his to enjoy, but he did not enjoy it. The portrait of the Pharisees continues. They claimed to be so close to God, when actually they were so far from Him. The Father's blessings were available to them, but they would not receive them.

"It was meet [fitting] that we should make merry, and be glad: for this *thy brother* was dead, and is alive again; and was lost, and is found" (v. 32, author's italics). Though the Pharisees scorned the publicans and sinners, they were still their brothers or the object of paternal, divine love. God is love. And God would deny Himself if He did not rejoice over the salvation of one sinner who is the object of His love.

The story ends here with no hint that the elder brother changed his mind and attitude, which is the essence of true repentance. The Pharisees kept on despising publicans and sinners. God in His Son kept on receiving them and saving those who believed.

This beautiful story ever stands as a condemnation of those who, like the Pharisees, hold themselves aloof from the Father's love and despise those who are less righteous outwardly than they are. But it also stands as a beacon light of hope to guide those who are lost in the far country of sin back to the Father's house.

Luke 16:1-13

The Shrewd Steward

The figure of the younger son wasting his father's goods suggested what has been called the parable of the unjust steward. Jesus Himself called him such. But he is also said to have acted "wisely" or "shrewdly." So we may more likely call him "the shrewd steward."

Whereas the three parables in Chapter 15 were spoken to the Pharisees and scribes, this one was given to the disciples. If we press every point in the parable we get into moral difficulty. For thus it would appear that Jesus approved of the actions of the steward. It is well, therefore, to recall that a parable is designed to teach one great truth. In this case it is found in verse 9.

A certain rich man had a steward (v. 1). He was a slave who had been made "house manager" over his owner's goods. This steward was "accused" unto his owner that he had wasted his goods. The word "accused" means to slander by gossip. So evidently such gossip came to the ears of the rich man.

He must have believed the gossip. He may even have investigated and found the report to be true. For he called the steward to him, demanding to know why this report (v. 2). He called on him to render an account of his stewardship. And evidently he knew what the report would show. For he said, "Thou mayest be no longer steward."

Knowing that he was soon to be relieved of his responsibility, the steward began to think of his future. "What shall I do?...I cannot dig; to beg I am ashamed" (v. 3). He was not strong enough to do manual labor. His pride would not permit him to become a beggar. Finally the man reached a conclusion. "I am resolved" might well be rendered, "I've got it! I know what I will do" (v. 4). He suddenly remembered his owner's debtors. So he decided to make a deal with them, to put them under obligation to him, so that when he was dismissed they would let him live with them.

No sooner resolved than did he act. Calling his owner's debtors he made his deal (vv. 5-7). One owed one hundred measures of oil. So he reduced the figure by half. Note that he told the debtor to sit down "quickly" and write in the lower amount (v. 6). Haste was of the essence. Another owed one hundred measures of wheat. He told him to write eighty or a reduction of twenty per cent.

When the owner heard about this he "commended the unjust steward [or steward of unrighteousness], because he had done wisely" (v. 8). He did not commend his unrighteous deed but the fact that in his situation he had acted shrewdly. This makes quite a difference. It removes any basis to charge Jesus of approving by implication an unrighteous act. The entire point hinges on the wise use that an unrighteous man made of his unrighteousness. He looked beyond the present to the dividends of the future.

Then Jesus drew the lesson out of the parable. "For the children of this world are in [*eis,* unto] their generation wiser than [shrewder beyond] the children of light" (v. 8). The children of this world are stewards of unrighteousness. The children of light are stewards of righteousness. And the former use their stewardship unto their own more shrewdly than do the latter.

Applying the lesson Jesus said, "Make to yourselves friends of [*ek,* by or out of] the mammon of unrighteousness; that, when ye [it] fail [s], they may receive [welcome] you into everlasting habitations" (v. 9). As the shrewd steward used the mammon of unrighteousness in an unrighteous manner in order to insure a welcome into the houses of those who benefited from his evil deed, so the followers of Christ should use this mammon of unrighteousness (or riches) to insure that they will be welcomed into heaven. Not that this will insure their going to heaven. As children of light they are already going there. The point is that upon arrival they will be welcomed by those who are already there as the result of the *children's* proper use of their stewardship.

Note the words "when ye fail." The best manuscripts read "when it shall fail" (aorist tense with a future effect). The reference is to the "mammon of unrighteousness" or money. Wealth will come to an end, at least our stewardship of it will do so—at death if not before. In fact "it" may even be enlarged to include all the stewardship of life, our opportunities to use present powers for future effects. Note also *"they* may receive you . . ." (author's italics). The "they" refers to those who are in heaven because of a proper use of our present stewardship. The figure is a glad welcome in heaven by those who are there because of our efforts on earth.

From this parable Jesus drew one of His most significant lessons of life. One who is faithful in little things is faithful in greater ones (v. 10). So many people speak of doing great things but are not willing to do faithfully the little task. A person proves his ability to handle great responsibilities by being faithful and successful in handling the lesser ones. Conversely a man who is unjust in little things will also be unjust in greater matters (v. 10). An embezzler usually begins by taking small amounts of money and then works up to larger amounts. So-called little sins become larger ones. Therefore, if one is not faithful in the unrighteous mammon, or in the use of money, how can he expect God to trust him to do spiritual things? (v. 11). A person who robs God by withholding his tithes and offerings will not develop spiritually. The right use of wealth is not a condition of salvation. But a wrong use of it may be an evidence that one is not truly a Christian. Material possessions are not ours but God's. So if you are unfaithful in the use of His things, "who shall give you that which is your own" (v. 12), or salvation?

This point is emphasized in verse 13. Literally, "No domestic servant can be a slave to two owners." Each demands absolute obedience, and it cannot be given to both. "Either he will hate the one, and love the other; or else he will hold to the one, and despise the other." "Hate" and "love" carry the idea of choice. So each one must choose. Either he must choose God and reject mammon, or do the opposite. No man can have two gods. "You cannot be a slave to God and to mammon" (v. 13).

Those who worship mammon serve it absolutely. Those who worship God must do the same. Unfortunately those who serve mammon put to shame those who serve God. This is a fitting finale to the parable of the shrewd but unjust steward.

Luke 16:14-31

The Rich Man and Lazarus

The Pharisees reacted adversely to the parable of the shrewd steward and the lesson about God and mammon which Jesus drew from it. For they were "lovers of money" *(philarguroi)*. They "*were hearing* all these things and *were scoffing* at him" (v. 14). The italicized words show that all through Jesus' teaching they were listening and sneering, or turning up their noses at Him. In so doing they sought to justify their attitude before men. But God knew their hearts. And such an outward attitude of righteousness coming out of evil hearts was an "abomination in the sight of God" (v. 15). There was withering scorn in Jesus' words as He exposed their detestable attitude.

The law and the prophets (the Old Testament) were in authority until the coming of John the Baptist. Since then the kingdom of God had been preached, and men were seeking to force their way into it (v. 16). But these Pharisees were despising it. Furthermore, by their covetousness they even violated the law. But regardless of their attitude toward both the kingdom and the law, the law was still in force (v. 17). It was easier for heaven and earth to pass than for one small letter of the law to fall. To illustrate this truth Jesus referred to the seventh commandment. Whatever men said or did they might scorn the law, but adultery was still adultery (v. 18).[1] The Pharisees might scoff at Jesus, they might violate the tenth commandment against covetousness, but they would not escape the judgment. To illustrate this Jesus gave the parable of the rich man and Lazarus.

A certain rich man lived in luxury (v. 19). All that money could provide was his. He was clothed in an outer garment of purple, which was worn only by the wealthy and princes. He also wore "fine linen" for his undergarments. This was Egyptian flax. Vincent says, "Some of the Egyptian linen was so fine that it was called *woven air*." Furthermore, he "fared sumptuously every

---

[1] For a full discussion of this law see my *Matthew, op. cit.,* pp. 255 ff.

day." This means that he *made merry brilliantly*. It is an excellent picture of the Pharisees as it shows the wrong use of money and opportunity.

By contrast there was also a beggar named Lazarus who was placed at the rich man's gate (v. 20). Apparently each day that he fared sumptuously the beggar was at his gate, placed there for the very purpose of getting help. So the rich man had ample opportunity to use some of his wealth to relieve the poor man's lot. And he certainly needed relief. His body was full of sores, perhaps the result of malnutrition. He desired even the crumbs which from time to time fell from the rich man's table (v. 21). Whether he got them is not told. But the assumption is that he did not. Dogs came and "kept licking" (imperfect) his sores. This could mean that they added to his misery or that this was his only comfort. If the latter be true, and probably is, this heightens the picture. The rich man utterly ignored this fellow human being, but wild dogs at least paid him some attention. This is the condition of the two men in this life. But then the scene suddenly changes.

For the beggar died, and was carried by angels to Abraham's bosom (v. 22). This was a Jewish concept of Paradise. Being in Abraham's bosom suggests the honored place at the heavenly feast (cf. John 13:23). So he received a very special welcome into heaven. Outside the rich man's gate on earth, he was hungry and ignored. Reclining on Abraham's bosom in heaven, he was feasting and honored.

"The rich man also died, and was buried" (v. 22). One gets a jolt even as he reads this. What a difference from the death of Lazarus! "And in hell [*hades*], he lifted up his eyes" (v. 23). *Hades* is the abode of the dead. "Hell" as a place of punishment renders *Gehenna*. But *Hades* is simply the abode of the dead with no reference to spiritual condition. Both Lazarus and the rich man were in *Hades*. For both died. But what a difference: the one in Abraham's bosom and the other in torment. This latter thought carries the idea of *Gehenna*. So immediately upon death each received his respective reward—heaven or hell.

While they were separated the rich man still could see "Abraham afar off, and Lazarus in his bosom." And this sight only added to his misery. So he cried, "Father Abraham, have mercy on me" (v. 24). Note the Jewish attitude toward Abraham as "father." And he cried for mercy, but was beyond its reach. He was being tormented in the flame, or hell fire. So he begged Abraham to "send Lazarus, that he may dip the tip of his finger in water, and cool my tongue." The one to whom he refused mercy he now wants to show mercy toward him. Lazarus had begged in vain for crumbs. Now the rich man begs in vain for a drop of water. No words were ever spoken which so clearly showed the reversal of conditions in the after life as over against those in the present life.

Abraham told the rich man to *remember* (v. 25). And that memory must have been the hottest fire of all. Memory of a lost opportunity which now was gone forever. For the conditions which existed in the after life could not be changed (v. 26). A great gulf separated Lazarus and the rich man, greater by far than the social gulf which had separated them on earth. Lazarus could not go to his aid. Neither could the rich man go where Lazarus was. Lazarus was in heaven to stay; the rich man was in hell to stay.

Realizing finally that his case was hopeless, the rich man remembered his five brothers back on earth who evidently were now as he once had been (vv. 27-28). So he pleads that Lazarus may be sent to warn them not to come to this place of torment. But Abraham reminded him that they had "Moses and the prophets" (v. 29; cf. v. 16). Let them hear them. The rich man said, "Nay, father Abraham; but if one went unto them from the dead, they will repent" (v. 30). They will change their minds, hearts, and attitudes. But Abraham replied, "If they hear not Moses and the prophets, neither will they be persuaded, though one rose from the dead" (v. 31).

With consummate skill Jesus had run the entire gamut. The Pharisees will not hear Moses and the prophets. Neither will they repent even if one rises from the dead.

It can hardly be a coincidence that Jesus called this beggar Lazarus. This was the name of a man whom Jesus did raise from the dead (John 11). Did the Pharisees believe him? They did not. Instead they sought to kill him in order to remove the evidence of Jesus' greatest miracle.

But even beyond this was God's greatest miracle when He raised Jesus from the dead. Did they believe Him? They did not. They even lied about it in order to disprove it and its witness.

If the parable of the prodigal son is the most beautiful short story in the world, this one must be the most meaningful. It had a message for the Pharisees in Jesus' day. And it thunders its warning through the ages at all who keep on hearing the gospel yet keep on scoffing at it.

Luke 17:1-10

The Christian Motive

Luke closes Jesus' extended session of teaching by reporting four items which at first glance appear to be unrelated. But they may be gathered together under the heading of "the Christian motive." Some of these sayings appear elsewhere in Matthew and Mark. For this reason some hold that Luke simply inserted them into his Gospel without regard to either time or place. Plummer says that they have no connection with the larger body of teaching which precedes them (chapts. 15-16), and that they are not related to one another.

However, it does seem possible to relate them in both regards. Jesus had been speaking first to the Pharisees and then to His disciples, each lesson growing out of the preceding one. Largely the theme had been a contrast between the attitude of the Pharisees and the attitude of God, or of His people. The contrast between earthly and heavenly values is sharply drawn in the parable of the rich man and Lazarus. Now in Luke 17:1-10 Jesus concluded this entire section of teaching by setting forth the motive which should characterize the Christian in his life as over against that which was present in the lives of the Pharisees. While the Pharisees are not mentioned, their attitude lurks in the background to enrich the meaning of Jesus' words.

This Christian motive may be seen in four categories as Jesus speaks of the sin of tempting others, the obligation to forgive, the power of faith, and the proper basis of service.

First, the Christian should beware of the sin of tempting others to sin (vv. 1-2). Jesus recognized the fact that it is impossible or inallowable to insist that offenses or causes of stumbling will not come. Satan will see to that. But this gives no man the right to be the occasion of such. And since Jesus was talking to His disciples we may consider this warning as directed especially to His followers. "But woe unto him, through whom they come." It would be better for him if he were put to death by hanging a millstone about his neck and casting him into the sea (v. 2). This rather than to cause to stumble one of these "little ones."

Was Jesus talking about children? He could have been. What a sin it is to lead little children astray! But more likely "little ones" refers to any weak, struggling Christian who is striving to grow and develop as a child of God. When one becomes a Christian he is born again as a babe in Christ. From that point on he is to grow in grace, spirit, and stature in the Christian life. For one to put a stumbling stone in his path is a grievous sin indeed. For a Christian to do so does not negate his salvation. But it destroys his usefulness as a Christian. Physical death is sweet as an alternative to this. How we should guard our actions and attitudes lest we become guilty of such spiritual sins!

Second, the Christian should beware of an unforgiving spirit (vv. 3-4). This is one of the greatest stumbling blocks which we cast into the path of these "little ones." So many Christians who scrupulously refrain from committing sins of the flesh are the greatest of sinners in committing the spiritual sin of unforgiveness. Such an attitude is so foreign to one who has received the infinite forgiveness of God.

So Jesus said, "Take heed to yourselves" (v. 3). "If thy brother may sin." "Against thee" is not in the best manuscripts. It may be a sin against you or it may not. In a sense every sin of the Christian is against every other Christian, for it shames the body of Christ and hinders the work of all other Christians. But the point is, "if thy brother sin." "Brother" here does not refer to one's blood brother but to his Christian brother.

Now Jesus said that when one Christian sees another Christian sinning he should rebuke him. To ignore the sin is to sin against him in turn. We are to watch over one another in brotherly love. And to rebuke in this manner a fellow Christian who sins may lead him to repent and to turn away from the wrong path. The Christian, therefore, should not in Pharisaical self-righteousness look with scorn upon a sinning brother. Neither should he tell others about the sin. He should tell it to him. In Matthew 18 Jesus goes into greater detail. If after telling the man and he does not repent, then other Christians should be enlisted to help deal with him. If still he refuses to repent, it becomes a matter for the entire congregation. It may be that his unrepentant attitude is evidence that he is not a Christian at all.

But in this passage Jesus assumes that he repents when rebuked by one other Christian. In such case the Christian is to forgive him. This does not mean that one Christian, even a priest, can absolve him of his sins. Ultimately this can be done only by God in Christ. But in his own heart the Christian can and should forgive him, and not hold it against him.

Furthermore, if seven times in one day he sins "against thee" *(eis se,* here these words are genuine), and repents each time, you are to forgive him (v. 4). The rabbis taught forgiveness up to three times. However, Jesus is not dealing in mathematics but in spirit. The point here is unlimited forgiveness. Paul says that Christian love *(agapē)* "thinketh no evil" (I Cor. 13:5). Literally, "Love does not keep books on the evil done against it." We are not to list *debits* and *credits* in our book of forgiveness. We are to forgive as God in Christ forgives us.

Such a prescription was too much for the apostles. So they said to Jesus, "Lord, increase our faith" (v. 5). Literally, "Lord, immediately add to our faith" (aorist), so that they might live up to Jesus' demand for unlimited forgiveness. They had had differences even among themselves and knew how difficult it is to forgive.

Third, the Christian should recognize the power of faith in this regard (v. 6). The apostles wanted more faith. But faith is not quantitative, it is qualitative. Their prayer should have been, "Lord, improve our faith."

Jesus said, "If ye had [have] faith as a grain of mustard seed." The conditional sentence of the first class assumes that they do have. But let us be certain that we know what Jesus actually said. He did not say "faith as big as a grain of mustard seed." In terms of quantity it would be small indeed. Any Christian has that, or else he would not be a Christian. Jesus said "faith *as* a grain of mustard seed" (author's italics). He was speaking not of the *size* of faith but of its quality or the kind of faith one has.

Now what kind of faith is "as a grain of mustard seed"? It is a living faith, a working faith, or one which produces results. Put a mustard seed into the ground and cover it up, even put a hard clod on top of it. What happens? The life in the seed goes to work. If it cannot grow through the clod, it grows around it, and up, until the living plant appears on the surface.

Now Jesus said that if you have such a faith you would say to a sycamine tree, "Be thou plucked up by the root, and be thou planted in the sea; and it should [would] have obeyed you" (v. 6). Does this mean that you could do this miraculously? If so, what a discouragement this would be to all of us. For in such fashion we cannot even transplant violets in a garden, to say nothing of transplanting trees from the land into the sea.

"As a grain of mustard seed" should help us here. A faith that works can do this. If necessary it will get a shovel, dig up the tree by the roots, and by some hydraulic method plant the tree in the sea. The apostles wanted faith to enable them to live up to Jesus' teaching on forgiveness. To do so they did not need twice the amount of faith which they had. They needed to use the faith which they possessed. In other words they had to work at the task of developing a forgiving spirit. It is not easy, but it can be done if we work at it hard enough.

But just suppose that the apostles did all that Jesus said. They did not become stumbling blocks to other Christians. When sinned against they not only sought to help the sinner, but forgave him when he repented. Should they expect to be rewarded for such? Or should they do these things merely as a part of their Christian living? So

Fourth, Jesus set forth the proper motive for Christian service (vv. 7-10). He posed a situation in which each of them had a slave. When the slave had finished his day's work would he be honored and served by his owner? Rather the owner would expect the slave to prepare and serve his meal to him. Afterward the slave would be permitted to eat. Would the owner thank the slave for his faithful service, for doing what he was commanded? Jesus said, "I think not" (v. 9). Why? Because the slave had only done his duty.

"So likewise ye, when ye shall have done all those things [of which Jesus had spoken] which are commanded you, say, We are unprofitable [useless] servants: we have done that which was our duty to do" (v. 10). Until one has done more than is expected of him or that which is commanded of him he can expect no merit or reward. The Christian who serves for this purpose only has even fallen short of God's will for him.

Service should be rendered for the joy of serving. Any lesser motive is unworthy of the Christian calling.

Luke 17:11-19

The Blessedness of Gratitude

According to John's Gospel it was at this point that Jesus raised Lazarus from the dead. Thereafter, He retired to a remote area of Judea for a brief stay. It was now only a few weeks before Passion Week. So Jesus went north through Samaria into Galilee in order to join a caravan bound for Jerusalem for the feast of the Passover. The time was in the spring of A.D. 30. It is at the point of Jesus' departure from Judea to Galilee that Luke takes up the story (17:11).

Upon His arrival in Galilee Jesus entered into a certain village. There He was met by ten lepers. In keeping with regulations they "stood afar off" (v. 12). But they kept calling out to Him, "Jesus, Master [*Epistata*], have mercy on us" (v. 13). Jesus told them to go and show themselves unto the priest. This He did before healing them. Even though He proposed to perform a miracle, He did not ignore the Mosaic law which required healed lepers to be pronounced clean by a priest. Even as they went, they were cleansed (v. 14). They demonstrated their faith in Jesus' word, and He honored their faith. So eager were they to get to the priest that they did not even thank Jesus.

But one of them, seeing that he was cleansed, "turned back, and with a loud voice glorified God" (v. 15). He fell down on his face before Jesus, and thanked Him (v. 16).

Luke notes that "he was a Samaritan" (v. 16), implying that the others were Jews. Here once again the Evangelist introduces the element of surprise. A Samaritan showing gratitude to Jesus, a Jew, while the nine Jews appear as ingrates.

However, to Jesus this was no occasion for surprise but for sorrow. "Were there not ten cleansed? but where are the nine?" (v. 17). How often this question must be asked by Him even now as the recipients of His goodness still are ingrates! It is pathetic to hear Him note that the only one who turned back to give glory to God was "this stranger," or foreigner (v. 18). This very word "foreigner" *(allogenēs)* is found on the limestone block from the temple of Israel in Jerusalem. It was placed in the Court of the Gentiles next to the entrance to the Court of the Women or an area into which only Jews could go. "Let no foreigner [*allogenē*] enter within the screen and enclosure surrounding the sanctuary." A foreigner doing this was subject to the penalty of death. Alas, a foreigner might not be permitted in the Jewish part of the temple, but one found grace with the Lord of the temple.

For Jesus said to him, "Arise, go thy way: thy faith hath made thee whole" (v. 19) . *Sesōken,* the perfect form of *sozō,* could mean to heal of disease or to save. Since all ten were healed of leprosy, evidently it means here to save from sin. The nine ingrates were cured of leprosy, nothing more. And they might contract it again. But this grateful *foreigner* received more. He was saved from sin. And the perfect tense means that he would never be lost again. He was twice blessed: healed in his body and saved in his soul. And he was a Samaritan!

Luke 17:20-37

The Nature of the Kingdom

Expectancy was in the air. For almost three and one-half years Jesus has been preaching the kingdom of God. The Passover feast was drawing near. And it appeared that Jesus was planning to attend it. Jewish nationalism ran unusually high at this time. For the Passover commemorated God's deliverance of His people from Egyptian bondage. At this season the Jews always expected another such deliverance from their oppressors. Jesus was said to be the Christ. And popular opinion thought of the Christ in political and military terms. If Jesus were such a Christ would He set up His kingdom at the coming Passover in Jerusalem?

These thoughts may have been in the minds of a certain group of Pharisees. So their inquiry may have been sincere. Or it may have been designed to get Jesus to set a date when He would establish His kingdom. And expecting Him to fail in such an attempt, His enemies would have their evil designs served. So these Pharisees demanded to know "when the kingdom of God should come" (v. 20).

Their question did serve one good purpose. It gave Jesus the opportunity of teaching the true nature of the kingdom. He said that the kingdom of God does not come with *close observation* (v. 20, *paratērēseōs*). This word was used by medical writers for closely watching the symptoms of heart disease. Jesus said that there was no need for close observation, because the kingdom would not come with outward evidences. It will not be *here* or *there,* but within the heart (v. 21). Actually the kingdom would not be in the unbelieving hearts of the Pharisees. But it would be in the hearts of believers.

Then Jesus directed His remarks to His disciples. To them He said that the kingdom itself would be set up silently and without visible signs. The signs which men desire will be seen only at His second coming. "The days will come [after His ascension], when ye shall desire to see one of the days of the Son of man, and ye shall not see it" (v. 22). Others will say that it is *here* or *there,* but the disciples should not follow after them. They were not to be rushing after those who set times and places for His return (v. 23). His return will be seen by all, even as lightning is seen flashing through the sky (v. 24). Before His second advent there must come the cross (v. 25). This is not to say that He would return immediately thereafter. But they were to expect no great external display in the near future, such as the Pharisees were seeking.

Life will go on its normal path until suddenly the end. This Jesus illustrated with the example of the flood and the destruction of Sodom. In the days of Noah they "went on eating, drinking, marrying, and being given in marriage" (v. 27). All of these verbs are imperfect forms showing the process in the past. Then suddenly Noah "entered into the ark, and the flood came, and destroyed them all." These verbs are aorist forms depicting the suddenness of the succeeding actions. The same was true in the days of Lot (v. 28). "They did eat . . . drank . . . bought . . . sold . . . planted . . . builded" (imperfects). Then suddenly Lot "went out of Sodom . . . rained fire and brimstone . . . destroyed" (aorists). Both examples show life going along its normal path until suddenly the end! It will be the same with the coming of the Son of man (v. 30). Life as usual, then suddenly He will appear.

When that happens there will be no time left in which to gather one's goods (v. 31). What need will we have for them anyway? "Remember Lot's wife," said Jesus (v. 32). She hesitated, looked back, and was turned into a pillar of salt (Gen. 19:26). But the point here is simply that of suddenness and haste.

Those who are the Lord's will welcome His return. Those who are lost will seek to save their lives by fleeing. But the saved need have no fear, and the lost will have no hope (v. 33). There will be a separation between the two, as the saved will be taken by the Lord and the lost will be left (vv. 34-36). This figure should not be taken literally. Jesus' point is that at His return they will be separated according to their spiritual condition.

When the disciples asked, "Where, Lord?" (v. 37), He set no place but a condition. "Wheresoever the body is, thither will the eagles [vultures] be gathered together." This was a common sight in the Middle East then as it is now. In short, Jesus said that when the conditions are right He will appear.

Jesus never spoke of His second coming in terms of time or place but of condition. It is His followers' business not to try to figure out the former but to be used of Him in creating the latter.

Luke 18:1-8

The Necessity for Prayer

"And he spoke a parable unto them to this end, that men ought always to pray, and not to faint" (v. 1) . Continuous praying is an absolute necessity for the followers of Christ. "Ought" renders an infinitive *(dein)* which expresses a moral and spiritual obligation.

Why did Jesus say this at this time? He had been speaking of His second coming, certain as to fact but indefinite as to time. In view of this, and especially the false reports as to His return having taken place, the disciples are not to be discouraged but are to pray constantly for strength and guidance. Furthermore, Jesus had spoken of His rapidly approaching death (17:25) . When that event occurs the Shepherd will be taken from the sheep. They will be as lambs among wolves. So specifically in that experience, and other trials of persecution, the *sheep* are constantly to call upon God in prayer.

The words "to faint" suggest such great trials. For they render a word *(enkakein)* which means to give in to evil, to lose heart, or to play the coward. All of these meanings enhance Jesus' words about prayer. Men are not to do these things but are to rely upon prayer for strength, encouragement, and bravery. That the apostles needed such an exhortation is seen in their conduct when Jesus was arrested. But that they kept praying and received the answer is evident in their conduct following Pentecost.

It was to encourage them to be persistent in prayer that the Lord spoke the parable of the unjust judge (vv. 2-5) . This judge was evidently a Gentile, probably an appointee of Herod Antipas, or of the Romans. Among the Jews such a case would have been taken before the elders. If arbitration were necessary it would have been done by three people: one appointed by the plaintiff, one by the defendant, and a third appointed independently. Paid magistrates were notoriously corrupt. Without a bribe from the plaintiff it was almost impossible to get a case heard before them. Barclay notes that they were popularly called "robber judges."

This particular judge "feared not God, neither regarded man" (v. 2). Neither the voice of God nor the voice of man meant anything to him. The only language which he understood was that of money.

Now a poor, helpless widow "kept coming to him" (imperfect) saying, "Avenge me of mine adversary" (v. 3). Actually she asked protection "from [*apo*] my adversary." But the judge "kept on not willing" (imperfect) to heed her plea. His persistence in refusing matched her persistence in pleading. But finally he gave in. Not because he feared God or cared about the widow, but because she kept troubling him about her case and annoyed him or wearied him, did he decide to grant her request (vv. 4-5).

Then Jesus applied the lesson (v. 6). If a judge characterized by unrighteousness will finally grant a request, shall not God avenge His own elect who cry unto Him day and night? (v. 7). The King James Version adds "though he bear long with them." But the best manuscripts read "And he is longsuffering over them." "Night and day" suggests continued pleading as in the case of the widow. This does not mean that God is indifferent to our cries. To the one praying it may seem that He delays His answer. But He is longsuffering upon us. It may be that even though we pray, our hearts are not conditioned so as to receive the answer. We often say that our prayers are not answered. But "no" is an answer. What we mean is that we do not always get what we want. Actually God has one of three answers to every prayer: "no," "yes," or "wait." He may say, "No," immediately, because we either ask in the wrong way or for the wrong purpose, or else because it is not best that we receive that for which we pray. God may say, "Yes," immediately. But He may say, "Wait." He may not relieve us from some trial, but instead give us grace within it, which is far better (cf. II Cor. 12:8-9). Or He may wait until in His wisdom it is time to grant our prayer, either because we are spiritually ready to receive it or because He knows that conditions are right for us to do so.

Jesus added, "I tell you that he will avenge them speedily" (v. 8). Not necessarily the moment that we first ask. But when He is ready to avenge His elect, He will act quickly, without delay. We should keep on praying, but should leave the time and answer in God's hands. After all, is not that the meaning of "Thy will be done"?

Finally, Jesus asked a puzzling question. "Nevertheless when the Son of man cometh [at the end of the age], shall he find faith on the earth?" (v. 8). Does this suggest widespread unbelief when Jesus returns? Is His mediatorial mission to end in such failure? This is hardly the meaning of the question. The Greek text says "the faith," or a particular kind of faith. This seems to refer back to the original statement that men should always pray and not play the coward. The widow typifies the faith in prayer to which He refers. So His question evidently means "shall he find the kind of faith which produces persistent prayer in time of trouble."

So this closing question in the light of verse 1 is almost a command. It will help us in facing the challenges of the evil one if we so regard it—and obey it. Evidently this was in the mind of Joseph Scriven when he wrote:

> Oh, what peace we often forfeit,
> Oh, what needless pain we bear
> All because we do not carry
> Ev'rything to God in prayer!

Luke 18:9-14

The Pharisee and the Publican

There are those who insist that this parable was not spoken immediately after the parable of the unjust judge. According to them Luke merely placed it here since it taught another lesson in prayer. Luke does not say one way or another. But the word "and" *(kai)* seems to relate the two parables. There is more reason to say that Jesus spoke the latter parable in this context than to say that He did not. In His audience were Pharisees (17:20) whom evidently Jesus had in mind in the parable. For He spoke it to certain ones who considered themselves to be self-righteous and who despised or set at naught all others outside their class (v. 9).

Among the Jews there were three daily prayer times: 9:00 A.M., noon, and 3:00 P.M. They regarded prayers prayed in the temple as being more effective than others. It would be a common thing, therefore, that "two men went up into the temple [*hieron,* temple area] to pray" (v. 10). Jesus identifies them as a Pharisee and a publican, the two extremes in Jewish society.

The Pharisee, standing in a prominent place so as to be seen, "prayed [imperfect, 'was praying'] thus with [*pros,* face to face] himself" (v. 11). He did not pray to God. Instead he carried on a soliloquy within his own soul. Though he addressed God, all that came thereafter was a recital of his own virtues. He was quite satisfied with himself. He felt no need to pray other than the fact that the hour of prayer had come. And he made sure at that time to be where he would be seen. In fact, he evidently felt that God was quite fortunate to have such a one who deigned to pray at all.

The only thing in his prayer worthy of the name was that he said, "God, I thank thee." But even that was a selfish and proud thanksgiving. "I thank thee, that I am not as other men" (v. 11). His was a prayer of scorn for others. He recited only the sins of which he was not guilty. Other men were extortioners, unjust, and adulterers. But he was righteous. Rabbi Simeon ben Jochai said, "If there are only two righteous men in the world, I and my son are these two; if there is only one, I am he!" This was the attitude of this Pharisee.

In his proud prayer he singled out one particular man for special scorn: "Or even as this publican," or "this one, the publican," or tax-collector. He implied that he was guilty of all three of the above-mentioned sins. And he may have been.

Having vented his spleen upon all other men, the Pharisee cited two of his many virtues (v. 12). "I fast twice in the week." Only one fast was absolutely obligatory during the year, that on the day of Atonement (cf. Lev. 16:29). But those who wished to obtain special merit fasted on Mondays and Thursdays. Barclay calls attention to the fact that these were market days which guaranteed a large crowd in Jerusalem. Those who observed these fasts whitened their faces and wore old clothes in order to call attention to their pious acts.

"I give tithes of all that I possess" (v. 12). The law required tithes of all produce. But this Pharisee tithed even small garden herbs (Matt. 23:23). He did more than the law demanded. But the true reading is "all that I get." He tithed his income but not his capital. The implication of his recital of these two virtues is that God owes him something.

But "the publican, standing afar off" (v. 13). Note the contrast. "Standing" here is a different form of the verb from "stood" in verse 11. The latter denotes a prominent position in contrast to the former. "Afar off" does not refer to the temple but to the Pharisee. He did not feel worthy to be near so righteous a man. Both were in the Court of Israel, but the publican probably stopped just inside the entrance. He did not feel worthy to lift his eyes toward heaven. In his grief for his sins he "kept on smiting" (imperfect) his breast as he said repeatedly, "God, be merciful to me a [the] sinner." Not one word is said about his virtue. Whereas the Pharisee confessed other men's sins, the publican confessed his own. Note "the sinner." The Pharisee regarded himself righteous and all other men sinners. But the publican thought of himself as the only sinner in the world. The Pharisee compared his life with those of other men. The publican compared his life only with the righteousness and holiness of God. Any man who does other than as the publican did is merely praying to himself.

Actually the Pharisee was too proud to pray; he could only remind God of the reward due to him. But the publican was so convicted of his sins that he could not keep from praying, not for reward but for mercy. The Pharisee said that if God is just He will reward me. The publican said that if God were only just He would cast his soul into hell. So he cried out only for mercy.

Jesus took note of all these things when He said, "I tell you, this man [publican] went down to his house justified rather than the other [Pharisee]" (v. 14). The publican prayed for mercy and received forgiveness. The Pharisee indulged himself in a soliloquy. And had not the temple been destroyed by Titus, his *prayer* might still be bouncing around within its walls. But it never arrived before the throne of grace.

How we should ponder the lesson of this parable! Do you see yourself in it? "For every one that exalteth himself shall be abased; and he that humbleth himself shall be exalted" (v. 14).

Luke 18:15-17

The Child and the Kingdom

A comparison between Luke and the other Synoptic Gospels shows that this event occurred somewhere in Perea. Jesus was on His final journey to Jerusalem. He had been teaching a lesson on the controversial subject of marriage and divorce (cf. Matt. 19:1-12; Mark 10:1-12). His teaching was interrupted by those who "were bringing" (imperfect) their infants to Jesus in order that He might touch them (v. 15). It was customary to bring babes to the rabbi for blessing on their first birthday. But the disciples "kept on rebuking" (imperfect) them. Either they were endeavoring to protect Jesus from undue labor, or they discounted the importance of children. Or, more likely, they resented this interruption of so interesting a teaching. But whatever their reason they mistook Jesus' attitude toward little children.

For Jesus called both the parents and children unto Himself. "Called" is an indirect aorist form which expresses this thought of calling to Himself. Then He said, "Suffer [permit] little children to come unto me, and forbid them not [stop forbidding them]: for of such is the kingdom of heaven" (v. 16). Thus Jesus rebuked the disciples for rebuking the parents.

Jesus was on His way to Jerusalem to die. The strain of the coming ordeal was already showing in His manner. But nothing was so important but that He had time for these little ones. After all, what could they know about a cross? They were like any children, unaware of the troubled issues of life, yet in them was bound up the potential of the future. It was even of such as these that the kingdom of heaven could be likened. This does not mean that the kingdom is composed entirely of children, but of those with the traits of a little child.

A child lives in a world of wonder and mystery, yet a world which he accepts by faith. Adults are so prone to lose this sense of poetic wonder to live in a drab, prosaic world. Little do they realize that religion itself is fraught with mystery which defies our pat answers. When the pat answers do not come, we are tempted to doubt. But a child walks by faith when he cannot walk by reason. He lives the simple life where God is real. His heart is so tender that when he disobeys, he is unhappy. Most of all he wants to please God, and is ready to repent when shown his sin. And he accepts by faith the forgiveness which God gives, even as by faith he trusts implicitly his parents to provide for his needs.

"Whosoever shall not receive the kingdom of God as a little child shall in no wise enter therein" (v. 17), said Jesus. Thus He made the child the model for those who would enter into the kingdom. So often in seeking to determine if a child understands the plan of salvation, we treat him like an adult. We expect adult answers from childlike hearts. A child's simple, "I love Jesus and want to live for Him," may express a profounder Christian experience than reams of theological debate and explanation. Jesus said that we have the whole thing backward. Instead of expecting an adult experience in the child, we should strive to bring about a childlike experience in the adult.

Luke 18:18-30

The Price Tag of Life

Travelling through Perea Jesus was met by a "certain ruler" (v. 18). What kind of ruler he was is not stated. Some think that he was the ruler of a synagogue. But Plummer dissents without further specification. Matthew notes that he was a rich young man.

That he was a young man with high ideals is quite clear. He was seeking eternal life. And he was earnestly and enthusiastically doing so. Mark 10:17 says that he came running and kneeled before Jesus. He asked, "Good Master [Teacher], what shall I do to inherit eternal life?" Literally, "By doing [aorist participle] what shall I inherit eternal life?" The aorist tense shows that he thought in terms of some one great deed, perhaps some outstanding benevolence. He was prepared to pay for it.

But Jesus answered by endeavoring to set his thinking straight. "Why callest thou me good? none is good, save one, that is, God" (v. 19). He had called Jesus "good Teacher." No pupil ever addressed a rabbi as "good." So the young man paid Jesus the supreme compliment. But he called Him only a "Teacher." Jesus reminded him that only God is absolutely *good*. Thus either he had used the term loosely, or else he must think of Jesus as more than a great Teacher. By subtle suggestion Jesus was leading him to think of Him as deity, not simply as a great man.

In direct answer to the youth's inquiry Jesus reminded him of the Ten Commandments (v. 20). "Thou knowest the commandments." "Knowest" *(oidas)* means a thorough, perceptive knowledge. Then Jesus quoted five of the commandments. Matthew 19:19 adds the comprehensive one about loving one's neighbor as one's self. Note that these were the commandments having to do with man's relation to other men. He said nothing about the first four which concern one's relation to God.

The young man replied that "all these have I kept from my youth up" (v. 21). He implied that all of his life he had maintained good relations with other men. Perhaps he had lived by the letter of these laws. But one wonders about their spirit. Had he really loved other men, especially the poor unfortunates, and tried to use his wealth to relieve their misery? Furthermore, there is a note of disappointment in his reply. He had thought of some unusual deed, but Jesus spoke of the humdrum facts of life. Like Naaman the leper, he must have felt that the answer was too simple.

Hearing the young man's reply Jesus said, "Yet lackest thou one thing" (v. 22). Matthew reports the ruler as saying, "What lack I yet?" (19:20). This is implied by Luke in verse 21. So Jesus said that *one* thing was lacking. He should sell his goods and distribute the proceeds to the poor. Thus he would have treasure, not on earth alone, but in heaven. "And come, follow me" (v. 22).

Did Jesus mean that he should become a pauper, and then follow Him? This understanding of Jesus' words is to look only at the surface. Up to this point Jesus had said nothing about the man's relation to God, only to men. In effect, in verse 22 the Lord was reminding him of the first four commandments. He had made a good score with regard to men. What about his relation to God? In essence his goods were his god. So if he would inherit eternal life he must remove that god and worship God alone. This he would do as he renounced dependence upon his wealth and followed Christ in faith. He was to serve God with his wealth by serving man with it.

This is a challenge to every man of means. But it applies to those of lesser wealth also. You can hold one small coin so close to your eye as to shut out the view of a mountain. Worldly possessions great or small may shut one off from faith in God and absolute obedience to Him. That which separates you from God may be something other than money. It may be intellectual pride or some other thing which absorbs your interest. But whatever it is Jesus says that you should remove it, and follow Him.

Hearing Jesus' demand, the young man became exceedingly sorrowful *(perilupos,* v. 23*)*. He was literally surrounded *(peri)* with sorrow *(lupē)*. "He was very rich." We would say that he was a multimillionaire. And he was unwilling to part with his god to serve the living God.

Matthew records that the young man departed from Jesus (19:22). We may well imagine that Jesus also was "very sorrowful" as He saw him leave. This is involved in His words "how hardly shall they that have riches enter into the kingdom of God!" (v. 24). Not because they are rich, but because they trust in their riches. Indeed, "it is easier for a camel to go through a needle's eye, than for a rich man to enter into the kingdom of God" (v. 25). This was probably a current proverb for picturing the impossible. No matter how wealthy one is, he cannot be saved on the basis of his wealth. Money is not legal tender in heaven. A rich man, like a poor man, must be saved as a sinner, by grace and not by merit.

Upon hearing this, those about Jesus asked, "Who then can be saved?" (v. 26). Wealth was considered to be a sign of God's favor. If such could not be saved, then what manner of person could? It is so difficult for men to realize that one may be up and out as well as down and out. A man's salvation is gauged not by his financial balance sheet, but by whether his name is written in the Lamb's Book of Life. But Jesus added a word of hope. "The things which are impossible with men are possible with God" (v. 27). What man cannot do through his money or other merit, God can do by His grace. The difficulty is not with God. For His grace is abundant to all who believe. The difficulty is with the man who finds it hard to divest himself of all dependence upon his riches, to admit that he is a lost sinner, and to turn to God in repentance and faith.

We are not surprised to hear Peter say, "Lo, we have left all, and followed thee" (v. 28). He was thinking of their reward. But in all honesty it must be admitted that to leave one's nets and boats was one thing; to leave one's multi-millions was another. So, heavenly reward was not to be reckoned on a dollars and cents basis. However, Jesus assured him that God in His own time and way would reward His people in this life, and, most of all, in the hereafter with life eternal (vv. 29-30).

No man should expect to inherit eternal life by any great deed that he does. Neither should he follow Christ merely for the sake of reward. Nor should he question God's benevolent will with regard to either time or eternity. But all should follow after Him in faith, knowing that God's greatest gifts are not monetary but spiritual. To everyone who comes to Him through faith in His Son God gives the true riches. And such will be "very rich" indeed.

Luke 18:31-34

The Shame and the Glory

The caravan in which Jesus was travelling was nearing the border of Judea. Soon they would be in the territory where the power of the Jewish leaders was greatest. Every step brought Jesus nearer to His "waiting cross" (Barclay). Never does His courage appear greater than as is seen in His resolute journey toward Jerusalem.

Jesus knew the coming ordeal, but His disciples were not aware of it. Repeatedly in the past He had told them about it. But so foreign from such was their concept of the Christ that they could not grasp it. Therefore, once again Jesus took the Twelve aside to seek to impress upon them the gravity of the situation (v. 31).

Heretofore He had spoken about what the Jewish rulers would do to Him. But now Jesus added the note that the Gentiles also would be involved (vv. 32-33). He will endure the greatest shame, being mocked, spit upon, and scourged. In the end He will be put to death. But all of this is necessary in order that the prophecies about the Suffering Servant shall be fulfilled. Both Jews and Gentiles will think that they are venting their spleen upon Jesus, when all the while unknowingly they will be fulfilling the Word of God.

But the shame will give place to glory. For when sinful men have done their worst, God still will triumph over them. For Jesus "the third day . . . shall rise again" (v. 33). On that glad day the earthly humiliation will give place to heavenly glory. The greatest glory will be that He who created all things will then be the Redeemer of all who come to Him in faith.

But the Twelve "kept on not perceiving" (imperfect). The saying of Jesus "was hid from them." "Was hid" is a perfect form expressing complete misunderstanding. It is so easy for us to sit in judgment upon the Twelve as we enjoy our vantage point beyond the resurrection. But do we really understand, even now? The greatness of God's love, mercy, and grace still confounds us. To mount the throne by the way of the cross is still a paradox.

Yet history proclaims that it is true. And Scripture teaches us that we too must tread the path over which Jesus walked. If we seek to save our lives, we shall lose them. Only by losing ourselves completely in the service of Christ shall we find our lives in values which abide in eternity. We must suffer with Him if we would be glorified with Him.

Luke 18:35-43

The Persistent Beggar

Finally Jesus crossed the Jordan river into Judea. A short distance west of the river stood the site of old Jericho, and a little beyond that the new or Roman Jericho. The caravan had passed through the former and was nearing the latter. Alongside the road a blind man sat begging (v. 35). Matthew notes two such men. But Mark and Luke refer to only one, probably centering on the more prominent one. Mark adds that his name was Bartimaeus (10:46).

Hearing the multitude passing by, he asked what it was (v. 36). When he heard "that Jesus of Nazareth passeth by" (v. 37), he shouted, "Jesus, thou son of David, have mercy on me" (v. 38). He evidently had heard that Jesus had healed blind men. And his designation of Jesus shows that he regarded Him as the Christ. Jesus must have been teaching as He walked. The man's loud cry made it difficult to hear Him. So those in the front part of the caravan told him to be quiet (v. 39). But this only made him cry more insistently. He "kept crying" (imperfect) so much the more. The word for *cry* in verse 39 is different from the one in verse 38. The latter was merely a shout to gain attention. The former denotes an ungovernable emotion, or a scream. He kept screaming, "Thou son of David, have mercy on me" (v. 39).

Hearing these cries, Jesus stopped and commanded that the beggar be brought to Him (v. 40). When the man stood before Jesus He asked, "What wilt thou that I shall do unto thee?" (v. 41). Doubtless He knew what the beggar desired. But He wanted him to ask in order that when he received it he would believe the source whence it came. The man replied, "Lord, that I may receive my sight" (v. 41). The Greek is more pathetic. "Lord, that I may see again." He had been begging for alms. But now such things faded into insignificance. He only wanted to see again. With his sight he would not need alms. Furthermore, life would again be filled with beauty—sunrise and sunset, flowers and green fields, the faces of loved ones.

Note Jesus' reply. "See again" *(anablepson,* aorist imperative, v. 42). "See again immediately!" A miracle! "Thy faith hath saved thee" (v. 42). "Hath saved" *(sesōken,* perfect) could mean permanent, complete physical healing or permanent, complete spiritual salvation. Both are probably true in this case. Certainly the former was true. For "immediately he saw again" (v. 43). The latter also was true. For "he kept on following him" (imperfect), glorifying God. Also the people who had been so indifferent to the poor beggar's need now joined in praise to God.

The man had but one chance to be healed. He made the most of it. Despite discouragement he persisted until he saw again. And the first thing that he saw was the glory of God in the face of Jesus Christ!

Luke 19:1-10

The Little Man Who Stood Tall

Jesus was eager to get to Jerusalem. In all likelihood He would have gone straight through Jericho without stopping. But as was usual He never passed by one in need. In contrast to the poor beggar asking alms, this case involved one who was rich from the profession of demanding taxes. However, his need was equal to, if not greater than, that of blind Bartimaeus. For he was blind in his soul.

Jesus had entered and was passing through the Roman Jericho (v. 1). In the city was a man named Zacchaeus (v. 2). He was a rich "chief publican" *(architelōnēs)*. This is the only time that this word is found. But like "chief priest" *(archiereus)* it means "chief" *(archi)* "publican" *(telōnēs)*. Jericho was an important tax collecting point, not only because of many passing caravans but because of many products which were sold in the area. So evidently Zacchaeus was a tax commissioner over other publicans.

A crowd travelled with Jesus to which was added the curious of Jericho (v. 3). Zacchaeus was small of stature. Therefore, he was unable to see above the crowd, despite the fact that "he kept seeking" (imperfect) to see Jesus, "who he was." He perhaps had heard of Him, even that He associated with people of his kind, so he wanted to see what manner of person He was.

Failing to see through the crowd, he ran ahead of the group and climbed into a sycamore tree, literally, a fig-mulberry *(sukomorean, sukon,* fig, *moron,* mulberry) tree (v. 4). It was a wide, open tree with low limbs which enabled this short man to climb into it. When Jesus arrived at the tree, seeing Zacchaeus in it, He said, "Zacchaeus, make haste, and come down; for to day I must abide at thy house" (v. 5). Literally, "in your house it is necessary [moral and spiritual necessity] me to abide." Of all the houses in Jericho He chose the home of this chief publican. He did not stop merely for rest but for a moral and spiritual purpose. Even though He often accepted invitations, this is the only recorded instance where Jesus offered Himself as a guest. He had a purpose in doing so.

Zacchaeus could hardly believe his ears. Jesus entering his house! A despised publican's house? But he did as Jesus said. He hurriedly descended from the tree and "received him joyfully," or rejoicing as he welcomed Him into his house (v. 6).

The crowd was indignant (v. 7). And especially the residents of Jericho. There was perhaps not one but who had been robbed by this chief publican through exorbitant taxes. "They all murmured." This is an imperfect middle form of the verb *diagogguzō*. The very sound of the word is that of humming bees. They kept buzzing angrily among themselves that Jesus would grace the home of this "sinner."

But a different scene was transpiring within the house (v. 8). Zacchaeus stood facing Jesus as he spoke. The word "behold" suggests a sudden resolution. "Lord, the half of my goods I give to the poor; and if I have taken anything [condition of the first class assumes that he had] from any man by false accusation, I restore him fourfold." This restoration was far more than the law required. So his act went beyond legalism. It indicates that Zacchaeus was a changed man.

And Jesus recognized this fact. "This day is salvation come to this house, forsomuch as he also is a son of Abraham" (v. 9). Zacchaeus might be despised by his neighbors. But his profession had not cancelled his birthright. He was not so low but that he could respond to the grace of God.

When was Zacchaeus actually saved? While he was in the tree? Between the limb and the ground? In his house? Who can say? But saved he was. For that day "salvation to this house came" *(sōtēria tōi oikōi toutōi egeneto,* aorist). For only salvation could produce such a change in him. The people buzzed angrily that Jesus would show such concern to this chief publican. Perhaps they expected Him to lecture him about the evil of his ways. Had they lived today they probably would have wanted Jesus to join their picket line carrying a sign reading "Unfair to helpless taxpayers." But Jesus did more. He went into his home and won him to Himself. And when he returned to the street He presented them not with an indignant, conniving publican but with a redeemed tax commissioner, a philanthropist and an honest man.

This is the business of Jesus. It should be the business of all who follow Him. "For the Son of man is come to seek and to save that which was lost" (v. 10).

Luke 19:11-27

The Responsibility of Privilege

Jesus was still in Jericho, but was soon to depart on the final phase of His journey to Jerusalem. The crowd was excited with the expectancy that He would upon arrival there set up His kingdom. In order to offset this excitement Jesus spoke the parable of the pounds (v. 11). In it He did two things. He exhorted the disciples to be faithful in the discharge of their duty; He also warned the Jewish leaders as to their continued opposition to Him.

A certain nobleman went into a far country to receive for himself a kingdom (v. 12). This is suggestive of the trips made to Rome by Jewish rulers to be confirmed as the chosen representative of the Empire in Palestine. Herod the Great had made such a journey in 40 B.C. when he was confirmed as king of Judea by the Roman senate. Jesus' figure is especially reminiscent of the contest between Archelaus and Herod Antipas in 4 B.C. Shortly before his death Herod the Great changed his will, leaving Judea to Archelaus instead of to Antipas. When the former went to Rome for confirmation the latter went also to contest it. Furthermore, the Jews sent an embassage to oppose Archelaus. The Roman Caesar Augustus confirmed the will, but only gave Archelaus the title of ethnarch. Should he prove himself he later was to be called king. But he failed to do so, and was deposed in favor of a Roman governor.

When the nobleman left he entrusted to ten of his slaves equal sums of money, ten pounds each or about $15.00 (v. 13). He did not divide among them all of his estate, to each according to his ability, as in the parable of the talents (cf. Matt. 25:14 ff.). He merely wanted to test these particular slaves, so he only gave them small but equal amounts. And he did so with the instruction, "Occupy [trade or do business] till I come" (v. 13).

However, as in the case of Archelaus, this nobleman's citizens hated him. So they sent a message after him saying, "We do not wish this one to reign [be king] over us" (v. 14). In the parable the "slaves" correspond to the disciples and the "citizens" represent the Jews as a people.

But despite opposition the nobleman received his kingdom (v. 15). Upon his return he called for an accounting by the ten slaves. The first reported that he had increased his pound to ten pounds (v. 16). But note that in each case the slaves called them "thy pound." It still belonged to the nobleman, and was only held in trust by the slave. As a reward the nobleman gave the slave authority over ten cities, one for each of the added pounds. The second slave reported that his pound had gained five pounds (v. 18). So he received authority over five cities (v. 19). Each of these slaves was rewarded according to his faithfulness.

But the third slave (the account does not run through the entire ten) had a different story to tell (vv. 20-21). Instead of trading with his pound, he carefully wrapped it in a napkin and put it away for safe keeping. He did not squander it, but neither did he use it. This he did because he feared his owner. He considered him to be a harsh man who took unfair advantage in order to make a profit. Whether or not this was true is not said. But in view of the attitude of the first two slaves, it most likely was not true of him. The point is not to show the character of the nobleman but that of the slave.

Nevertheless, he took the slave at his own word (v. 22). He judged him by his own statements. Even if he were that sort of man and the slave feared to lose the pound in trading, at least he should have deposited the pound in the bank (v. 23). Then he would have received interest on his money. The word "bank" means "table," here a money-changer's table. The English word "bank" comes from the word "bench."

Rather than rewarding the fearful slave, the owner ordered his pound taken from him and given to the one who had gained ten pounds (v. 24). The crowd had been following Jesus' story eagerly. So almost without thinking they reminded Him that this man already had ten pounds (v. 25). Jesus replied with a rule of life. The faithful man receives more, but from the unfaithful will be taken even that with which he has been trusted (v. 26). The latter is a case of forfeited stewardship.

Now the lesson of the parable is quite simple. The nobleman is Jesus who will go away after the resurrection in order to claim His kingdom. Thus Jesus showed that the kingdom would not be set up immediately upon His arrival at Jerusalem. He even implied an interval of undetermined length between His ascension and second coming. During that interval He will entrust to His followers certain responsibilities. And upon His return He will reward the faithful. The fact that the third slave lost his pound does not mean that the fearful disciple will be lost. He was still his owner's slave or disciple. What he lost was his reward in heaven.

But what about Jesus' enemies? They will be slain (v. 27). In spiritual terms, they will be cast into hell. To be sure, their city and nation will be destroyed in history. But Jesus looked beyond history to the end of time. And in the long look of history the *enemies* are not Jews only. They are all who say in their hearts, "We will not have this man to reign over us" (v. 14).

Disciples should be faithful to Jesus. Enemies should become friends of Jesus. For He has gone "into a far country to receive for himself a kingdom, *and to return*" (v. 12, author's italics).

VIII
The Gathering Gloom

Luke 19:28-48

The Royal Entry

It is only about twenty miles from Jericho to Jerusalem. The road winds through a wilderness country, uphill most all the way. So having finished His teaching in Jericho Jesus "was going [imperfect] before, ascending up to Jerusalem" (v. 28). The imperfect tense pictures every step of the journey as Jesus eagerly went before the crowd on the final trip toward the city of His destiny. If we had only Luke's account we would suppose that He arrived in the Jerusalem area on Sunday morning. But John tells us that He arrived "six days before the passover" (12:1), or on Friday before Passion Week. Jesus probably spent from Friday afternoon until Sunday morning in Bethany.

Luke takes up the narrative at this point with his customary "and it came to pass" (v. 29). Jesus was near the towns of Bethphage and Bethany which are located just over the brow of the Mount of Olives eastward away from Jerusalem. It was from Bethphage that He began what is popularly called "The Triumphal Entry" into Jerusalem.

In ancient times a victorious king or general returning from battle made a triumphal entry into his capital city. Amid great rejoicing on the part of the people he entered the city riding on a white horse followed by conquered enemies, perhaps a king or general. As he did so he distributed gifts among the people. However, the entrance into Jerusalem by Jesus carried no such note. More likely Paul describes His *triumphal entry* into heaven after the resurrection and ascension (cf. Eph. 4:8-9). The entrance of Jesus into Jerusalem may more fittingly be called His "Royal Entry." For in keeping with Jewish custom He came riding upon an ass as a king coming in peace (cf. Zech. 9:9).

Why did Jesus make such an entry? From John we know that Jesus had repeatedly taught in Jerusalem as He revealed Himself in His true relation to God and to the Jews. But her leaders had rejected Him, even endeavoring to kill Him. When the message of the Old Testament prophets had been rejected, they often acted it out in symbolic form. Therefore, we may understand Jesus' entry into Jerusalem after this fashion. Actually it was His final challenge to the city as He presented Himself as the King of Peace. Either the city would receive Him or it must reject Him. The time for a showdown had come.

Why did He choose the Passover season for such a challenge? Because at this time He would find the city crowded with Jews both from within and from without Palestine. Every adult male Jew living within twenty miles of Jerusalem was required to attend the Passover. Every Jew, regardless of where he lived, hoped to attend one Passover during his lifetime. Thirty years after this particular Passover a Roman governor took a census of the lambs slain at such a feast. The number was two hundred and fifty thousand. Since one lamb was required for ten people, this would mean that two and one-half million Jews were involved. This suggests the number of Jews who were challenged by Jesus on that day. And the decision to receive or to reject Him involved both Palestinian Jews and those from the Dispersion. So in reality Jesus presented Himself to world Jewry.

This was no impulsive act on Jesus' part. For it shows deliberate preparation. He had arranged, probably on Saturday, for a man to have a donkey tied at a given time and place. A pre-arranged signal had been set by which the owner would know to whom he should surrender the animal. Why this secrecy? Jesus knew that the Jewish rulers had given orders for His arrest (John 11:57). He also knew that already treachery was in the heart of Judas. To reveal His plans ahead of time, even to the Twelve, would have endangered His purpose.

Therefore, on Sunday morning from Bethphage He sent two of His disciples after the donkey (vv. 29-30). They were to go "into the village over against you," probably to Bethany. There they would find "a colt tied, whereupon yet never man sat." The animal being tied suggests previous preparation. If anyone asked why they loosed the donkey they were to reply, "Because the Lord hath need of him" (v. 31). This answer was the signal. So they went and found it as Jesus had said (vv. 32-34). Having secured the donkey they brought him to Jesus, placed their garments upon him, and sat Jesus thereon.

The procession started toward Jerusalem (v. 36). And as they went along, the people "kept spreading" (imperfect) their garments on the ground before the donkey, thus making a royal path over which Jesus might ride. John says that some pulled branches off the palm trees for the same purpose (12:13).

The multitude caught the significance of the act. As Jesus rode down the western slope of Olivet toward Jerusalem, the people began to rejoice and praise God for all the mighty works of Jesus which they had seen (v. 37). They proclaimed Him as the Christ as they shouted the Messianic words, "Blessed be the king that cometh in the name of the Lord: peace in heaven, and glory in the highest" (v. 38). From the four Gospel accounts we learn that a group coming out of the city met the procession going into the city. And together they accompanied Jesus into Jerusalem as they shouted their praise (cf. Matt. 21:9; Mark 11:9; John 12:18). It was a joyous occasion indeed as the people, despite the parable of the pounds, expected the immediate establishment of the kingdom.

But a group of Pharisees was unhappy about the whole affair. Their plans to seize Jesus had gone awry. Instead of leading Him a prisoner into the city, they saw Him as the popular hero being ushered into Jerusalem by this wildly rejoicing multitude. Even so, they sought to stop this Messianic demonstration by demanding that Jesus rebuke His followers (v. 39). Jesus replied, "I tell you that, if these should hold their peace, the stones would immediately cry out" (v. 40). This could have one of two meanings. Robertson says that this word about the stones' crying out was a proverb expressing an impossible happening. He could not stop the crowd even if He wished to do so. Or it could mean that the hour of His revelation as the Messiah had come. If men failed so to declare Him, inanimate nature would do so.

The attitude of these Pharisees demonstrated that once again Jerusalem would reject Jesus. So as He drew near and saw the city, He "wept over it" (v. 41). Literally, "He burst into tears." He lamented over Jerusalem as He said, "If thou hadst known, even thou, at least in this thy day, the things which belong unto thy peace! but now they are hid from thine eyes" (v. 42). Literally, "If knowing in this day, even you, the things toward peace. . . ." Jerusalem had had other days of opportunity, and had rejected them. Now this is the last one, and the things necessary to her peace are hidden from her eyes. Jesus is her Prince of Peace, but she will refuse Him. In her blind search for a political and military Messiah she will stumble on to her ruin.

"For the days shall come upon thee, that thine enemies shall cast a trench [cast up a bank] about thee, and compass thee round, and keep thee in on every side, and shall lay thee even with the ground [raze to the ground], and thy children within thee; and shall not leave in thee one stone upon another; because thou knewest not the time of thy visitation" (vv. 43-44).

Here Jesus clearly described the terrible siege of Jerusalem by the Romans toward the end of the Jewish War (A.D. 66-70). Rebellion was in the city's heart, and it would bring her to her ruin.

Presently Jesus was inside the city. There He entered the temple and cleansed it a second time (cf. John 2:14 ff.). Mark 11:12, 15 ff. places this event on Monday. Luke merely records it without regard to time. Some hold that there was but one such event, and that either John or the other Evangelists have erred as to the time. But there is no reason why Jesus would not assert His authority over the temple at both the beginning and the end of His ministry.

The "Bazaars of Annas" were infamous. What had begun as a service to the worshippers had become a vicious racket. It was difficult for them to bring animals to the temple for sacrifice. This was especially true of Jews from outside Palestine. So animals were provided for sale, probably in the Court of Gentiles, and at an above-the-market price. Furthermore, every adult male Jew was supposed to pay the half-shekel temple tax, and in that Jewish coin. Up to a certain time it could be paid in one's village. Thereafter, it must be paid at the temple. Those from outside Palestine paid it at the temple. Since they had foreign coins they had to exchange them for the Jewish coin. An exorbitant rate of exchange was charged. The profit from these services was supposed to go into the temple treasury. But in time much of it began to line the pockets of those who rendered the services. Crooks usually attract crooks. So one tradition says that the temple had even become a place where thieves met to plan their crimes.

Despite the fact that about three years previously Jesus had driven these evil men and their products from the temple, now they were back again. And at this season they were doing a land-office business. So when Jesus entered the temple, instead of finding an atmosphere of sanctity He was greeted with that which prevails even today in an Oriental bazaar. Instead of the odor of burning incense there was the stench of animals. In the place of prayers He heard the noise of animals and the bargaining cries of those who bought and sold. A Gentile who might have wandered in would have been repelled rather than drawn to the worship of Jehovah.

So Jesus was filled with righteous wrath. He began to cast out those who sold and those who bought (v. 45). He overthrew the tables of the money-changers and the seats of those who sold doves (Matt. 21:22; Mark 11:15). This hardly fits the picture of the "gentle Jesus, meek and mild." It was the boiling-over wrath of a righteous God against those who so defiled His holy place.

As He cleansed the temple Jesus said, "My house is the house of prayer: but ye have made it a den of thieves" (v. 46). Judaism never appears worse than it does here. And it received the condemnation of God Himself!

Thereafter Jesus taught daily in the temple (v. 47). All the while the Jewish rulers sought to destroy Him, but they could find no opportunity to do so, since the people gathered about Him to hang on His every word (v. 48).

The stage had been set. Jesus had thrown down the gauntlet to His enemies. Before the week was out they thought that they had won. But their *victory* was short-lived indeed. And so is every man's experience who defies the Holy One of God.

Luke 20:1-47

The Day of Controversy

In the closing verses of Chapter 19 Luke made the general statement regarding Jesus' activity during these opening days of Passion Week, the Jewish rulers' efforts to destroy Him, and His hold upon the people. In Chapter 20 he gives certain details concerning these matters. If Jesus' enemies were to accomplish their evil designs, they first must cause Him to *lose face* with the multitudes.

So "it came to pass that on one of those days" (Tuesday) Jesus was teaching and evangelizing in the temple (v. 1). There He was accosted by the "chief priests and the scribes . . . with the elders." The "chief priests" was a group composed of the High Priest, former High Priests, and their families. Together with the scribes (Pharisees) and elders they comprised the Sanhedrin, the ruling body among the Jews. Thus this was an official delegation bent upon getting some official charge to make against Jesus.

They demanded to know by what *kind* of authority He was doing "these things, and whence came this authority?" (v. 2). "These things" is a comprehensive term involving all of Jesus' works, including His miracles of healing. But in the immediate context three things stand out: the Royal Entry, the cleansing of the temple, and the present teaching. The Royal Entry had definite Messianic overtones. Jesus had exercised an authority over the temple which, according to the Jews, belonged only to a prophet, the Messiah, or to God Himself. Which one of these authorities did Jesus claim? The Jewish rulers did not care particularly if Jesus claimed to be a prophet. They certainly did not recognize Him as God. So the question really narrowed down to whether or not He claimed to be the Messiah.

As for His teaching that also was a vital matter. The Sanhedrin held that an accredited teacher must be appointed by them, by a group of rabbis, or by some individual rabbi. They knew that they had not appointed Jesus as such. So they demanded to know who had done so. They wanted to know the *what* as to His authority, and the *who* as to whence He received it.

In their questions they thought to place Jesus in a dilemma. They were aiming at an admission from Him that He was the Christ. Since to them the term carried a nationalistic, political, and military meaning, should Jesus claim to be the Christ they would have an accusation to present before the Roman governor. And Rome would not take lightly such a charge.

However, Jesus did not take their bait. Instead He asked them a question which placed them in an impossible dilemma (v. 3). "The baptism of John, was it from heaven, or of men?" (v. 4). So they reasoned among themselves (vv. 5-6). If they should say, "From heaven," Jesus would ask why they had not believed him. To say, "Of men," would endanger them before the people who regarded John as a prophet. So they sought refuge in agnosticism. "They answered not to know whence." The infinitive "to know" *(eidenai)* means a conviction arrived at after perceiving experiential knowledge until it became a conviction of the soul. If after all this time, while the populace regarded John as a prophet, they either had not bothered to study the matter or else had not yet arrived at a conclusion, how could they pose as judges concerning Jesus? So He exposed them as being incompetent to judge Him.

It is a strange thing that the word "agnostic" has come to apply to one who claims superior intelligence and who scorns men of faith, when the word itself comes from the Greek word for experiential knowledge *(gnōsis)* prefixed by the *alpha privative (a)*, the result being a word meaning "no knowledge." So an agnostic really is an ignoramus, a know-nothing. He may have a mass of information, but he has not thought through it to a conclusion or to a conviction.

Some truths do not submit to rationalism. In the final analysis they must be perceived through faith. The people had examined the evidence about John, had made the leap of faith, and were persuaded that he was a prophet of God. The scholars had become entangled in their system of thought, and had become lost far from the goal of truth. They simply did not know the truth about John. Yet they claimed to be the interpreters of God's Book. They were in the same state about Jesus. Not bothering to perceive Him, they could only oppose Him. In all likelihood had the people been left to themselves they would have received Jesus as the Christ. But they were led astray by their spiritual and intellectual leaders. It is so often the case that "babes" have a greater spiritual comprehension than do the "wise and prudent" (cf. Matt. 11:25).

Jesus refused to tell the *authorities* about His *authority* (v. 8). But in His question He had implied more than they knew. Jesus did not base His authority upon John the Baptist. But if the Sanhedrin insisted upon some earthly source of authority, John would be the only one. For he had baptized Jesus. So even if they pressed that point, the people themselves would claim that Jesus' authority was from heaven, since they so regarded John's authority. The Sanhedrin was left in a dilemma indeed. However, Jesus was not through with them. Ignoring them for the moment He spoke a parable to the people. A man had a vineyard (cf. Isa. 5:1ff.). He leased it out to husbandmen, and then went on a long trip (v. 9). At the time of harvest he sent a slave to collect his revenue, but the husbandmen beat him and sent him away empty-handed (v. 10). A second slave received the same treatment, only this time they added insult to violence (v. 11). A third was given even worse treatment (v. 12). Whether these slaves were sent all at the same harvest is not stated. It may have been a succession of harvest times. This latter idea is more in keeping with the meaning of the parable.

Finally, the owner, as a final effort, decided to send his "beloved son" (v. 13). Surely they will reverence him, or will give the revenue to him. However, when the husbandmen saw him coming they reasoned in quite another manner. Since he was the heir, if they killed him they would inherit the vineyard (v. 14). This was their reasoning, not that of the owner. It never occurred to them that they would incur the wrath of the longsuffering owner. But such is the stupidity of sin. Nevertheless, they violently cast the "beloved son" out of the vineyard and killed him (v. 15).

"What therefore," asked Jesus, "shall the lord of the vineyard do unto them?" Matthew places the answer in the mouths of the husbandmen (21:41). But Luke follows Mark (12:9) in putting it in Jesus' mouth (v. 16). But all three agree that Jesus applied it to Scripture.

Jesus said, "He shall come and destroy these husbandmen, and shall give the vineyard to others" (v. 16). Note that *he shall come*. After his beloved son there will be no other intermediaries. The people were rapt with attention. "And when they heard it, they said, God forbid" (v. 16). "God" is not in the best manuscripts. They simply said, "May it not happen" *(mē genoito)*. "Let such a thought die aborning!" We would say, "Perish the thought!" It was an extreme expression of a wish to negate a thought. Now who were the "they"? The people only, or does it include the Jewish rulers also? It could be either or both, perhaps the latter.

Then Jesus quoted Psalm 118:22. "The stone which the builders rejected, the same is become the head of the corner" (v. 17). In the original, "the" is absent before "stone." But the sense is "the stone." For the rabbis regarded this psalm as being Messianic. So in that case there could be only one such stone. This quotation was intended to prove the statement made in verse 16 about change in the stewardship of the vineyard. If this were not true, how would the scribes interpret the psalm? By their own teaching the Messiah would be rejected by the "builders," but later would become the stone which would join together two walls. These two walls suggest the Old and New Revelations which would find their true meaning in the Messiah.

Jesus then applied the lesson. "Whosoever shall fall upon that stone shall be broken; but on whomsoever that stone shall fall, it will grind him to powder" (v. 18). Those who stumble over Christ will be harmed thereby. And many in Jesus' day, and since, have found Him to be a stumbling stone.

Then the figure changes from a man stumbling over the stone to the stone itself falling on someone. This suggests a headstone high up on the wall. If men try to pull it down it will fall upon them. While many Jews were stumbling over Jesus, the Jewish leaders actually were trying to pull Him down out of the wall of God's redemptive purpose. They were representative of the Jewish nation. So the One whom they are endeavoring to pull down will actually fall upon them in judgment. *To grind to powder* really means *to scatter as dust or chaff*. That on which the stone falls will be crushed into dust which, in turn, will be blown away. Here then is another prophecy of Jesus concerning the complete destruction of the Jewish nation. And with that the Headstone will go on uniting the wall which will be built by other husbandmen in the vineyard of God.

The chief priests saw through the parable that it was directed to them and their nation (v. 19). God had made the Israelite nation the husbandmen in His vineyard of spiritual ministry to all nations (cf. Exod. 19:1ff.). But they had not rendered to Him His expected revenue. Repeatedly He had sent His prophets to call them back to their covenant with Him, but to no avail. The nation had ignored, insulted, beaten, and even killed them.

Now this longsuffering God finally had sent His beloved Son. And soon they will kill Him. This will be their final rebellious act. Their very effort to pull Jesus down and out of God's redemptive purpose will result in the crushing and scattering of their nation. Henceforth God's purpose will run through a new people, the true Israel, the followers of Christ, the Christian people made up of redeemed Jews and Gentiles (cf. I Peter 2:4-10). A comparison of the language in Exodus 19:5-6, Luke 20:16-18, and I Peter 2:4-10 reveals this to be true.

So on this Tuesday of Passion Week Jesus clearly rejected the Jewish nation which had rejected Him. And the delegation from the Sanhedrin understood His words. But for their fear of the people they would have arrested Him on the spot. However, even though they had lost this one battle they did not surrender. They kept pressing their attack through first one group and then another as they sought to break Jesus' hold on the people and to get some charge to present to Pilate (v. 20). Luke records two such attempts.

First, a group of Pharisees and Herodians (cf. Matthew and Mark) tried their hand (v. 21). No two groups could have been further apart politically. The Pharisees hated the Herods and wanted to restore the nation of Israel under Jewish rule. The Herodians were dedicated to restoring to power the Herods, who were not pure Jews. But they found a common cause in their hatred for Jesus.

So after feigning friendliness toward Jesus they asked Him a question. "Is it lawful for us to give tribute unto Caesar, or no?" (v. 22). Neither group wanted to do so, but that was not the point. They asked Jesus a loaded question, thinking that He would be in trouble however He answered it.

If He said, "No," they could accuse Him before Pilate of teaching sedition. Two things the Romans required above all others: to keep the peace and to pay taxes. To accuse Jesus of teaching against paying taxes would have been a serious charge indeed. If He said, "Yes," then the people would have resented Him. For they violently hated the idea. They would thus have considered Jesus a traitor to His own people.

However, there was an even more serious matter involved. For Jesus to have taught that they should pay taxes to a Gentile nation would have been tantamount to a denial of His Messiahship. According to the Jews the Messiah would set up His own kingdom. He certainly would not countenance the payment of taxes to another power.

However, Jesus was not drawn into their trap (v. 23). Instead, He asked His questioners to show Him a *dēnarius,* a Roman coin worth about seventeen cents (v. 24). Even if Jesus had such a coin He did not use it. He made them produce one. The fact that they had one showed that they recognized the power of Rome over them. Furthermore, even the Jews admitted that the right to coin money gave one the right to levy and to collect taxes. So Jesus then asked as to whose image was inscribed on the coin. They admitted that it was that of Caesar, probably Tiberius Caesar.

Then Jesus answered their question. "Render therefore unto Caesar the things which be Caesar's, and unto God the things which be God's" (v. 25). In other words every man has two obligations, one to his nation and the other to his God. He should discharge both obligations. Of course, the first obligation is to God. But no righteous man will refuse to do his civic duty when it does not conflict with his loyalty to God.

Our Lord not only answered His tempters. In the process He laid the foundation for the principle of the separation of Church and State. Neither should replace or control the other. They may and do have mutual obligations. The State should maintain a society in which the Church is free to do its work. The Church should produce the kind of character which will mean good citizenship. Men may debate about the *gray* areas between these two units of society. But one sharp dividing line certainly exists. Neither should control the other or invade its domain bodily. Where each recognizes its responsibility and discharges it, all the while respecting the role of the other, the result is a blessing to both.

Jesus' answer was too much for His critics (v. 26). There were too many thorns in it for them to take hold of it before the people. The Lord had defeated them again. Robertson says that "they became silent as they went back with the 'dry grins.' "

Second, a group of Sadducees confronted Jesus with a question (v. 27). Another strange guest crowded into bed with the Pharisees and Herodians. For unlike either of these they were in favor of Roman rule as long as they remained in power under their rule (cf. John 11:48). Furthermore, they were at opposite ends of the theological school from the Pharisees. They were liberals while the Pharisees were ultra-conservatives. Among other things, the Sadducees denied the resurrection from the dead. In Galilee they had joined the Pharisees in opposing Jesus. But when He raised Lazarus from the dead within sight of the temple, they took charge of the plan to destroy Him (John 11:49-53). Now after the Pharisees and Herodians had failed so miserably, they tried their hand.

The problem which they presented to Jesus was perhaps one which they had used repeatedly to taunt the Pharisees about their belief in the resurrection. The problem was based on Deuteronomy 25:5-6 (cf. Gen. 38:8). If a man died childless, his brother was to marry his widow and provide him with an offspring (v. 28). Suppose that there were seven brothers (vv. 29-33). The first died childless. Each of the other brothers in succession married the widow, but all died childless. Finally the woman died. Now "in the resurrection" whose wife should she be (v. 34)?

In reply Jesus cited no one brother. Instead He pointed out that while marriage is an earthly institution, there is no such in heaven (vv. 34-35). All those there are "sons of God" and "sons of the resurrection" (v. 36). Thus Jesus went to the heart of the Sadducees' denial of the resurrection. They based this denial on the claim that the five books of Moses, which alone they regarded as Scripture, do not teach the resurrection. But Jesus cited Moses himself as an authority for it. At the burning bush he quoted God as saying that He is the God of Abraham, Isaac, and Jacob (v. 37). All of these patriarchs had been dead for years. Yet God spoke of them as living. Thus God is not the God of the dead but of the living (v. 38). So there is a life beyond death.

Certain Pharisees present were delighted to hear Jesus cite the Mosaic writings to teach the resurrection. Even though they hated Jesus they complimented Him on His words. But it was really a dig at the Sadducees. Since the Pharisees had failed so miserably in trying to trap Jesus, they were delighted to see that the Sadducees did no better. And after that neither group dared to ask Jesus any other question (v. 40).

Now it was His turn to ask a question. "How say they that Christ is David's son?" (v. 41). "Son of David" was a Messianic title. Yet in the Psalms David called Him "my Lord." "The Lord said unto my Lord, Sit thou on my right hand, till I make thine enemies thy footstool" (vv. 42-43). If, therefore, David called Him "Lord," how can He also be his son? The Jewish rulers made no reply. They had none to make. Did they catch another point? They were Jesus' "enemies." The time will come when they will be His footstool.

The people had listened carefully to the battle of wits and words. Now as a parting shot at His routed foes Jesus warned the people against the scribes (Pharisees). Matthew 23 gives in greater detail Jesus' excoriating condemnation of these "hypocrites" in the most unmerciful words ever to fall from His lips. It was the righteous anger of a broken heart and a refused love.[1] These were the last recorded words that Jesus ever spoke to them other than brief words spoken at His trial. Even those He spoke because He was required to testify under oath. Truly, then, their *house* was left *unto them*.

[1] See my *Matthew, op. cit.*, pp. 314 ff.

Luke 21:1-4

The Measure of a Gift

Following the long debate with the Jewish leaders Jesus lingered in the Court of the Women in which the debate may have taken place. He was tired from so strenuous an effort. So He "sat down" (Mark 12:41) over against the "treasury" with His head resting in His hands. "And he looked up, and saw the rich men casting their gifts into the treasury" (v. 1).

In the Court of the Women were thirteen trumpet-shaped receptacles into which the people deposited their gifts. These gifts were used for various purposes: e.g., to buy wood or incense for the altar or to maintain the golden vessels in the temple. Each receptacle bore a label denoting for which of these its contents would be used. A regular procession of givers went by casting in their large gifts.

Finally, Jesus saw a "poor widow" casting in "two mites," or *lepta*. A *leptos* was a very thin coin worth about one-eighth of a cent. So she gave one-fourth of a cent. This was the smallest gift which was legal to give. But she did not out of a stingy heart give the least possible sum. She gave all that she had. She was a "poor" widow. This renders a Greek word whose basic meaning is to work for a living. Mark uses a word *(ptōchē)* describing her as a woman of abject poverty. Luke also uses this word for "poor" in verse 3.

Jesus made no mention of the large gifts of rich people. But calling His disciples (Mark 12:43), He pointed out the widow's gift. "Of a truth" (v. 3) suggests that He is about to make a statement which is contrary to ordinary opinions. As indeed it was. "This poor [beggarly] widow hath cast in more than they all." For out of their *surplus* they had given a sum which they would hardly miss. But the widow out of her "penury" (lack or *deficit)* had cast in all of her "living," or livelihood. She worked for a living (v. 2). But her earnings were not enough for her needs. So she also had to beg (v. 3). Yet out of her deficit income she gave, even though it meant taking bread out of her mouth.

Jesus did not seek to prevent her from giving. To have done so would have deprived her of a blessing. She had a right to express her love for God. She might, as the result of her giving, have an empty stomach. But she had a full soul. So Jesus commended her for her act. He did not look at the amount of the gift but at the greatness of her love. God weighs our love and sacrifice rather than counts the sum which we give. A person should not consider the size of his gift to God only by what he has before he gives, but also by what he has left after he gives.

The writer commended a man for a large sum of money which he gave through his church. He replied, "Pastor, I do not deserve your commendation. For it involved no sacrifice on my part. During this year I have worn fine clothes, lived in a fine house, eaten good food, bought my wife a new car, and have taken her on a trip to Europe. I have deprived myself of nothing. There are many people who have given more than I have. Perhaps it is some poor widow who gave a much smaller amount but at a greater sacrifice." He had caught the spirit of Jesus' commendation to this poor widow who gave two mites.

By contrast is the man of wealth who gives miserly, yet says that he has given the "widow's mite." Until one has given his all to the point of penury he has no right to claim such an honor.

Luke 21:5-38

The Olivet Discourse

After Jesus had commended the widow for her sacrificial gift, He left the temple never to return[1] (cf. Matt. 24:1; Mark 13:1). In view of the many unhappy experiences He had had in this area, this final scene is a ray of benevolent light cast upon a dark scene (cf. also Luke 2:46-49).

As they were departing from the temple area the disciples remarked about how the temple "was adorned with goodly stones and gifts" (v. 5). Some of these stones were enormous in size. The columns of the portico were over forty feet high, each composed of one piece of marble. The "gifts" were things devoted to God, and given by princes and other wealthy people. Josephus describes one such, a gift from Herod, which was a golden vine with branches as tall as a man. Tacitus mentions the great wealth of the temple.

Herod's temple was a gorgeous structure indeed. He began its construction in 20-19 B.C. It was not completed until A.D. 64, just six years before it was destroyed by the Romans. It was built out of white marble, and its front was covered with plates of gold. When the sun shone on this gold it gave off such a fiery splendor that one had to turn his eyes from it as he would from looking directly into the sun. Its rising marble terraces Josephus described as a snow-covered mountain. One can well understand the Jews' pride in this temple.

But Jesus shocked the Twelve by telling them that the day would come when every stone of the temple would be thrown down (v. 6). Apparently they remained silent until they stopped to rest on the slopes of the Mount of Olives across the Kidron valley overlooking the temple (Matt. 24:3; Mark 13:3). They evidently thought that such a cataclysm meant the upheaval connected with the setting up of the kingdom of God (Second Advent), when the present temple would be replaced by a more

---

[1] He was brought to the general area for the Jewish phase of His trial. Luke 21:37-38 is a summary statement of His teaching activities on Monday and Tuesday of Passion Week.

glorious one. So they asked Jesus, "Master, when shall these things be? and what sign will there be when these things shall come to pass?" (v. 7). Matthew 24:3 records their question more distinctly, but the contents are the same.

The reply which Jesus gave to their question has caused no end of difficulty in interpretation. Some take the whole to refer to Jesus' second coming. But to do so is to miss the point of the Lord's words. It will help us to keep clearly in mind that Jesus divides the disciples' question into two distinct parts. "When shall these things be?" (destruction of the temple). "And what sign will there be when those things shall come to pass?" (Second Advent). While the Twelve thought of them as one event, Jesus pointed out that they are really two separate events.[2] We may divide His answer thusly: warning against false signs (vv. 8-11); tribulation in service (vv. 12-19); the destruction of Jerusalem (vv. 20-24); the Second Advent (vv. 25-31); summary warnings and instructions (vv. 32-36).

Warnings against False Signs (vv. 8-11)

In this section Jesus is dealing with false signs which will be interpreted as heralding His Second Advent. He warns His followers not to be deceived thereby. That these warnings are necessary is seen in the fact that through the centuries these very things have been cited as evidences that the return of the Lord is near.

"Take heed [beware] that ye be not deceived" (v. 8). The word "deceived" *(planēthēte)* means more than a mere mistake. It refers to a fundamental departure from the truth. Our word "planet" comes from this word, since the ancients thought of the planets as wandering bodies. Then Jesus warned against three distinct things which could lead them astray.

One was false Christs (v. 8). The word "Christ" is not in the Greek text, simply "I am" *(egō eimi)*, but the reference is to "Christ." This is not to be confused with *Antichrist*. The reference is to individuals who from time to time will appear claiming to be the Christ. And there have been "many." This was especially true in the generation following the life of Jesus. They were a major factor in stirring the Jewish people into rebellion which brought on the war with Rome (A.D. 66-70) that ended with the destruction of Jerusalem, the temple, and the Jewish nation as such. Jesus said that His people are not to follow them.

---

[2] See my *An Exposition of the Gospel of Matthew,* Chapters 24-25.

Another false sign would be disturbances in the social order (vv. 9-10). The followers of Jesus are not to be terrified when they hear of "wars and commotions," or unsettled conditions. Again this warning was most timely. For such conditions have always, even in our time, been pointed out as signs of the second coming of Christ. Jesus said that such things would happen merely as a part of history. "But the end is not by and by," or "immediately" *(eutheōs)*.

Still another false sign would be disturbances in nature (v. 11). Earthquakes, famines, pestilences, and disturbances in the sky will be interpreted as omens of the end of time. But like nations and kingdoms warring against one another, these things will merely be a part of the normal trends of life. They are not signs of the immediate return of the Lord.

Tribulation in Service (vv. 12-19)

The immediate concern to Jesus' followers should not be the Lord's return or the above-mentioned false signs. "Before all these" (v. 12) refers to priority in time. On the night before His death Jesus will warn the disciples of tribulation which they will endure (John 15:18 ff.). It is to this that He refers here. They will be persecuted by both Jews and Gentiles (v. 12). But it will result in their bearing a witness to both their faith and the gospel itself (v. 13). Particularly in the case of Paul it afforded him the opportunity to preach before governors, kings, soldiers, and, perhaps, even emperor Nero himself.

When these things occur they are not to worry about words to be spoken in their defense. Through the Holy Spirit Jesus will give to them words which their hearers can neither withstand nor explain away (vv. 14-15; cf. 12:11-12; John 15:26 f.).

The followers of Jesus can expect betrayal within their own families (v. 16). But even though they will be hated by all non-Christians, they will know the protection which only the Lord can give (vv. 17-18). Jesus was not speaking of physical but of spiritual safety. He had just spoken of some being put to death. But their souls would be safe. What courage would be required if Christians knew that no physical harm would befall them? They would be like the little boy who said, "I wouldn't mind going to war and being a hero, if I knew that I would not be hurt."

"In your patience possess ye your souls" (v. 19). Literally, "ye shall acquire your souls," or "lives." Of course, this does not mean that thereby they will be saved from sin. But they will achieve the true purpose for which they live. The word "patience" *(hupomonē)* could be rendered "patient endurance." But even that does not do the word justice. This word was used for a military citation. A *patient* soldier was one who could take all that the enemy threw against him, and still have enough reserve strength to counter-charge to victory. This is the idea in Jesus' use of the word. Let the enemies of Christ do their worst. If the disciples can take it and still possess the reserve strength to counter-charge to victory, they will live victorious lives in the service of Christ.

The Destruction of Jerusalem (vv. 20-24)

Jesus was now ready to answer the former question. "When shall these things be?" The destruction of the temple. When they should see Jerusalem "being encompassed" by armies, then they would know that her *desolation* is near (v. 20). The disciples had been thinking that Jerusalem would soon be glorified as the capital city of the kingdom of God. Jesus says that it will soon be destroyed, along with the temple. In His laments over the city He had spoken of such an event. Now He describes the armies as they are surrounding the city for a final siege.

Note that Jesus did not name the date even though it was less than a generation away. He described the condition. Some critics insist that these words were written after the event, but were not spoken by Jesus. However, if one admits the element of prophecy at all, such a time element is unnecessary. Certainly such ability to foresee the future should not be denied to the Son of God.

When they shall see the city *being surrounded* they are to flee before the encircling maneuver is completed, else it will be too late (v. 21). Those in Judea are to flee to the mountains. Those in the city are to get out. Certainly no one outside the city should try to enter it. It is a matter of record that when this condition occurred Christians fled to Pella in Perea (Eusebius). He attributes their act to knowledge of this prophecy by Jesus.

This will be a terrible time of vengeance upon Jerusalem (v. 22). Eusebius quotes Josephus (though no record of Josephus in this regard is known) as saying that Jerusalem was destroyed to avenge the death of "James the Just, who was a brother of Jesus, that is called the Christ. For the Jews slew him, although he was a very just man." But Jesus had said that this would come upon Jerusalem to avenge all of the martyrs' blood spilled throughout the Old Testament (cf. Matt. 23:35-36).

It will be a terrible time for women who are with child or who have suckling children (v. 23). It will be difficult for them to flee from the city. In the carnage which will accompany the fall of the city many will fall by the sword and others will be taken captive (v. 24). Josephus says that 1,100,000 perished in the siege and that 97,000 were carried into captivity. Doubtless this is an exaggeration by the Jewish historian. That many people could not have stood within the walls of the city. But allowing for his tendency to exaggerate numbers, still the number must have been very great. Plummer suggests the number of slain to be 70,000.

Jerusalem will "be trodden down of the Gentiles, until the times of the Gentiles be fulfilled" (v. 24). The meaning of these words has been the subject of much debate. Plummer lists several possible meanings, but suggests two probable ones. (1) The season for the carrying out by Gentile nations of divine judgment upon the Jews. (2) The Gentiles' possessing the same privileges which the Jews had forfeited. Robertson says, "What this means is not clear except that Paul in Romans 11:25 shows that the punishment of the Jews has a limit." Bruce *(Expositor's)* is inclined to regard Jesus' words as referring to the Gentile *day of grace.* They were to have theirs as the Jews had had theirs. Thus he agrees with Plummer's second suggestion. In a sense all three of these scholars agree. The writer finds himself in accord with them.

But in his opinion "until" does not point to a time when Jerusalem will become the earthly capital of the kingdom of God. In Romans 9-11 Paul distinguishes between national Israel and spiritual, or true, Israel. He points out that this true Israel has always been the remnant through which God's purpose runs. Peter shows this *true priest-people* to be the Christian body composed of both Jews and Gentiles (I Peter 2:4-10). The "until" points to that time when, somehow in God's economy, great numbers of Jews will receive Christ as their Messiah and Saviour. But even then their turning to Him will not be on a national basis. It will be an individual experience. For Peter said, "But we believe that through the grace of the Lord Jesus Christ we [Jews] shall be saved, even as they [Gentiles]" (Acts 15:11).

The Second Advent (vv. 25-31)

Now Jesus turns to answer the latter question: "What sign will there be when these things shall come to pass?" (v. 7). Thus He shows that what the Twelve thought of as one event will be two separate events.

Employing apocalyptic language Jesus speaks of disturbances in the heavens and on the earth (v. 25). Probably the best reading would be, "Upon the earth distress of nations in perplexity like the roaring of sea and waves," or like a sea in a storm. Men's hearts will faint from fear and expectation because of what is happening on the earth and in the sky. It is not clear just how this is to be taken, literally or figuratively. But either way it speaks of disturbances which shall reflect themselves in the hearts of men. In view of Jesus' teaching elsewhere to the effect that life will go in its usual way until suddenly the end, these disturbances must be coming suddenly and will be of short duration before the Lord appears.

"And then shall they see the Son of man coming in a cloud with power and great glory" (v. 27). Then, and not until then, will this occur. The fact that Jesus used the future third person plural instead of the second person suggests that the Twelve will not live to see this. Of course, Jesus taught that His return is always imminent. His followers are to live in constant expectancy. In Matthew's account (24:30) after reciting the disturbances in the heavens he records, "Then shall appear the *sign* of the Son of man in heaven" (author's italics). He adds that the tribes of the earth will mourn (disturbances on earth) and "they shall see the Son of man coming in the clouds of heaven with power and great glory" (24:30). So the *sign* of His coming will be His appearance itself. The disturbances will be harbingers of that event. Of course, these disturbances will be of such nature that they will clearly foretell the Lord's appearance.

Naturally our curiosity desires more detail. But when dealing with prophecy, especially where it is couched in apocalyptic language, it is difficult to be exact as to details. But our Lord told us all that we need to know about His return. He never spoke of it with respect to time, but condition. His followers in every age are to be expectant. They are not to be led astray by false signs, but are to be looking for the true signs. When they appear they will be so definite that those who look for Him in faith and hope will recognize them. The nearest that Jesus ever came to stating a time is, "And this gospel of the kingdom shall be preached in all the world for a witness unto all nations; and then shall the end come" (Matt. 24:14). But even here the emphasis is upon condition, not a definite date. We are to be busy at creating the *condition*, leaving the *time* in the mind and heart of God.

While the disturbances preceding the Lord's return will be the cause of despair among the unsaved, they will be a source of hope and joy to the Lord's people. "And when these things begin to come to pass, then look up, and lift up your heads; for your redemption draweth nigh" (v. 28). Here again Jesus speaks to the disciples as though they will see this. This should not be construed as an error on Jesus' part with respect to the time of His second coming. Rather it emphasizes the element of expectancy. Some generation of Christians will be living on the earth at that time. This was such a generation when Jesus spoke these words.

The point is that His return will be the occasion of great joy to His people. "Redemption" perhaps has a threefold meaning here. It speaks of release from the burdens of toil and tribulation endured in the Master's service. It will vindicate their faith in the eyes of a world which has rejected both Him and them. It will be the final act in the Lord's work of redemption. The souls of His people were redeemed on Calvary, and became a reality to them the moment that they trusted in Him. At His return their bodies will be redeemed (Rom. 8:23-25), either in the bodily resurrection of those who have died prior to that time, or in the immediate change which will transform those who are alive at that time from bodies of flesh and blood into spiritual bodies (I Cor. 15:35-57; I Thess. 4:14-18). This redemption of the body will provide us with the kind of bodies suited to the conditions under which we shall live in eternity (I Cor. 15:38 ff.). The nearest that we can come to describing our resurrection bodies is to say that they will probably be similar to the body which Jesus had after His resurrection.

Jesus concluded His answer to this question by giving the parable of trees (vv. 29-31). When trees put forth their leaves "ye see and know *of your own selves* that summer is now nigh at hand" (author's italics). You know it of your own selves without being told by another. The drawing near of summer is self-evident. Likewise, "when" (*hotan,* primarily refers to condition) we see the disturbances described by Jesus, we shall know of ourselves that "the kingdom of God is nigh at hand." Here Jesus spoke of the consummation of the kingdom, not of its beginning. The disciples expected an immediate consummation of the kingdom. But Jesus pointed to a future consummation. However, He still spoke to the disciples in terms which would leave them, as well as us, in a state of expectancy. The second person plural forms of the verbs are applicable to any generation living at any time. The second coming of Christ is ever the abiding blessed hope of those who look for Him in faith.

Summary Warnings and Instructions (vv. 32-36)

This closing summary is a point of debate among interpreters. Especially is this true of verse 32. "This generation shall not pass away, till all be fulfilled." Was Jesus speaking of His second coming? If so, then one is forced to conclude that He was in error in thinking that it would occur during that generation. To get around this difficulty some identify "this generation" with those living at the time that the disturbances occur. However, this puts an undue strain upon Jesus' language.

The difficulty disappears when we keep in mind that Jesus was answering two distinct questions. The former had to do with the destruction of Jerusalem and the temple. It is natural, therefore, to relate verse 32 to that matter. For before that generation passed away the city and temple were destroyed (A.D. 70). As the disciples looked upon them it must have seemed incredible that such would occur. So Jesus reinforced His words by adding, "Heaven and earth shall pass away; but my words shall not pass away" (v. 33). He had predicted the fate of Jerusalem, and it would take place. If the disciples thought of the city and temple as permanent, what about the natural universe? Even that will pass away in God's own time. But Christ's words abide forever, not only the words so recently spoken but every one of His words.

This statement forms a natural transition from the former to the latter question asked by the disciples. For Jesus' words about His second coming are abiding also. But note the change in tone. With regard to the destruction of Jerusalem, it would occur during "this generation." But now Jesus changed to "lest at any time," or "lest haply" (v. 34). This could apply to *any generation*. So Jesus issued a blanket warning to the Twelve and to any other succeeding group of His followers. They should guard against "surfeiting" (the nausea which follows a debauch), "drunkenness" and "the cares of this life" (not necessarily sin but any anxiety of this life) which would prevent their being constantly watchful as to the Lord's return. It is a question as to which produces the other. Sinful living and earthly cares dim the sense of hope and expectancy with respect to the Lord's return. And in reverse order a loss of expectancy concerning the latter leads to the former. Peter writes of those who are "scoffers, walking after their own lusts [desires], and saying, Where is the promise of his coming . . ." (II Peter 3:3-4). The second coming will be as a "snare" or something unexpected (v. 35). This snare will be like a net which will settle down quickly on all who "dwell on the face of the whole earth." Jesus' return not only will be sudden, it will also be universal.

Verse 36 ties this entire discourse into one neat bundle. Literally, "But be sleeplessly alert in every season, praying constantly in order that ye may prevail [have strength against] to flee from all these things, the ones about to happen, and to stand before the Son of man." Now this entire verse could apply to the second coming of Christ. But it makes even better sense to apply the first part ("watch . . . worthy") to the rapidly approaching destruction of Jerusalem and to the second coming, the second part ("to escape . . . pass") to the destruction of Jerusalem, and the third part ("to stand . . . man") to the return of the Lord.

"All these things, the ones about to happen" certainly suggest the fall of Jerusalem much more than the uncertain time of the second coming. Earlier in the discourse Jesus had counselled flight from Jerusalem when they saw the armies encircling the city (vv. 20-21). The words "to escape" (KJV) render the infinitive *ekpheugō*. *Pheugō* means to seek safety in flight. The prefix *ek* means "out of." Where would one seek safety in flight out of the coming of the Son of man? No, Jesus told the disciples to be sleeplessly alert in every season, praying continuously that they might have strength to flee out of Jerusalem and its environs when they saw "these things, the ones about to happen," the destruction of Jerusalem, heralded by the encircling armies.

Then He dealt with the second coming: "and to stand before the Son of man" when He appears. Note the two infinitives "to flee out of," and "to stand." So these infinitives set forth two distinct ideas. As they are to be prayerfully alert in every season with respect to escape from Jerusalem, also they are to be prayerfully alert in every season that they may have strength to stand blamelessly before the Son of man when He returns. If one is ready, not only through regeneration but through faithful service also, there will be no dread to stand before the Lord when He returns.

For those outside of Christ His return will be a time of inexpressible horror. For those *in Christ* it will be one of unutterable joy. Which will it be for you?

Luke 22:1-6

The Defection of Judas

Events were rapidly moving toward a climax. It was late on Tuesday of Passion Week. "The feast of unleavened bread was drawing near [imperfect]" (v. 1). For the benefit of his Gentile readers Luke adds the explanatory note that this feast "is called the Passover." The Jewish leaders "continued seeking [imperfect] how they might kill" Jesus (v. 2). They were determined to do so, but how to accomplish it was a problem. "For they kept on fearing [imperfect] the people." They had planned to seize Him upon His arrival in the vicinity of Jerusalem (John 11:57). But their plans had gone awry. The royal entry and subsequent events had shown the great hold which Jesus had upon the people. Seeing this the Jewish rulers had decided to wait until after the Passover (Matt. 26:3-5). After the feast there would be far fewer people in Jerusalem. Most of those remaining in the city would be Jerusalemites. And the rulers could control them better than they could those from Galilee and elsewhere. Furthermore, the revolutionary atmosphere would abate following the feast, and especially so should Jesus not make the expected move to establish His kingdom.

However, help from an unexpected source changed their plans for delay. In their fondest dreams the rulers did not anticipate help from within Jesus' intimate circle of the Twelve. But they did not know Judas Iscariot as Jesus knew him. Luke says that Satan entered into Judas (v. 3). Satan had been toying with Judas for a long time. Jesus was aware of this at least one year before His death (John 6:70-71). But up until this time apparently Judas had sought to resist him. However, he now opened the door of his life, and the Adversary entered.

Judas will forever remain a mystery. It is quite clear from the Gospel record that he never did really become a disciple of Jesus. Yet He chose him as one of the Twelve. We can only surmise that Judas possessed qualities or abilities which, if surrendered to Jesus, would have made him a useful servant of Christ. Even so, Jesus would not coerce his will. What Judas did with his life was his choice to make. Satan also saw qualities in Judas which he could use. And Judas withheld himself from a committal to Jesus. What is even worse, he committed himself to Satan.

He seems to have been possessed by selfish ambition. Thinking that Jesus was going to establish an earthly kingdom, he wanted a place of prominence and power in it. We may well imagine that he was a prime instigator of the effort to make Jesus a king following the feeding of the five thousand. At His Royal Entry Jesus had a golden opportunity to proclaim His kingdom. When He did not do so, according to Judas He had missed His chance. Rumors were rife as to the Sanhedrin's purpose to seize Jesus. So it was only a matter of time until they would accomplish their nefarious purpose. Therefore, Judas decided that he might just as well try to get something out of the debacle.

According to Matthew 26:14 and Mark 14:10 (compared with John 12:2-8) Judas went directly from the home of Simon the leper to make a bargain with the chief priests to betray Jesus. He had been stung by Jesus' rebuke about his criticism of Mary's act of love. He was in an inner rage over this. In such a condition he opened the door to Satan.

Was Judas responsible for his act? Some have supposed that he was born for such an act, that he was merely a puppet in God's hands. But God does not deal thusly with men. To suppose this is to make God, not Judas, responsible for this most ignominious of acts. Others hold that he was simply a puppet in Satan's hands. When Satan entered into him he was no longer responsible for his deeds. Still others suggest that Judas meant well. He thought to crowd Jesus into a corner, thinking that rather than to die He would destroy His enemies and establish His kingdom. But when the entire record is considered we cannot escape the fact that Judas acted as a responsible individual. What he did, he did deliberately and with a venomous purpose. His act was his own, and the consequences for himself were of his own making. In the light of the Gospels it is impossible to absolve him of guilt.

It was on Tuesday night that Judas made his bargain with "the chief priests and captains" (v. 4). The "captains" were the officers in charge of the temple guard. They were brought in on the consultation, since they would be involved in the arrest of Jesus. Their assistance naturally pleased the chief priests (v. 5). So they covenanted to give Judas a sum of money. Luke does not mention the amount. Matthew 26:15 says that it was thirty pieces of silver (cf. Exod. 21:32; Zech. 11:12): the price of a slave! It amounted to a little less than twenty-five dollars. There is no darker picture in the annals of men than this. Religious leaders acting thus – and with one of Jesus' intimates at that!

Judas agreed to be the cat's paw of the Sanhedrin. And he "kept seeking" (imperfect) a *good chance (eu,* good, *kairos,* season or time) to betray Jesus unto them "in the absence of the multitude" (v. 6). He would hand Him over to them during the feast in spite of the people, and without a tumult.

Where did the chief priests get the money with which to pay Judas? Most likely it came out of the sacred treasury, money dedicated to the service of Jehovah. They used God's money to betray God's Son, and in the name of *religion!* Evil compounded with evil!

Luke 22:7-38

The Upper Room

We have no record as to what Jesus did on Wednesday of Passion Week. He probably remained in or near Bethany, resting, and teaching His disciples. Finally, "the day of unleavened bread" arrived, "when the passover [lamb] must be killed" (v. 7). This would be Thursday, the 14th of Nisan. The Passover itself was the 15th of Nisan which began at sunset on Thursday.

As with the royal entry so with the passover meal, Jesus had made previous preparations as to the place where He and the Twelve would eat it. But these plans He kept to Himself. He must not permit Judas to know in advance where He would observe this feast. Sometime around noon on Thursday He sent Peter and John to prepare the meal in the appointed place (v. 8). In response to their inquiry as to the place Jesus told them to go into Jerusalem. There they would see a man carrying a pitcher of water. They were to follow him, and he would lead them to the house. They were to ask the owner of the house to show them the guestchamber that Jesus had engaged in which to eat the passover with His disciples. It was there that they were to prepare the meal (vv. 10-12). In that day the better class of homes had two rooms, the one built upon the other, with the entrance to the upper room being made by way of outside stairs. The upper room was the "guestchamber."

Now it is of interest to note the man carrying a pitcher of water. None of the Gospels names this man. Matthew speaks of "such a man" *(ton deina)*. These words are found in the papyri in the sense of "Mister X." Modern Greek so uses them. Water carrying was a woman's task. So a man carrying a pitcher of water would be readily identified. This evidently was a previously arranged sign by which the man and the two disciples would be brought together. In all likelihood "Mister X" himself did not know the reason for his action until Peter and John talked with him at the home (v. 11). The home probably was that of Mary, the mother of John Mark.

So when they had ascertained the place, the two disciples proceeded to prepare for the meal. Certain food must be procured: e.g., unleavened bread, bitter herbs, wine (cf. Matt. 26:29), and certain sweet fruit preserves. A lamb must be purchased also. This would have to be approved by the priest as being without blemish, and then be slain in the courts of the Temple. The slaying of lambs was done on the 14th of Nisan between 2:30 and 5:30 p.m. The lamb was then roasted, and the food prepared for the table in the guest room.

Shortly after sunset Jesus and the other disciples arrived at the room and all twelve with Him reclined on couches about the table (v. 14). Before they began eating Jesus spoke of His intense desire to eat this meal with His disciples before He suffered. For He would not do so again until the heavenly feast in the kingdom of God (vv. 15-17).

At this point Luke records his account of the institution of the Lord's Supper. But the chronology of Mark places it later, after the departure of Judas (cf. John 13:27-30). In all likelihood Mark's chronology at this point is correct. In fact the sequence of events in the upper room, following the other Gospels, calls for a rearrangement of some of Luke's material. It does no violence to it to do so, but rather makes clearer the entire account.

The heart of Jesus was filled with desire to eat the passover and with the knowledge of what awaited Him on the morrow. But the Twelve were concerned with one thing only. Who would have the places of honor about the table? They were actually in contention over the matter as to "which of them should be accounted the greatest" (v. 24). So Jesus used the occasion to teach them a lesson in true greatness. Gentile or pagan kings lord it over their subjects, and the ones exercising authority over them are called "benefactors," or doers of good (v. 25). Tersely Jesus made a contrast between earthly and heavenly standards of greatness. Literally, "But ye not so" (v. 26). "Ye" is in the emphatic position. In the Christian fellowship the "greatest" shall be as the "younger," or "junior." He who aspires to being the "chief" let him be as a menial servant. Certainly by earthly standards the guest at the table is considered greater than those who serve the table. But Jesus, the Host at this meal, said, "In the midst of you I am as the one serving" (v. 27). The disciples had been with Jesus in His trials (v. 28). Despite their many shortcomings they had been faithful. So He appoints to them a kingdom, even as the Father has done for Him (v. 29). Therefore they will share with Him in the honor and power of this kingdom (v. 30). They are suffering with Him; they will be glorified with Him (cf. Rom. 8:17).

It was probably at this point that Jesus washed the disciples' feet (John 13:1-20). Thus the Host performed this most menial task for His guests (v. 27). In so doing He did not give a third ordinance to us. Rather He taught us a lesson in showing true greatness through humble service.

Having finished this object lesson Jesus again reclined at the table. It was then that He threw a bombshell into their midst by revealing that one of the Twelve would betray Him into the hands of His enemies (v. 21). Literally, "But, behold, the hand of the one betraying [present participle] me with me upon the table." Judas was then in the process of betrayal even while he ate with Jesus. This statement did not point out his identity. It merely showed the intimacy which was being betrayed. To be sure Jesus was going to the cross according to God's will. But "woe unto that man by whom he is betrayed" (v. 22). This clearly shows that Judas is not absolved of his guilt.

All of the disciples had their hands on the table. So they began to inquire among themselves which one should do this thing (v. 23). While the Eleven had never entertained such an idea, their questions show how little they really understood themselves. The human heart is indeed deceitful. Who can know it? Perhaps there were many glances of suspicion which passed between them. Finally, according to Matthew and Mark they [the Eleven] began to ask, "Is it I, Lord?" (Matt. 26:22). Had Judas remained silent this would have looked bad for him. So at the last he asked, "Is it I, Rabbi?" (Matt. 26:25 RV). Note the change from "Lord" to "Rabbi." Judas addressed Jesus only as "Teacher." He did not acknowledge Him as Lord. John 13:23-30 relates that Jesus clearly identified Judas as the betrayer. John had asked Jesus to point out the guilty one. Jesus did so by giving Judas a piece of bread dipped in gravy. In the middle of the table there was a bowl of gravy into which all were dipping their bread. At times during the meal the host would show special honor to a guest by giving him such a piece of bread. Jesus did this to Judas. Was this one last effort to get Judas to turn from his evil deed? At any rate, only John and Judas knew the significance of the act. It was at this point that the betrayer departed to fulfil his evil bargain.

After Judas left the upper room Jesus warned the Eleven against the danger of their deserting Him in the ordeal which was rapidly approaching. Especially did He single out Simon Peter. "Simon, Simon, behold, Satan hath desired to have you, that he might sift you as wheat" (v. 31). He had Judas lock, stock, and barrel. Now he also wants Peter. But Jesus assured him that He had prayed for him that he would be faithful (v. 32). He knew, however, that Peter would stumble and fall. He would deny Jesus. But, unlike Judas, Peter was a true disciple, and he would repent and receive forgiveness. And when he has *turned back* he is to strengthen the other disciples.

True to his nature Peter assured Jesus that he would remain true even if it meant prison and death (v. 33). Doubtless he meant it at the time. But Jesus knew him better than he knew himself. So He told him that before daylight the next morning he would deny Him three times (v. 34).

At this point Jesus said one of the strangest things which ever fell from His lips. He reminded the Eleven that in the past when He sent them forth to preach they carried no money bag, or any extra provisions, yet they lacked nothing. To which they all agreed (v. 35). "Then said he unto them, But now [in contrast with the former time], he that hath a purse, let him take it, and likewise his scrip: and he that hath no sword, let him sell his garment, and buy one" (v. 36). A literal translation is even more emphatic as to what Jesus said. "But now the one having a money bag let him take [aorist imperative] it, likewise also a wallet, and the one not having [either] let him sell immediately [aorist imperative] his outer garment and immediately buy [aorist imperative] a sword."

What are we to understand by these words? To those who regard Jesus as an absolute pacifist they pose a serious problem. For here He clearly told His disciples that if they had no money they should sell their outer garments and purchase swords. And the fact that both "sell" and "buy" are aorist tenses suggests that they should do so that very moment. It is impossible to tone down this statement. Neither can we dismiss it as not being a genuine saying of Jesus. Bruce is right when he says, ". . . let him sell his upper garment, however indispensable for clothing by day and by night. A *sword* the one thing needful. This is a realistic speech true to the manner of Jesus, and what is rare in Luke, given without toning down, a genuine logion without doubt" *(Expositor's, in loco)*.

It will help us to understand this statement if we consider the next verse. "For I say unto you, that this that is written must yet be accomplished in me, And he was reckoned among the transgressors [lawless ones]: for the things concerning me have an end [goal]" (v. 37). Jesus quoted Isaiah 53:12 which speaks of the manner of the death of the Suffering Servant. And it "must" *(dei,* moral and spiritual necessity) "be accomplished" *(telesthēnai,* from *teleō,* to bring to final and complete fulfilment) in Jesus. For the things concerning Him have a *goal (telos,* also from *teleō).* The word "reckoned" ("numbered" in Isaiah) means to be placed on a list. In this case Jesus must be listed for death along with "the lawless ones," or criminals, the two robbers.

Now where does this leave us? Jesus knows that He is going to die the next day, and in a manner prescribed by God. But already Judas had left to bring the temple police. Even then they might be on their way to seize Jesus. He is ready to die, but not by mob violence in the street. Furthermore, before He is ready to be taken, He has before Him the agony of Gethsemane. After that He will willingly submit to His captors. But not before. So Jesus was telling the Eleven to get swords immediately that they might guard Him until He was ready to be taken.

Some interpreters endeavor to tone down these words by saying that Jesus was simply warning His disciples about persecution which they would endure in the future. If so, then He clearly told them that along with their money bags and wallets they were to carry swords as they went forth to preach the gospel. Evidently they did not so understand His words. For they certainly did not carry swords even for defensive purposes. If we take these words out of their context, then they really have no meaning at all. But if we accept them at face value within the context of this night when evil prowled the streets of Jerusalem, then they take on both a pragmatic and a spiritual meaning.

We do violence to the over-all picture of Jesus if we see Him only as meek and mild. When it was called for He was capable of righteous wrath. To be sure these words of our Lord should not be interpreted as sanctioning armed aggression. Neither did He counsel spreading the gospel by the sword. But defensive action is quite another matter. There are some things worth fighting and dying for. Jesus had no sympathy for the "better to be Red than dead" philosophy. His own redeeming death proves this. He was not afraid to die. But He would die in a certain way and for a definite purpose. Until He was ready to die thus He must be protected. Satan wanted Jesus to die, but not on a cross.

Jesus would die according to the will of God, not that of Satan.

The Eleven understood Jesus to be talking about real swords. For they said, "Lord, behold, here are two swords" (v. 38). They probably belonged to the owner of the house where they were gathered. The word "behold" suggests that the swords were in the upper room, and had just come to the notice of the disciples. Jesus replied, "It is enough." Two would be sufficient. They did not need armor for all of the disciples. They were not about to storm the Tower of Antonia or to start a military revolution. Two swords were sufficient for protection. What happened to these two swords? Peter had one in the Garden of Gethsemane. But where was the other one? When Jesus arrived in the garden He left eight disciples near the entrance. Were they an outer guard? Did they have one sword, even as Peter in the inner guard had the other?

Furthermore, in this light we can understand Peter's action in using his sword in Gethsemane. During Jesus' prayer period he had been asleep most of the time. He did not know that Jesus was ready to be taken. So when the temple police arrived he did exactly what he understood that he was to do. He sought to protect Jesus. But Jesus told him to put up the sword. Protection was no longer necessary, and Peter would simply get himself killed for nothing.

But let us return to the scene in the upper room. It was at this point following Jesus' words about the sword that He instituted the Lord's Supper. Luke's account of this is quite simple, and is very similar to the one given by Paul in I Corinthians 11:23-25. It is worthy of note to point out that only the Eleven were present with Jesus at this time. The Lord's Supper is for baptized believers only. Most likely Judas had been baptized. But he was not a believer.

So in this little circle the Lord simply took some unleavened bread, gave thanks, broke the bread, and gave some to each disciple. He said, "This is my body which is given for you: this do in remembrance of me" (v. 19). Then He took "the cup," saying, "This cup is the new testament [covenant] in my blood, which is shed [poured out] for you" (v. 20).

Jesus did not say that the bread and fruit of the vine "became" His body and blood. "This is [*estin*] my body" The word "is" is omitted but implied with regard to the blood. These elements were simply representative or symbolic of Jesus' body and blood. This Supper is not a sacrament but a memorial designed to bring to mind that which Jesus did for our redemption. Animal blood was used in the sealing of a covenant. The old covenant had been sealed thus. But the new covenant is sealed by the blood of the Son of God. And less than twenty-four hours from the time Jesus gave this simple, beautiful ordinance, He poured out His blood to seal it.

John records further teaching of Jesus in the upper room and on the way to Gethsemane. But Luke simply says that from the upper room Jesus led the Eleven out of the city to the Mount of Olives. Under the cover of darkness through the streets of a sleeping city the Lord moved toward His rendezvous with destiny.

Luke 22:39-46

The Struggle in Gethsemane

There was no longer any need for Jesus to maintain secrecy as to His whereabouts. Therefore, when He left the upper room He went to His customary place of prayer when He was in the vicinity of Jerusalem (v. 39). It was a garden called Gethsemane, located somewhere on the Mount of Olives. This garden probably belonged to some wealthy friend of Jesus. The name "Gethsemane" means "oil press." Therefore, it evidently contained many olive trees. The location of this garden cannot be ascertained with exactness. Today such a garden is located at the base of the mountain just across the Kidron brook, east from St. Stephen's gate. From this garden one gets a marvelous view of the Gate Beautiful which now is walled up, but which in Jesus' day led into the city in the area of the temple. In this garden are several ancient olive trees. The Church of All Nations is built therein and over the Rock of Agony, said to be the rock on which Jesus leaned as He prayed. Even if this is not the exact location, the garden of Gethsemane must have been somewhere nearby.

Matthew and Mark give many details of the agony in Gethsemane which are omitted by Luke. For instance, Luke does not tell that Jesus left eight disciples near the entrance, and took Peter, James, and John farther into the garden. Neither does he go into the details of the three prayers of Jesus. He records two distinct times of prayer. But he does include the basic elements of these prayers, and also adds details omitted by the others.

Arriving at the place of prayer, Jesus urged the disciples to pray, or to keep on praying that they not enter into temptation (v. 40). Matthew and Mark add "watch," or be on guard. Then He went about a stone's cast farther, kneeled down, and "kept on praying" (imperfect). This verb form suggests more than just one petition. He prayed, "Father, if thou be willing, remove this cup from me: nevertheless not my will, but thine, be done" (v. 41).

To what does the "cup" refer? Most certainly it was not physical death. Jesus did not fear death. He had known that it lay before Him, and resolutely walked the road that would lead to Calvary. Furthermore, He knew that beyond Calvary was the resurrection. So we must look elsewhere for the meaning of the "cup." Some suggest that He prayed that He would not die in Gethsemane, but would live to go to the cross. However, this hardly satisfies the situation. In all likelihood the "cup" referred to that which His death embodied, that He should become sin. As He stood on the very brink of this awful experience His holy soul drew back from the horror of becoming the very essence of sin. If there were any other way by which man could be saved – but, if not, then He was ready for God's will to be done.

That a tremendous struggle went on in Jesus' soul is quite evident. Was He struggling with the temptation of Satan to turn back from the cross? Hardly. For Satan does not appear in so holy a scene. Was it a struggle between Jesus' will and that of the Father? Not so. For there is no semblance of rebellion on Jesus' part. He simply prayed that if God's will could be otherwise.... But always it was, "Nevertheless not my will, but thine, be done." The struggle was within Jesus' own will with reference to His becoming sin.

That the struggle was great is seen in the fact that an angel from heaven appeared to strengthen Him (v. 43). Luke alone mentions this. At the close of the three temptations in the wilderness angels came and ministered unto Him (Matt. 4:11). While the angel no doubt strengthened Jesus in spirit, the primary reference is to physical strength. Hobart points out that, outside of the Septuagint, this verb in the transitive sense, "to strengthen," is found only in Hippocrates and Luke. Luke, the physician, takes note of this bodily need. Luke further adds to this thought as he notes that Jesus was in "agony" *(agōniai,* v. 44). This word carries the idea of a great contest. Field insists that this word contained the idea of fear. So in an agony of holy fear at the thought of becoming sin Jesus prayed even more earnestly, "And his sweat was as it were great drops of blood falling down to the ground" (v. 44). Jesus broke out in a bloody sweat. "Drops" *(thromboi)* really means "clots" of blood. This word was common in ancient medical works, but Luke, the physician, alone uses it in the New Testament. He vividly portrays the great struggle through which Jesus was passing.

Finally, the victory won, Jesus arose from prayer (v. 45). Returning to the disciples He found them "sleeping for sorrow."

Prolonged sorrow produces sleep, and Luke is careful to spare the disciples the shame of sleeping on guard during this fateful experience of their Lord. But he does add that Jesus mildly rebuked them for sleeping, and urged them once again to rise and pray lest they should fall asleep on such an occasion. But he that is without sin, let him cast the first stone. For we still are asleep at our post while Jesus continues to agonize over a lost world.

Luke 22:47-53

The Betrayal by Judas

When Judas left the upper room he doubtless went straight to the house of Caiaphas. He was now ready to earn his *pay*. The arrest of Jesus would have to be done by the temple police, since it was to be carried out under orders from the high priest. However, in order to prevent a tumult among the people should they learn of the arrest, even at such a late hour, a detachment of Roman soldiers was procured from the Tower of Antonia. It took time to assemble the guard.

Probably Judas first led them to the house where Jesus had eaten the passover meal. Failing to find Him there he surmised that He would be in Gethsemane. For Judas was familiar with this place where Jesus often prayed. It must have been sometime after midnight when he and his armed band arrived at the garden.

They arrived just as Jesus was speaking to His drowsy disciples (v. 47). Judas was in the lead. By previous arrangement he was to point out Jesus by kissing Him (cf. Matt. 26:48). He probably kissed Jesus on the hand, since this was the customary way for a disciple to greet his teacher. Both Matthew and Mark say that he "kissed him much." Such perfidy under the feigned gesture of joy! There is both rebuke and pathos in Jesus' words: "Judas, betrayest thou the Son of man with a kiss?" (v. 48).

Things happened so quickly that the Eleven were stunned. But they rallied to the occasion. "Lord, shall we smite with the [a] sword?" (v. 49). They were asking for instructions. Was He now ready to be defended? Only Luke records this question. But one, Simon Peter, did not wait for an answer. Instead, he "smote the servant of the high priest, and cut off his right ear" (v. 50). Only Luke mentions that it was his *right* ear. It is John who names Peter, and also gives "Malchus" as the servant's name.

Assuming that Peter was right-handed, he evidently aimed at Malchus' head. But the servant dodged expertly. Instead of losing his head, he lost only his right ear.

It was at this point that Jesus told Peter to put up his sword

(Matt. 26:52). In doing so, He probably saved Peter's life. Then He healed the ear, a fact mentioned only by Luke (v. 51). Matthew also notes Jesus' word about being able to call upon twelve legions of angels to come to His aid, if He desired them. One legion, six thousand angels, for each apostle, including Judas! But Jesus no longer needed protection. He was now ready to go to the cross.

Then Jesus chided the chief priests, elders, and temple police for coming after Him with an armed band as though He were a thief (v. 52). "Swords and staves" would include both Roman soldiers and temple police respectively. But note also that only Luke mentions the presence of the chief priests and elders. They had come along to be sure that the mission succeeded. Jesus asked why they came at this night hour. While He was *daily* in the temple they had not bothered to arrest Him. There was irony in this question. The very reason why they chose this time to seize Jesus was to avoid any trouble with the people. Dark deeds are done under the cover of darkness.

"But this is your hour, and the power [*exousia,* tyranny] of darkness" (v. 53). What a tremendous statement! Evil ever works in the world. But it is always under the restraining hand of a benevolent God. Here, however, Jesus mentioned the "tyranny," or unrestrained power of darkness, or of evil. Evil challenged God's power. So now God removed His restraining hand. Let evil do its worst! Let it even kill the Son of God! God will still triumph over the forces of evil. Evil may have its hour of darkness now. Only thus can we understand the unrestrained evil conduct of those who brought Jesus to His death. But God will have His greatest hour when He raises His Son from the dead to be the Saviour of a lost world.

IX
The Trial, Crucifixion, and Burial of Jesus

Luke 22:54-62

The Denial of Peter

When Jesus was arrested all of the disciples fled. Their avowals of loyalty even unto death were soon forgotten. John records that Jesus was first taken before Annas, the former high priest. There may have been two reasons for this. The treachery of Judas had caught the Sanhedrin unprepared. It is possible that while that body was being assembled Annas was assigned the task of securing some charge to bring against Jesus. Furthermore, Annas stood well with the Romans. Any charge supported by him would carry weight with Pilate. When Annas failed to evoke from Jesus any word with which they might charge Him, He was sent to appear before the Sanhedrin.

Luke omits this particular event, and simply notes that they took Jesus to the high priest's house (v. 54). This statement could mean the appearance before Annas, since he may have occupied the same home with Caiaphas, his son-in-law.

At any rate Luke also notes that Peter followed Jesus and the band from a distance (v. 54). John also notes that another disciple, probably John himself, gained entrance to the house while Peter stood outside the gate. But through the influence of this disciple he was allowed to enter the courtyard of the high priest's residence.

It was April, and the night was cool. So those in the courtyard kindled a fire (v. 55). As they sat about the fire Peter was in their midst with his face to the fire. A certain maiden thought that she recognized him. So after gazing steadfastly at him, she finally said, "This man was also with him" (v. 56). But Peter denied this, saying, "Woman, I know him not" (v. 57). After a little while another, this time a man ("another" is masculine), said, "Thou art also of them" (v. 58). Matthew and Mark both mention a maiden as saying this. But probably a man also made this accusation, following the lead of the maiden. This time Peter replied more bluntly. "Man, I am not" (v. 58).

It appeared that they would let the matter drop. But about an hour later another said with confidence, "Of a truth this fellow was with him: for he is a Galilean" (v. 59). Matthew implies this last remark when he says, "For thy speech bewrayeth [betrayeth] thee" (26:73). Galilean speech differed from that of Judea. Evidently Peter had joined in conversation with those about the fire. And they noticed his Galilean dialect. Peter replied, "Man, I know not what thou sayest" (v. 60). Matthew and Mark give the added note that Peter also began to swear. His fisherman's vocabulary came to the surface. If his speech betrayed him he would show them some language which would prove that he was not a disciple of Jesus.

Why did Peter deny his relationship to Jesus? Quite obviously he was aware of the intent of those who arrested Jesus. And they would be just as eager to seize His followers. Furthermore, Peter had resisted the officers with violence. His act in cutting off Malchus' ear would likely not be ignored by the high priest (cf. John 18:26). So Peter denied Jesus in an effort to save his own skin. He was quite a different man from the boasting disciple in the upper room.

Just as Peter uttered his third denial he heard a rooster crow. And Jesus evidently heard it also. For He was now before the Sanhedrin, and could be seen by Peter. When the rooster crowed, Jesus turned and looked at Peter (v. 61). Actually, He glanced at him. But Peter caught the point. For suddenly there rushed to his mind the words of Jesus, "Before the cock crow, thou shalt deny me thrice" (v. 61).

Jesus' glance plus the memory broke Peter's heart. Unlike Judas who merely regretted (cf. Matt. 27:3, "repented" means regret with no change of heart) his act, Peter was filled with godly sorrow, the sorrow which leads to true repentance. So he "went out, and wept bitterly" (v. 62). Literally, "he burst into tears."

This is a sad sight indeed. In the crisis he failed to stand up for his Lord. Yet Jesus knew his heart. And the hour will come when Jesus will make a special appearance to Peter after His resurrection (Luke 24:34). Later in Galilee (John 21) He will show him that he is fully forgiven and given a special commission to feed Jesus' sheep. Weak though he was, Peter was a trusted and valuable servant of Christ. Before we condemn him, we should recall how often we have denied Jesus—and did not weep!

Luke 22:63-71

The Trial before the Sanhedrin

The trial of Jesus actually was composed of six phases, three Jewish and three Roman. The Jewish phases were (1) before Annas; (2) before the Sanhedrin before dawn; (3) before the Sanhedrin after dawn. The Roman phases were (1) before Pilate; (2) before Herod Antipas; (3) before Pilate a second time.

The denials of Peter probably took place during the first appearance before the Sanhedrin. Jesus had already been forced to testify under oath that He was "the Christ, the Son of God" (Matt. 26:63-64). This apparently occurred about the time that the rooster crowed. For when Caiaphas heard Jesus' testimony he accused Him of blasphemy. According to Jewish custom upon hearing blasphemy, Caiaphas tore his clothes. Then he asked for a verdict. The Sanhedrin unanimously declared Him worthy of death.

With this, bedlam broke loose. What had begun as an orderly court of justice (?) suddenly became a mob scene. The men that held Jesus began to mock Him and to beat Him (v. 63). They made sport of Him as they blindfolded Him, kept striking Him, and demanded that He prophesy as to who it was that struck Him (v. 64). All the while they spoke blasphemously of Him (v. 65).

Truly it was their hour and the tyranny of darkness. Unrestrained evil broke loose as it heaped insult after insult upon the Son of God.

According to Jewish law such a trial could not be held before dawn. So even though they had declared Jesus worthy of death, to make it legal the Sanhedrin assembled again after dawn. Jesus was brought before them to repeat the procedure which had transpired under the cover of darkness (v. 66).

"If thou art the Christ, tell us," they said (v. 67). The form of their statement assumed that He was. After all, He had said so under oath. Throughout His ministry Jesus had studiously avoided this title before the Jewish rulers. It was not until they put Him under oath that He admitted it. To have denied His Messiahship under such conditions would have been perjury. So Jesus admitted His true role, even though they would interpret it in political and military terms. Jesus' hour had come. He will die, but it will be the death, not of a lawbreaker, but of the Christ, the Son of God, a King.

However, since He had already admitted His Messianic role, and since He was not now under oath, Jesus refused to use the word again. Instead, He said, "If I tell you, ye will not believe: and if I ask you, ye will not answer me, nor let me go" (vv. 67-68). "Ye will not believe" uses the double negative *(ou mē pisteusēte)*. This was the strongest possible negative. After all, their minds were already made up. They were determined to kill Jesus. So further talk was unnecessary.

But they received more than they bargained for. For Jesus added, "Hereafter shall the Son of man sit on the right hand of the power of God" (v. 69). In reality Jesus said four things. In the title "Son of man" He admitted to being the Messiah. He also claimed equality with God. Again, He implied that even though they would kill Him He would live on in power and glory. Finally, He said that even though He now stood in judgment before them, the time was coming when He would be the judge as they stood before Him.

The Sanhedrin caught all four points. They summed them up in one question. "Art thou then the Son of God?" (v. 70). Their question invited an affirmative answer. It was the equivalent of a declarative statement on their part. So Jesus simply replied, "Ye say that I am" (v. 70). Therefore, He made them to admit His identity before they formally found Him guilty of death. It was a clever strategy on Jesus' part. He would die not merely upon His own admission to deity but also upon theirs.

According to them there was need for no other testimony. For they had heard Him themselves (v. 71). So they condemned Him by the words "of his own mouth." But He also condemned them by their words. They could not say that they did not proclaim the Son of God guilty of death.

The Jewish trial of Jesus was a farce. It was a kangaroo court, illegal in every respect. He was judged by those who accomplished His arrest. The trial was held at night. He was accused by false witnesses and forced to testify against Himself. Lest the older men influence the younger ones, the latter were supposed to vote on a verdict before the former. In this case Caiaphas voted first.

Under Jewish law a unanimous vote was to be the equivalent of "not guilty." This was not observed in Jesus' trial. Contrary to Jewish law Jesus was abused. The sentence of death could not be set on the same day as the trial. This also was ignored in Jesus' case. But, after all, when did unbridled evil bother with law and justice?

The more orderly procedure at the trial held after dawn cannot remove the awful blot upon justice which was made in the dark. The day dawned, indeed. But it was the dawn of the blackest day in the history of the world!

Luke 23:1-7

The First Appearance before Pilate

Luke does not say in so many words that the Sanhedrin pronounced Jesus as being worthy of death. But he implies it in stating that they led Him to appear before Pilate (v. 1). The entire Sanhedrin went along to accuse Jesus before the Roman governor.[1]

The Romans permitted the Sanhedrin to sit in judgment in civil and religious cases. But they retained unto themselves the right to inflict capital punishment. Therefore, even though they had judged Jesus guilty of a capital crime, the Sanhedrin had to bring Him before Pilate for formal sentencing.

Pilate was procurator of Judea A.D. 26-36. Evidently he was a man of ability or else he would not have been appointed to this position. Judea and Samaria formed one of the lesser Roman provinces which was placed under a procurator, who, in turn, served under the propraetor of Syria, a major province. The more peaceable provinces, e.g., Achaia, were ruled by proconsuls under the authority of the Roman Senate. The more belligerent ones which required large numbers of troops, e.g., Syria, were ruled by propraetors under the direct authority of the emperor. The lesser province of Judea and Samaria fell into this latter group.

Pilate had had bad relations with the Jews from the beginning. Shortly after taking office he set up winter quarters for his troops in Jerusalem. Since their standards carried images of Caesar, the Jews regarded them as graven images. It was only after a most violent protest from a Jewish delegation sent to Caesarea that Pilate removed them from the city. Later he placed gilt shields bearing images of pagan deities on the walls of Herod's palace in Jerusalem. Despite another violent protest he removed them only upon

---

[1] Luke 23:50 says that Joseph of Arimathea did not agree to the Sanhedrin's verdict. Since Mark 14:64 says that the verdict was unanimous, evidently Joseph and Nicodemus were not present. Probably knowing their feeling about Jesus, Caiaphas did not call them to the meeting.

orders from Tiberius Caesar himself. Pilate used money from the sacred temple treasury in an effort to build an aqueduct designed to improve the water supply of Jerusalem. This produced a great tumult in which Pilate's soldiers killed many rioters plus some innocent bystanders. Such deeds throw light on Luke 13:1. Philo tells of many abuses of authority by the governor, stating that he feared any appeal to the emperor by the Jews (cf. John 19:12). Therefore, he came to this supreme test with a sordid record.

It would be difficult to overstate the drama of the scene as Jesus stood before Pilate. The very God of the universe stood before the representative of the greatest ruling power on the earth. Pilate thought that Jesus was on trial before him, when all the while he was on trial before Jesus and before history.

Normally Pilate lived in Caesarea by the Mediterranean. He came to Jerusalem only when his duties demanded it. Such a time was the Passover, when due to the unusual revolutionary excitement among the Jews a greater number of troops in Jerusalem was necessary. When in Jerusalem Pilate lived in Herod's palace. Even though tradition sets the Roman trial of Jesus in the Tower of Antonia, the quarters of Roman soldiers, in all probability it is more natural to think of it as occurring in Herod's palace. At this early morning hour Pilate more likely would be at this place.

When the Sanhedrin appeared with their prisoner before Pilate they began to accuse Him in a manner designed to affect the governor. They accused Jesus of sedition, of forbidding the people to pay tribute to Caesar, and of claiming to be "Christ a king" (v. 2). The first two of these charges were pure falsehoods. The third was a definite perversion of Jesus' claim to kingship. They made no mention of religious charges at this point.

Apparently Pilate saw through the whole thing. But to show a semblance of interest he interrogated Jesus on the third charge, ignoring the first two altogether. He asked Jesus, "Art thou the King of the Jews?" (v. 3). The form of Pilate's question invited an affirmative answer. So Jesus replied, "Thou sayest," or "You say that I am."

The governor was not impressed. So he said to the chief priests and to the people, "I find no fault in this man" (v. 4). His legal decision was one of acquittal. And the matter should have ended there.

But the accusers more vehemently accused Jesus. They said that Jesus was stirring up the people, "teaching throughout all

Jewry, beginning from Galilee to this place" (v. 5). Hearing the word "Galilee," Pilate inquired if Jesus were a Galilean (v. 6). For this possibility suggested to him a way out of his predicament. He had Jesus on his hands, but wanted to be rid of Him. Galilee was under the jurisdiction of Herod Antipas, who at that time was in Jerusalem (v. 7). So ascertaining that Jesus was a Galilean, the Roman governor sent Him to Herod.

He sought a loophole through the letter of the law. His act was not prompted by any consideration for Herod's authority. They were on bad terms with one another, probably stemming from Pilate's harsh treatment of the Galileans in the temple (cf. Luke 13:1).

But Pilate was willing to seek haven in any port to escape the storm which swirled about him. Thus ended the first phase of Jesus' Roman trial. But the interval was to be of short duration. The Roman governor was not to escape his responsibility so easily. Pilate wavered on his first decision, and his hesitancy proved to be his undoing. One cannot *play the percentages* where Jesus is concerned—and win.

Luke 23:8-12

The Appearance before Herod Antipas

At long last Herod Antipas got his chance to see and hear Jesus. Apparently he had long since gotten over his morbid fear that He was John the Baptist come to life again. One wonders why he had not satisfied his curiosity merely by seeking out Jesus as He moved about his realm. Evidently he felt it to be beneath his dignity to do so. He had no spiritual interest in Jesus whatever. But for a long time he "was desirous to see him" (v. 8). He had heard many things about Jesus, including His miracles. So he kept hoping that he might see some miracle (sign, *sēmeion)* done by Him. To do so would give him momentary relief from the boredom which went with his position.

So when Jesus finally was led before him Herod *kept questioning* (imperfect) Him with many words (v. 9). What his questions were about is not stated. Evidently they were of such nature as to merit the scorn of Jesus. For "he answered him nothing." He maintained a dignified silence before this foxy puppet ruler.

As Herod questioned Jesus the chief priests and scribes stood by. When Jesus refused to answer, they broke out in the same vehement accusations which they had stated to Pilate (v. 10). Robertson says that they did so "like a pack of hounds with full voice [*eutonōs*]." They had their Victim *treed,* and did not want to lose Him.

But Herod brushed aside their accusations. To him the whole thing was just a show. He viewed Jesus with morbid curiosity as though He were something in a circus. He craved entertainment. And since Jesus refused to provide it by doing some *tricks* for him, he decided to provide his own at Jesus' expense.

Herod and his soldiers "set him at nought" (v. 11). This verb means to count as nothing or a zero, and to treat with utter contempt. So they mocked Jesus, perhaps taunted Him for His claim to kingship. Herod's crowning act was to dress Jesus in a brilliant, kingly robe, and to send Him back to Pilate.

Herod Antipas rendered no judgment at all as to Jesus' innocence or guilt. He simply made sport of the whole matter. This is a good indication of his evil and shallow character, as indeed it is of any man who treats Jesus with scorn. In all of this horrible picture no figure appears so ignominious as Herod.

Luke notes that on that day Pilate and Herod became friends (v. 12). Whatever may have been the cause of the breach between them, it was removed. Doubtless each man was jealous of his position and power. This would be true especially of Herod, the puppet king. The fact that the Roman procurator showed consideration for his authority over his own subject certainly pleased Herod. This was not the real reason why Pilate sent Jesus to him. But it healed the breach nevertheless. It is a part of the irony of the entire situation that He who came to reconcile men to God and to one another in righteousness should have been the means of reconciling these two men in their unrighteousness.

This was the only time that Herod Antipas ever saw Jesus. He had one chance to receive Him as his King. Instead he mocked Him in His kingship. Certainly this blasphemous deed will witness against him at the last judgment when he will stand before Him whom he held in contempt and regarded as a zero.

Luke 23:13-25

The Second Appearance before Pilate

Poor Pilate! He still had Jesus on his hands.

In a further effort to get rid of Him he called together the Jewish rulers and the people (v. 13). Evidently he hoped to find support from the people. He recounted the action thus far (v. 14). They had accused Jesus of sedition. He had examined Him, and had found no fault in Him with respect to their charges (Luke 23:2). Furthermore, he had sent Jesus to Herod (v. 15). The hearing before the tetrarch had produced no damaging evidence. So Pilate proposed to chastise Jesus, and release Him (v. 16). Chastise an innocent man? Pilate was unconcerned about legal rights. He merely wanted to appease this mob.

Verse 17 is not found in the best manuscripts. It was probably inserted from Matthew 27:15 and Mark 15:6 by some scribe in order to explain the meaning of verse 18. Matthew and Mark mention a custom of the Romans by which, to please the Jews, at the Passover they would release some prisoner of their own choosing. No record of this custom is found outside the Gospels. But it evidently was done nevertheless. Apparently Pilate had this custom in mind when he offered to release Jesus after whipping Him. And the Jews so interpreted his words.

For with one voice they cried, "Away with this one [*aire touton,* they did not dignify Jesus by calling His name], and release unto us Barabbas" (v. 18). Literally, "Take away this one and keep him away [present tense], and release immediately [aorist] unto us Barabbas."

Barabbas was an insurrectionist and a murderer (v. 19). He may have been one of the false Christs who proposed to be a military Messiah, the role which Jesus refused to fill. Like so many of them, he probably had simply degenerated into a bandit who had murdered in plying his trade as an outlaw. In all likelihood he was even then scheduled to be crucified along with two of his henchmen.

Matthew and Mark relate that Pilate gave the Jews their choice between Jesus and Barabbas. Luke's account fits into such a picture, even though he omits the details. Evidently Pilate felt safe in giving them this alternative. For reason dictated that they would not want this murdering outlaw turned loose upon society again. But mobs do not reason. So they chose Barabbas.

And their choice involved more than they knew. Origen reports having seen a copy of Matthew's Gospel which gives the robber's name as *Jesus Barabbas.* And this is most suggestive. For "Jesus" means "Jehovah is salvation," and "Barabbas" means "son of father."

Here were Jesus Christ, the Son of His Father, and Jesus Barabbas, the son of his father. Both offered the Jews a salvation. The One offered spiritual salvation from the bondage of sin; the other offered military and political salvation from the bondage of Rome. The One offered regeneration; the other offered revolution. The One offered to save the people by the shedding of His blood; the other offered to save them by the shedding of their blood. The fact stands that the Jews rejected Him who was the anointed of God to establish a spiritual kingdom; and they accepted their own kind of Messiah who by self-appointment proposed to establish an earthly political kingdom.

Even though Pilate failed in this first effort, he tried again. Perhaps the people would be doubly glad to have two prisoners released. So he proposed to release Jesus also (v. 20). However, to his consternation they *kept shouting* (imperfect), "Crucify, crucify him" (v. 21). Still trying, Pilate reavowed Jesus' innocence (v. 22). With a momentary show of strength, he proposed again to whip Jesus and then release Him. But like the rush and swirl of a tempest ("were instant") their loud cries rose about the governor "requiring that he might be crucified" (v. 23). And their loud demands prevailed. The representative of the greatest political and military power on earth gave in to this shouting mob. Roman justice never appears in a worse light! In this case the justice was no better than the man who was charged to administer it. And Pilate's record as procurator of Judea made him open to charges of misgovernment. His evil past caught up with him. He did not dare to resist this Jewish mob further. In truth they blackmailed him into submitting to their demand. So Pilate pronounced the final sentence that Jesus should be crucified (v. 24).

"And he released unto them him that for sedition and murder was cast into prison, *whom they had desired;* but he delivered

Jesus to their will" (v. 25, author's italics). No comments by the writer can add to this terrible picture.

But James Russell Lowell stabs us all awake in *The Present Crisis.*

> Truth forever on the scaffold, Wrong
> forever on the throne . . . .
>
> Then it is the brave man chooses,
> while the coward stands aside,
> Doubting in his abject spirit, till
> his Lord is crucified.

Luke 23:26-49

The Crucifixion of Jesus

A person condemned to death by crucifixion was required to carry his own cross to the place of execution. John 19:17 says that Jesus went out of the city bearing His cross. However, the ordeal through which He had gone had taken its toll. Therefore, He fell under the weight of the heavy cross. So according to Roman law another was pressed into service to bear the cross for Him.

This hapless victim was "one Simon, a Cyrenian" (v. 26). Cyrene was one of the major cities of North Africa. Its modern name is Tripoli. Since Simon was from Africa, some would identify him with Simon Niger who is also associated with Lucius of Cyrene (Acts 13:1). It is, therefore, held that Simon was a black man. However, this is only supposition. In all likelihood he was a Jew of the Dispersion, of the Jewish community which was located in Cyrene. Josephus tells of the origin of such a colony, and also quotes Strabo concerning it.

Simon probably had come to Jerusalem for the Passover. Every Jew of the Dispersion hoped to do this at least one time in his life. We may well imagine that he had skimped and saved for this one great opportunity. Luke mentions that he was "coming out of the country." This could hardly mean that he was just arriving in Jerusalem, since it was now the day after the passover meal, which had been eaten the previous evening. Due to the crowded conditions of the city at this season, many pilgrims spent the nights outside the city, and came in for the daytime activities.

Like any Jew, Simon must have resented the fact that he was made to carry the cross of a *criminal.* But sometime during the crucifixion, or else afterward, he evidently became a Christian. Mark 15:21 identifies him as "the father of Alexander and Rufus" who evidently were well-known Christians. Mark wrote his Gospel for the Romans. It is of interest, therefore, to read in Romans 16:13, "Salute Rufus chosen in the Lord, and his mother and mine." This could well be the same Rufus mentioned by Mark.

If so, then he was a Christian in Rome who was worthy of special note by Paul. Furthermore, his family was so dear to Paul that he called Rufus' mother (Simon's wife?) his own mother. So what at first appeared to Simon as a hated chore became a blessed experience to him and his family. Apparently by the time that Paul wrote Romans Simon had died, and his wife and son had moved from Cyrene to Rome.

Naturally, the procession to the crucifixion was followed by a crowd of people (v. 27). Among them were women who "bewailed and lamented him [Jesus]." "Bewailed" means that they were smiting their breasts as they cried aloud in lament. Luke alone reports this incident, which is quite in place in his "Gospel of Womanhood." Plummer notes that in the Gospels no woman is mentioned as being hostile to Jesus.

Since Simon was carrying His cross Jesus turned and spoke to these women. "Daughters of Jerusalem, weep not [stop weeping] for me, but weep [go on weeping] for yourselves, and for your children" (v. 28). The "days are coming" when it will be said, "Blessed are the barren, and the wombs that never bare, and the paps which never gave suck" (v. 29). Barrenness was usually considered as a shame for Jewish women. But Jesus pointed to the time when such would be happy that they never bore children. He spoke of a time when men would cry unto the rocks to cover them (v. 30). And the children which they never bore would be spared such an ordeal.

To what was Jesus referring? Certainly He spoke of some terrible judgment upon Jerusalem. Since He used the plural "days" this can hardly refer to the final judgment *day*. Evidently He spoke of the judgment upon the city as seen in its destruction by the Romans in A.D. 70. Jerusalem had rejected her Messiah-Saviour, and the rebellion in her heart brought on her destruction at the end of the Jewish war against Rome.

"For if they [Romans] do these things in a green tree, what shall be done in the dry?" (v. 31). This was a common proverb. Green wood is hard to burn, and so it suggests the innocent. Contrariwise, dry wood which burns easily suggests the guilty. If the Romans will do to Him in His innocence what they are doing, how much worse will be their actions toward those who are guilty of rebellion?

Along with Jesus there were two "others," evil doers, who also were led out to be put to death (v. 32). "Others" *(heteroi)* means others of a different kind. Jesus was dying innocently, but they were guilty of crimes worthy of death. Probably they were companions in crime with Barabbas who would have died with them had not Jesus become his *Substitute.*

Finally, they arrived at the place of execution. The Greek name for it is *Kranion,* the skull, suggesting the shape of the place. The Hebrew name is *Golgotha* (cf. Matt. 27:33; Mark 15:22; John 19:17). Luke gives it the Latin name *Calvary* (v. 33). Where was it located? Tradition places it on the site of the Church of the Holy Sepulchre. However, this is by no means a certain location. Hebrews 13:11-13 says that it was outside the gate, so it must have been outside the walls of the city. Archaeology is not certain where this wall was located at the time of Jesus' death. Another suggested site is Gordon's Calvary which most certainly was outside the city wall. Even today it has the shape of a skull. Perhaps we shall never know the exact spot. Possibly God does not intend that we shall know. But in all frankness in the writer's mind there is much to commend Gordon's Calvary as the likely spot.

Wherever it was located, it was here that Jesus was crucified between the two "malefactors" (v. 33). No more horrible manner of execution was ever devised. It was so terrible that Roman law forbade it for Roman citizens. According to Roman custom the upright piece of the cross was placed in a hole in the ground, and the cross piece was laid flat on the ground. Jesus was stripped naked. He was made to lie on the ground with His arms outstretched along the cross piece. To render Him helpless His arms and legs were jerked out of joint. After His hands were nailed to the cross piece, His body was raised until the beam was fastened to the upright pole. His feet about two feet above the ground rested on a little shelf, were crossed, and a spike driven through them into the upright pole. There He was left hanging throughout the ordeal. His body was so extended that His ribs might be counted. Every muscle and nerve was drawn tight so that the agony was beyond human endurance. Through bleeding and perspiration the loss of body fluid produced tremendous thirst. His entire body became fevered. His lips were parched, His tongue was swollen, His throat was dry, and His inflamed vocal cords produced only a rasping sound. It is impossible for language to describe the excruciating pain which accompanied crucifixion. It is no wonder that its victims usually struggled, cursed, and screamed as they were being nailed to a cross. But not so with Jesus.

Our Lord was on the cross from about 9:00 A.M. until 3:00

P.M. During this time He is recorded as speaking seven times. Luke records only three of these "crucial words from Calvary."[1] The first of these *sayings* was a prayer. While some of the oldest and best manuscripts of Luke do not include it, it is so like Jesus that it is generally accepted as being a genuine saying of the Lord.

"Then said Jesus, Father, forgive them: for they know not what they do [are doing]" (v. 34). "Said" is an imperfect tense, showing that Jesus "kept saying" this. It is possible that He began while the soldiers were preparing Him for crucifixion, and that He continued to pray even after He was nailed to the cross. The word "know" *(oidasin)* means more than mere experiential knowledge. It is such knowledge which has been perceived until it becomes a conviction of the soul, or soul knowledge. They did not really know what they were doing. Paul says that if the rulers had known *(egnōsan,* experiential knowledge) they would not have crucified the Lord of glory (I Cor. 2:8).

Now for whom was Jesus praying? Certainly He was praying for the four Roman soldiers who carried out the orders of Pilate. Most assuredly they did not know what they were doing. They were soldiers under military orders carrying out an assignment given to them by the Roman procurator. Jesus, therefore, also prayed for Pilate. But more, He prayed for those who had delivered Him to Pilate (cf. John 19:11). And what about the multitude which was a tool of the Sanhedrin? They all had a part in the crucifixion of Jesus. And for that matter, do not all men have a part?

Luke 23:38 notes that a superscription was placed over the cross of Jesus. Roman law required that the crime for which one was executed should be placed on the cross above the victim's head. In Jesus' case it read "THIS IS THE KING OF THE JEWS." The King James Version says that it was written in Greek, Latin, and Hebrew. But the best manuscripts of Luke do not have these words. However, they are genuine in John 19:20: "in Hebrew, ... in Latin, ... in Greek." These languages represent the three great streams of life in that day. And all had a part in the death of Jesus. Hebrew (institutional) religion rejected Him, Greek (pagan) culture ignored Him, Latin (Roman) government crucified Him. In this sense all streams of life, then and now, are guilty. So, in effect, we may say that Jesus prayed

---

[1] See my *The Crucial Words from Calvary,* Baker, Grand Rapids, 1958.

for all men, "Father, forgive them: for they know not what they do."

The key word in this prayer is "forgive" *(aphes)*. It means to let go or send away. It is used in the sense of waiving debts or taxes. But an interesting usage is found in Matthew 27:49, *"Let be* [wait], let us see if Elias will come to save him" (author's italics). In response to Jesus' cry a soldier was about to give Him a drink of vinegar. The others told him to *wait*. Here Matthew uses exactly the same form of the verb as is found in Luke 23:34. Therefore, in the light of Jesus' added words "for they know not what they do" may we not see the thought of "wait" in this prayer. After the resurrection they will have the "sign from heaven." Wait until after that to condemn them or to hold them guilty. After His resurrection they will *know* that they have crucified the Son of God. If then they do not repent, theirs will be a sin of full-knowledge. And, of course, in this light if a man today rejects Him, in the light of the resurrected and living Lord, it is also a sin of full-knowledge.

Though Jesus in mercy prayed this prayer for all men, it certainly does not mean a blanket forgiveness. Through His death and resurrection Jesus made it possible for God to deal with man in terms of grace rather than of law; the final result still depends upon the response which man makes to God's overture of grace.

All the while that Jesus was praying the soldiers were gambling for one of His garments (v. 34). They were permitted to divide among themselves the personal effects of the victim. Jesus had only the clothes that He wore. Normally a Jew's clothing consisted of sandals, a headdress, a girdle, an outer garment, and an inner garment. Each soldier took one of the first four items. John 19:23-24 notes that the inner garment was seamless. So rather than tear it the soldiers cast lots for it. They neither knew nor cared that they were fulfilling Psalm 22:18.

One of the saddest spectacles about Jesus' crucifixion was the conduct of those around the cross. Rather than to sit in reverent, sympathetic silence, they were as wild animals crying and taunting the Son of God (vv. 35-37). Even the dignified (?) rulers joined in this disgraceful scene, along with the mob and the soldiers. They challenged Jesus to come down from the cross. This was Satan's last effort to prevent Jesus from dying on a cross. He wanted Jesus killed. Indeed, he had repeatedly sought to accomplish this purpose. But he did not want Him to die on a cross. For this was God's design by which to save men and to defeat Satan.

But even in such a hellish scene there was a ray of heavenly light. The thieves on either side of Jesus joined in the insulting taunts of the mob (cf. Matt. 27:44). Finally, one of them "railed," or blasphemed, Jesus, saying, "If thou be Christ, save thyself and us" (v. 39). The "if" clause calls for an affirmative answer: Assuming that you are the Christ, "save thyself and us." "Save" in this sense means to save from death on the cross. This thief had no sense of repentance and faith unto spiritual salvation. He merely wanted to be saved from his present predicament.

But the other thief suddenly ceased to rail upon Jesus and began to pray. First, he rebuked the other thief, declaring that they were dying justly but that Jesus was dying innocently (vv. 40-41). And then his prayer: "Jesus, remember me when thou comest into thy kingdom" (v. 42, the best mss. do not have "Lord," but "Jesus"). He did not ask to be delivered from the cross, but to be remembered by Jesus when He came "into" His kingdom. He prayed for salvation from sin. The imperfect tense ("said") means that he kept repeating this prayer.

In a sense both of these thieves prayed. For they both asked Jesus to do something for them. The one introduced his *prayer* with a curse, asking only for physical relief. Jesus made no response to his request. The other began by confessing his sin, asking for spiritual salvation. The one thief entered hell with a so-called *prayer* on his lips. But the other's experience was quite different.

Jesus said, "Verily I say unto thee, To day shalt thou be with me in paradise" (v. 43). This thief asked for remembrance; he received fellowship. He asked to be remembered at some future time. He received the promise of fellowship that very day. And before the sun set that day he, arm in arm with Jesus, walked through the gates of glory!

It was now about the sixth hour, or noon (v. 44). "And a darkness came over the whole land until the ninth hour [3:00 P.M.], the sun's light failing" (vv. 44-45 RV). Nature itself rebelled at that which was happening to her God.

It was sometime during this darkness, probably toward the end of it, that Jesus cried, "My God, my God, why hast thou forsaken me?" (Matt. 27:46; cf. Ps. 22:1). Who can probe the deep meaning of this question? Jesus was suffering the very pain and desolation of hell for sinful man. G. Campbell Morgan notes that the beginning of sin is to forsake God; the end of sin is to be God-forsaken. And in some way unknown to us the Son, now become sin for us, was forsaken by the Father. Here Jesus drank the last bitter dregs of the "cup." It was for only a moment. But it was the infinite suffering of the infinite God for the infinite guilt of finite man.

John records that near the end of this period Jesus said, "I thirst" (19:28) and "It is finished" (19:30). Luke recognizes this last saying as he says that Jesus "cried with a loud voice" (v. 46). Then He said, "Father, into thy hands I commend my spirit" (v. 46). "Commend" renders a word meaning to place alongside. It was also a banking term meaning to place something on deposit for safe keeping and to be used for its intended purpose. So in a definite sense Jesus deposited His redemptive act in the hands of the Father for safe keeping and to be used for its intended purpose to save all who should believe in Him.

"And having said thus, he gave up the ghost" (v. 46). Literally, "He expired." Matthew 27:50 says literally, "He dismissed the spirit." When He had finished His work He bade His spirit to depart. King all the way! No man took His life from Him; He laid it down of Himself!

When Jesus died, "the veil of the temple [*naos*] was rent in the midst" (v. 45). The *naos* was the Holy of Holies in which God was said to dwell in mercy toward His people. Only the high priest was permitted to enter this *naos,* and that only once each year on the Day of Atonement. This Holy of Holies was separated from the Holy Place by a heavy curtain. Matthew and Mark note that this "veil" was torn in two from the *top* to the *bottom.* It was not an act of man but of God. Matthew also points out that the earth quaked, which may have caused the rent in the veil. The Jewish Talmud tells of the temple's quaking forty years before its destruction. This would mean A.D. 30, the year that Jesus died.

But there was more to this torn veil than a mere natural phenomenon. This veil barred man's approach to God's presence. But when Jesus died the way was opened by which sinful men might approach the throne of grace without fear (Heb. 4:16).

All of the strange things which happened at Jesus' death struck terror into the hearts of the people about the cross. Perhaps someone came running to Calvary with a report about the veil. At any rate the people suddenly realized that they had participated in more than the death of a mere man. It is no wonder, therefore, that they "smote their breasts, and returned" to the city (v. 48). Well they might demonstrate their extreme shock and grief. For they had participated in the tragedy of the ages.

But the centurion in charge of the crucifixion detail had quite a different reaction (v. 47). Seeing all of these things "he began to glorify God and kept on glorifying him" (imperfect). Said he, "Certainly this was a righteous man." Matthew notes that both he and the soldiers said literally, "Truly this was God's Son [*theou huios*]" (27:54). We can only hope that they also believed in Him as their Saviour.

Far out on the edge of the crowd, "afar off," stood a small band of Jesus' followers, including some women (v. 49). They were helpless to prevent Jesus' crucifixion. At the moment they could not even understand it. They could only watch and wonder. Truly they were now fasting as the Bridegroom was taken from them. But it would be a fast of short duration. For their deep sorrow would give place to extreme joy. Their puzzled wonder would flee before the light of full-knowledge as from those lips, now dead but soon to speak again, they would come to know the meaning of it all.

Luke 23:50-56

The Burial of Jesus

A major crisis will bring out either the best or the worst in a man. The latter is amply illustrated in the conduct of those who participated in the crucifixion of Jesus. The former is seen in the conduct of those who gave to Him a tender and loving burial.

Joseph of Arimathea (perhaps Ramah, Samuel's home) was a member of the Sanhedrin (v. 50). He is described as a *good* and *just* (righteous) man. Luke says that he "waited [was looking] for the kingdom of God" (v. 51; cf. Mark 15:43). Both Matthew and John agree that he was a disciple of Jesus, and Matthew notes that he was a man of wealth (27:57). John also says that he was a secret disciple out of fear of his fellow-members of the Sanhedrin (19:38). Furthermore, Luke points out that he did not agree in the Sanhedrin's action concerning Jesus' condemnation and death. Since that body's vote was unanimous, evidently Caiaphas, knowing of his feeling toward Jesus, did not call Joseph to the meeting of the Sanhedrin when Jesus was brought before them. It could be that his being omitted from the meeting revealed to him that his faith in Jesus was known to Caiaphas.

At any rate after Jesus' death Joseph came out boldly for Him. Despite the personal danger that his action involved, he went to Pilate and requested that he be allowed to bury Jesus (v. 52). Had not he or some other friend done so, Jesus' body probably would have been thrown into the Vale of Hinnom (Gehenna). It was customary to cast the unclaimed bodies of executed criminals into this garbage dump of the city.

At this point John brings Nicodemus into the picture as being allied with Joseph in this merciful act (19:39). Doubtless he also was omitted from the call of the Sanhedrin. His sympathy for Jesus was well known to that body (John 7:50-52).

So Joseph and Nicodemus took Jesus' body down from the cross, prepared it for burial, and laid it in Joseph's "sepulchre that was hewn in stone, wherein never man before was laid" (v.

53). John notes that this was a "new tomb" located in a garden adjacent to Calvary (19:41). When they had placed Jesus' body therein they rolled a great stone over the entrance to the tomb (Matt. 27:60).

As with Calvary so with the tomb, its location is not known with any degree of certainty. Tradition also places it within the Church of the Holy Sepulchre. But this tradition will either stand, or fall, with that concerning Calvary. Likewise there is Gordon's Tomb in a garden adjacent to Gordon's Calvary.

Comparing the two sites reveals an item of interest. As a member of the Sanhedrin Joseph was a married man, and may have had children. The tomb in the Church of the Holy Sepulchre has a place for only one body. On the other hand, Gordon's Tomb is divided into two sides. On one side are finished places for two bodies. Beyond a wall is a similar area *unfinished* as though the new tomb had been used unexpectedly before it was completed. Across its entrance is a groove in which the stone was rolled across the entrance. Of further interest is the fact that just in front of the tomb and to one side of the entrance recent excavations have unearthed the ruins of a small chapel dating from the Byzantine period which dates from the Fourth Century A.D. Evidently at that time this was considered to be a sacred shrine among the Christians. While these things are by no means conclusive, they are suggestive nevertheless.

The day of Jesus' death and burial has been a subject of debate. Some would insist that He died on Thursday afternoon at the hour when the paschal lamb was slain in the temple. It is also held that Thursday is necessary in order for Jesus to have been in the tomb three days and three nights (Matt. 12:40). However, the former idea is based more on sentiment than on fact. And the latter matter may be understood in another way.

Both Luke and John state that the death and burial took place on "the day of Preparation" (23:54; 19:42). "Preparation" *(paraskeuēs)* was a technical name for Friday. It is so used in modern Greek, much like the modern, popular designation of Monday as "Wash Day." Friday was the day when *preparation* (cooking, etc.) was made for the observance of the Sabbath on Saturday. John implies a hurried burial on "the Jews' Preparation" (19:42) in order that it might be done before the Sabbath. Luke 23:54 clearly says that "it was the day of Preparation, and the sabbath drew on."

So the evidence clearly favors Friday as the day when Jesus died and was buried. The Jews reckoned any part of a day as an entire day. Jesus was in the tomb a part of Friday (one day), all of Saturday (one day), and a part of Sunday (one day). It is to be expected that when Jesus spoke of Jonah's being in the fish "three days and three nights" He spoke in keeping with the custom of the time.

This position is further strengthened by the conduct of the women from Galilee (vv. 55-56). They followed Joseph and Nicodemus in order to ascertain where they placed the body of Jesus. Then they went to prepare "spices and ointments" for a further preparation of Jesus' body. But they "rested the Sabbath day according to the commandment" (v. 56).

Matthew 27:62-66 points out that the day after the Preparation the chief priests and Pharisees requested and secured a Roman guard to seal and guard the tomb of Jesus. They knew of Jesus' promise to rise on the third day. Their purpose was to prevent His disciples from stealing His body and falsely claiming a resurrection. In their zeal they unknowingly provided the most telling evidence for the bodily resurrection of Jesus from the dead. Before the Jewish rulers' eyes the tomb was sealed with the Roman seal, and the guard took its position.

Poor Roman soldiers! For never were such given so futile an assignment!

X
The Resurrection and Appearances of Jesus

Luke 24:1-12

The Empty Tomb

Many efforts have been made by skeptics to explain away the bodily resurrection of Jesus.[1] But in the final analysis they must face the fact of the empty tomb. All four Gospels relate that Jesus' body was placed in the tomb on Friday. All four record that it was empty on Sunday morning.

Luke says that very early on the first day of the week Mary Magdalene, Joanna, Mary the mother of James, and other women came to the tomb with spices which they had prepared (vv. 1, 10). Since the guard had been stationed on Saturday they were unaware of the fact. Mark notes their concern as to how they would get into the tomb (16:3). But when they arrived they found the tomb both open and empty (vv. 2-3). As they were perplexed about this two men, or angels, stood by them in shining garments (v. 4). It was they who had rolled away the stone. This was done not to let Jesus out. The exact time of His rising is not stated, but it took place after sunset on Saturday (Sunday) and before dawn. The stone had been removed in order to let the women into the empty tomb.

In fear the women bowed before these heavenly beings. But they said, "Why seek ye the living [the one living] among the dead? He is not here but is risen" (vv. 5-6). Never were more glorious words heard by human ears! The women came seeking the dead body of Jesus. But they failed in their search. And they were overjoyed by their failure. For instead of finding a dead Jesus they heard the assurance of a living Lord!

The angels reminded the women of Jesus' promise that He would rise on the third day (vv. 6-7). "And they remembered his words" (v. 8). It is strange that they had forgotten. Certainly the Jewish rulers remembered. It had been difficult all along for the disciples to grasp this grand truth. And the grief of recent days had dulled their senses.

---

[1] See my *An Exposition of The Gospel of Matthew,* pp. 413-418.

With unbounded joy the women rushed to tell the glad news to the Eleven and to the others (v. 9). Doubtless they spoke in excited tones. But even more than their excitement the message itself seemed to their listeners as "idle tales," or those of delirious women (v. 11). The word for "idle talk" *(lēros)* was a medical term meaning nonsense, or the wild raving of one in delirium or hysteria. So the disciples did not believe the report of the women. In fact, one of the greatest proofs of the resurrection of Jesus is that none of His followers expected it to happen.

Luke 24:12 is not found in the best manuscripts. But its contents are found in John 20:3-10. Peter and John rushed to check on the story of the women. Peter saw the empty tomb with the grave clothes arranged in orderly fashion. But it seems to have made no impression on him. It took a special appearance of Jesus to convince him that He was risen from the dead (Luke 24:34; I Cor. 15:5). But John, seeing the orderly arrangement, believed. He knew that the tomb was empty, not because of a grave robbery but because of the bodily resurrection from the dead.

The account in Luke is of especial significance. Every bit of his medical training would have prejudiced him against a bodily resurrection. Yet having traced all things accurately, he was so convinced as to its reality that he recorded one of the most beautiful and complete accounts of the fact that He who was dead is alive forevermore. This man of science, this historian of the first rank stands as a bulwark against those who would deny this miracle of miracles as Jesus was declared the Son of God with power by His resurrection from the dead.

Luke 24:13-35

The Walk to Emmaus

There is no more beautiful story in all literature than Luke's account of Jesus' appearance to Cleopas and another disciple. Who this other disciple was, no one knows. Many have been suggested, even Luke himself. But this is most unlikely. It could even have been the wife of Cleopas. Even though masculine forms are used to refer to them, this may be explained by the inclusive use of the masculine to refer to a husband and his wife. However, it is impossible to identify the other disciple.

It was late afternoon on resurrection Sunday. These two disciples were walking along the road to Emmaus, a village located about seven miles from Jerusalem. It is probably identical with the modern village of *El Kubeibeh,* located about that distance northwest of the city. As they walked along these disciples communed with one another and asked each other questions (v. 15). While they were so absorbed Jesus Himself drew near and walked along with them. Since they assumed that He also had come from Jerusalem, evidently He overtook them in the way. But for some reason they did not "fully recognize" Him (v. 16).

Jesus joined in the conversation (v. 17). Literally He asked, "What [are] these words that you are tossing back and forth to one another?" The best texts read, "And they stood still, looking sad" (v. 17). Cleopas answered, "You alone do you dwell in Jerusalem, and not know the things happening these days?" (v. 18, author's translation). Note the emphatic position of "you." Robertson translates this, "Hast thou been dwelling alone (all by thyself)?" It was incredible to Cleopas that anyone could have been in the city and not know of the crucifixion.

Certainly Jesus knew of which he spoke. Yet to draw him out He asked, "What things?" (v. 19). His question produced the desired result. For they both replied by recounting the crucifixion (vv. 19-20). And then they added this pathetic word: "But we trusted ['were hoping,' imperfect tense of *elpizō,* to hope] that he [and no other, Plummer] *is* the one about to redeem Israel" (v.

21). Some manuscripts read "was" *(ēn)* but the best ones read "is" *(estin)*. Does this express their hope before the crucifixion as though it were a present one? The fact of the empty tomb may have been keeping this a continuing hope.

Bruce in *Expositor's (in loco)* makes an interesting study of this along with the words "yea" *(alla ge,* v. 21) and "moreover" *(alla kai,* v. 22*)*. These various words suggest a conflict of emotions. "Does the *estin* in the previous clause mean that they think of Him as still living, hoping against hope on the ground of the women's report, mentioned in the following clause, and does the *alla ge* express a swing of feeling away in the opposite direction of hopelessness?=we hoped, we would like to hope still; yet how can we? He is dead three days, and yet again on the other hand *(alla kai,* v. 22) there is a story going that looks like a resurrection. How true to life this alternation between hope and despair!"

So these disciples brought Jesus up to date on all that had happened up until the time that they left the city. Certain women had brought the astonishing story that they had found the tomb empty, and that angels had told them that Jesus was alive. And others had gone to the tomb also to find it empty. But no one had seen Jesus since that time (vv. 22-24). They had left Jerusalem before the report of Mary Magdalene (John 20:18).

At this point Jesus interrupted them. "O fools [senseless ones, or ones without understanding], and slow of [in] heart to believe all that the prophets have spoken" (v. 25). Was it not morally and spiritually necessary for the Christ to suffer these things and to enter into His glory? (v. 26). Instead of these things being the cause of mingled emotions they should give them supreme joy. For all of this was a fulfilment of the teachings of Moses and the prophets (v. 27). What a lesson in interpretation they received as Jesus expounded to them the meaning of the Scriptures concerning Himself!

By this time they were near Emmaus (v. 28). The disciples had arrived at their home. Jesus did not presume upon their hospitality, so He was about to pass by. But He readily accepted their urgent invitation to abide with them (v. 29). It was near sunset when Jesus entered into their home. What a blessing they would have missed had they not invited Jesus to share their abode!

For as they sat down to eat, Jesus took bread, gave thanks, and *was giving* it to them (imperfect, v. 30). In that moment their eyes were opened, and they fully recognized Jesus (v. 31). It was the manner in which He broke the bread that revealed to them the identity of Jesus (v. 35). Why they did not know Him before is not stated, only that their eyes "were holden," or "were held." It must not have been His appearance, for others recognized Him on sight. But whatever it was, their eyes were opened to His identity. And with that recognition suddenly He "became invisible" to them (v. 31).

As soon as Jesus vanished they said to one another, "Was not our heart burning in us as he was speaking to us in the way, as he was opening to us the scriptures?" (v. 32, author's translation). So they rushed immediately back to Jerusalem, and found the Eleven and others with them (v. 33). But before they could tell their story the others said, "The Lord is risen indeed, and hath appeared to Simon" (v. 34). They said nothing about Jesus' appearance to Mary Magdalene, or to other women (Matt. 28:9-10). Simon Peter was so slow to believe. But Jesus' appearance to him convinced him. Now as Jesus had told him to do, his report had strengthened, or established, the faith of his brethren (Luke 22:31-32).

With that the two disciples of Emmaus added their words of great joy (v. 35). So many different reports could not be wrong. Jesus was alive indeed! But their greatest experience was yet to come.

Luke 24:36-43

The First Appearance to the Apostles

Even as the disciples from Emmaus were speaking to the group in Jerusalem, suddenly Jesus "stood in the midst of them" (v. 36). John tells us that the door was shut (20:19). So Jesus was in the room without opening the door. The best manuscripts do not have the words, "Peace be unto you," the customary Jewish greeting. But they are genuine in John's account of this appearance (20:19). So we may regard these words as having been spoken by Jesus.

Nevertheless, the group was terrified, thinking that they were seeing a spirit (v. 37). Hearing that Jesus was alive was one thing. But actually seeing Him was quite another matter. However, Jesus quieted their fears as He showed them His hands and feet which still bore the marks of the crucifixion (vv. 38-39). He encouraged them to handle Him in order that they might know by touch as well as by sight that it was He Himself. "For," said He, "a spirit hath not flesh and bones, as ye see me have" (v. 39, v. 40 not in best mss.).

Still it was too good to be true. Even though they were filled with joy and wonder, they did not yet have faith in the bodily resurrection of Jesus. Therefore, He gave them further evidence, as He asked for some food (v. 41). They had been eating broiled fish, so they gave Jesus a portion of it (v. 42, the best mss. omit any mention of the honeycomb). And taking the fish He ate it before them (v. 43). Here was positive proof of His bodily resurrection. This was no mere vision on the part of the disciples. Neither was He only a surviving spirit. He was the One who could be heard, seen, and felt; He ate food before them.

These are amazing evidences given by Jesus and recorded by Luke, the physician. The Lord submitted Himself to the test of three of the five senses. Some find objection to the idea that Jesus ate food. We are not to suppose by this that His resurrection body needed food. That is not the point. Jesus ate, not for His own benefit, but for that of His followers. His was a resurrection body that was *capable* of eating food. Thus the disciples were looking not at a spirit but at a real body.

Looking back we note several things about Jesus' resurrection body. It bore the wounds of Calvary. It was a real body of "flesh and bones." Even so, it was not subject to the degrees of time, space, or density. He appeared and disappeared. He entered closed doors without opening them. He was capable of eating food. He heard, saw, and spoke. He was capable of being handled and recognized. And He was a conscious, thinking being (vv. 44 f.).

Do these things cast any light upon the nature of our resurrection bodies? Perhaps so. But we must not press the point unduly. The most that can be said is that our resurrection bodies will be adapted to the conditions of life which we shall have in the hereafter (I Cor. 15:38-39). And in the bodily resurrection of our Lord is the assurance of our own resurrection (I Cor. 15:20).

Luke 24:44-49

The Second Appearance to the Apostles

No single Evangelist records all ten appearances of Jesus following His resurrection: Matthew, two; Mark, four (16:19-20 not in best mss.) ; John, four; Paul, not an Evangelist, four; Luke, five. It is of interest, therefore, that Luke, the physician-scientist-historian, leads the group in the number of these appearances.

Luke's report of the first appearance of Jesus to the apostles parallels that of John in which the latter points out that Thomas was absent. Subsequently there followed the appearance to the apostles with Thomas present, the appearance to the apostles on the shore of the sea of Galilee, and the appearance on a mountain in Galilee. Sometime during the forty days, probably in Jerusalem or Galilee, Jesus appeared to James (I Cor. 15:7). Then near the end of the forty days between the resurrection and the ascension He again appeared to the apostles in Jerusalem. This appearance is reported only by Luke (24:44-49; Acts 1:3-8). If we followed Luke's Gospel alone, this appearance would appear to be a part of the one on the night of resurrection Sunday. But comparing it with Acts it is clear that it comes just prior to the Ascension.

This appearance took place somewhere in Jerusalem, maybe in the upper room in which the last passover meal was eaten. But wherever it occurred, it was a glorious experience for the apostles as Jesus interpreted the Old Testament Scriptures in the light of what had happened to Him.

Jesus began by reminding them that before His death He had told them that it was *morally and spiritually necessary (dei)* that the things "written in the law of Moses, and in the prophets, and in the psalms" concerning Him should be fulfilled (v. 44). These three sections were used to designate all of the Hebrew Scriptures. "Then opened he their understanding [mind], that they might understand the scriptures" (v. 45). Was ever a group so fortunate as these? Every student of the Bible knows the joy of sitting at the feet of some great teacher. But here was the

Teacher about whom the Scriptures spoke. Not only His words but His deeds also were an interpretation of their meaning. The events of recent days made it so much easier for them to understand. But, even so, not until the Holy Spirit comes to guide them into all truth will they fully know the mind of Christ.

As Jesus opened their minds He declared that the Scriptures themselves taught that the Christ should suffer, and rise from the dead the third day (v. 46). This is the sum and substance of the Old Testament. Furthermore, this teaching included the fact that repentance and remission of sins should be preached in His name among all nations (v. 47). This preaching should be "in his name," on the basis of His redemptive work and of His authority as the Christ of God, crucified and risen from the dead (cf. Matt. 28:18 where "power" means "authority").

In the King James Version and others "beginning at [from, *apo*] Jerusalem" forms the close of verse 47. Perhaps the reading is better to say, "Beginning at Jerusalem ye are witnesses of these things" (v. 48). This does not infer a priority of the gospel for the Jews. They were simply to begin preaching where they were. From Jerusalem, their present location, this preaching was to be "unto all the nations" (vv. 47-48; cf. Acts 1:8).

To enable them to do this Jesus says, "And, behold, I send [am sending] the promise of my Father upon you" (v. 49). In the Greek text, "I" *(egō)* is written out for emphasis. "I, and no one else, am sending...."

On the night before the crucifixion He had promised the Holy Spirit. "And I will pray the Father, and he shall give you another [*allos,* another of the same kind as Jesus] Comforter, that he may abide with you for ever" (John 14:16). Jesus was going away, but they would not be left alone. Note that they are not to pray for the Holy Spirit. Jesus will *pray* the Father, and the Father will *give* the Spirit.

Now in Luke 24:49 He says that He will send the Holy Spirit. Truly He and the Father are one.

The disciples are not to go forth on their mission until the Holy Spirit comes in a special manifestation. He had been present all the while. But in the coming era He will be the presence of God with and in them. "But *you* tarry in the city until ye *get yourselves clothed* with power from on high" (v. 49, author's italics). Note the points of emphasis. Jesus said, "I am sending... but *ye* tarry... until ye *get yourselves clothed....*" It is Jesus' role to send the Spirit; it is the disciples' role to tarry. Until when?

Until they get themselves clothed with this power from on high.

It is unfortunate that the verb *endusēsthe* ("endued" or "clothed") is translated as a passive voice. It is a middle voice. It is something that the disciples are to do for themselves. They are not to wait for God to clothe them. They are to *get themselves clothed.* Now the Holy Spirit will come in power. But they must get themselves clothed with His power. This suggests that the Holy Spirit's power can be available, yet not be operative in them. So often we pray for the Holy Spirit to *come and take control.* He has *come.* There is no need to pray for that. What we, like the disciples, should do is to pray that we shall let the Holy Spirit take control, or become operative in and through us. When one is saved the Holy Spirit takes up His abode in him (cf. John 14:17). Thereafter, he has all of the Holy Spirit there is. But he must permit himself to be used of the Holy Spirit; he must get himself clothed with His power.

This is suggestive of what these early Christians did between the Ascension and Pentecost. They repented of their sins, and received God's forgiveness through Christ. They restored broken fellowships within their own ranks. They laid themselves upon God's altar in complete dedication. They opened their lives so as to become instruments of the Holy Spirit, so that when He came they were ready to be used of Him.

It was then, and then only, that they were ready to go forth from the city. And what wondrous works the Holy Spirit wrought through them! The same Holy Spirit is within Christ's people today. His power is available to each one of us. But are we available to Him? If we are to make the impact upon our world that they made upon theirs, we too must *tarry* until we *get ourselves clothed* with His power.

Luke 24:50-53

The Last Appearance and Ascension of Jesus

There is no way to determine the length of time between the previous appearance of Jesus and this one. From both Luke and Acts it could simply be a continuation of that which took place in Jerusalem. But in any event it is the last time that the apostles saw Him on this earth.

Many times Jesus had led His little band out of Jerusalem and up the Mount of Olives. Certainly they were not aware that this would be the last time. For in Acts 1:6 they are recorded as asking whether or not at this time He would set up His earthly kingdom. In spite of all that had happened, they were still unable to catch the full significance of the kingdom. In reply to their question Jesus told them that such knowledge was in the "authority" *(exousia,* out of the being) of the Father (Acts 1:7).

The Lord led the apostles up the Mount of Olives until they were "over against" *(pros,* face to face with) Bethany (v. 50 RV). There Jesus "lifted up his hands, and blessed them." As He blessed them He "suddenly parted from them" (v. 51, aorist active). The words "and carried up into heaven" do not appear in some of the best manuscripts. But that is the meaning nevertheless. In fact Acts 1:9 says that "he was taken up; and a cloud received him out of their sight" (RV).

The words "And they worshipped him" also are absent from the best manuscripts, although we may be certain that they did so. But they "returned to Jerusalem with great joy: and were continually in the temple, blessing God" (vv. 52-53). The despair which had weighted them down was fully lifted by the Ascension. And Luke ends his account with a note of joy and victory.

A. T. Robertson speaks for all believers everywhere when he closes his volume on *Luke (Word Pictures, in loco)* with words of life, light, and beauty. "The bells rang in heaven to greet the return of Jesus there, but he set the carillon of joy to ringing on earth in human hearts in all lands and for all time." Amen!